MW01622279

WINERY DOGS

OF WALLA WALLA

First Edition 2007

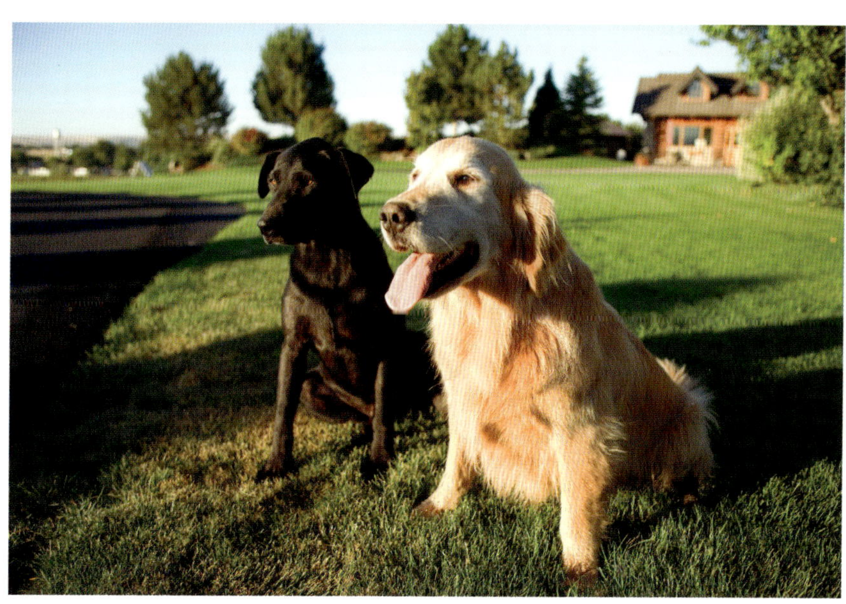

Barbara Whatley

Photography by Tim Hall

Winery Dogs of Walla Walla Publishing

Acknowledgements

Publisher	Winery Dogs of Walla Walla Publishing www.winerydogsofwallawalla.com
Production and Design	Barbara Whatley
Design Assistant	Samantha McEwen
Photographer	Tim Hall Photography www.timhallphoto.com
Text Authors	Individual Dog Owners
Text Editor	Carl Tyler
Printer	Printed in Korea by asianprinting.com

ISBN 13: 978-0-615-17165-4

Contact for wholesale sales
www.winerydogsofwallawalla.com

Ask for a book at your favorite winery, wine shop, bookstore, or pet store.

TO THE DOGS

This book is dedicated to our winery dogs - we share our lives with them and cherish them because they do the same for us. While each is different, they're all the same, blessing us with unconditional love and bringing a special kind of happiness to the experience of tending vineyards and making wine in the Walla Walla Valley.

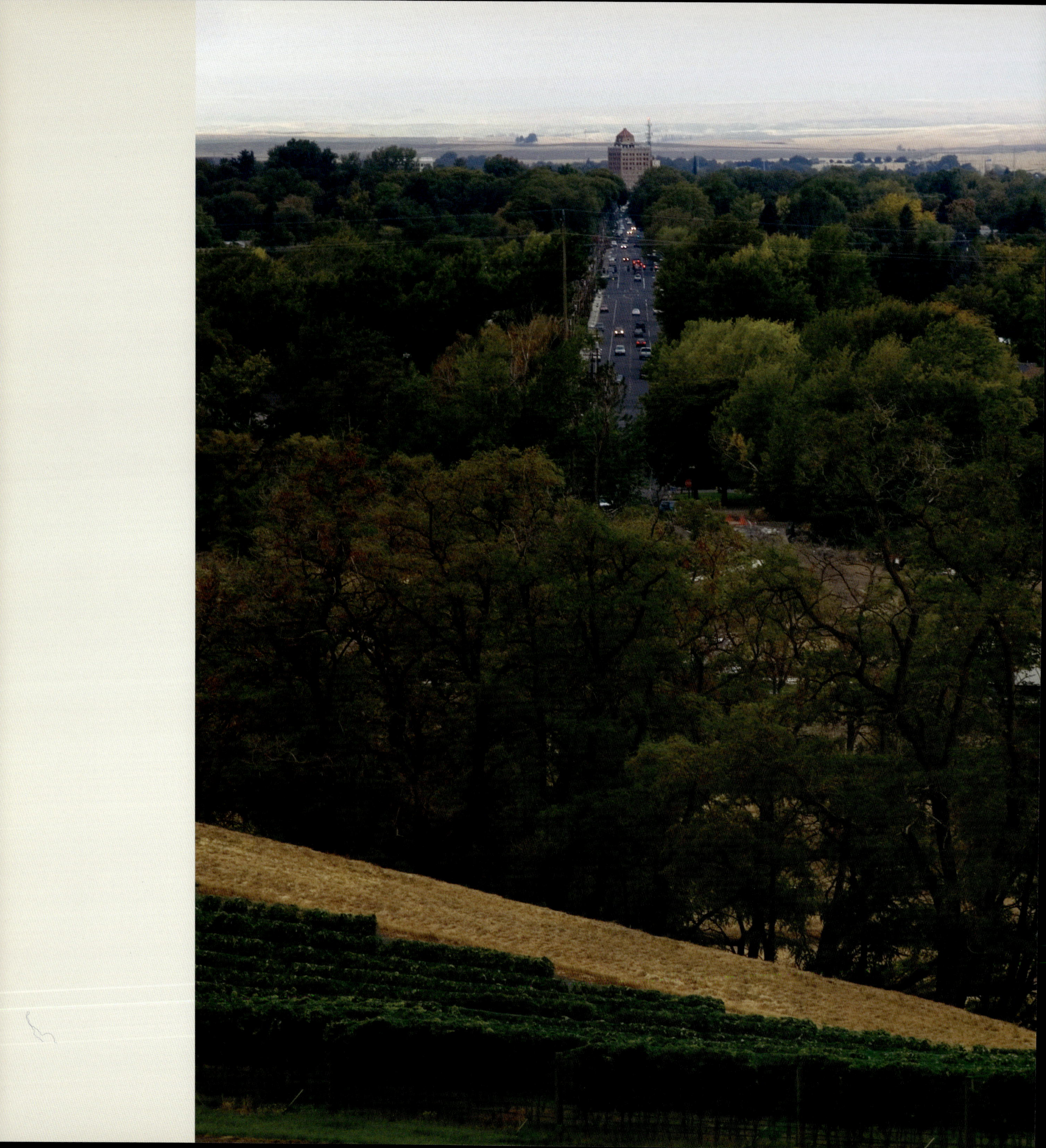

Contents

Acknowledgements	**2**
Dedication	**3**
Contents	**5**
Forward	**7**
Introduction	**9**
Area Map	**10-11**
Feature Pages	**12-123**
Winery Roster	**124-127**
Thank You	**128**

Styx

Winery Dogs of Walla Walla Publishing

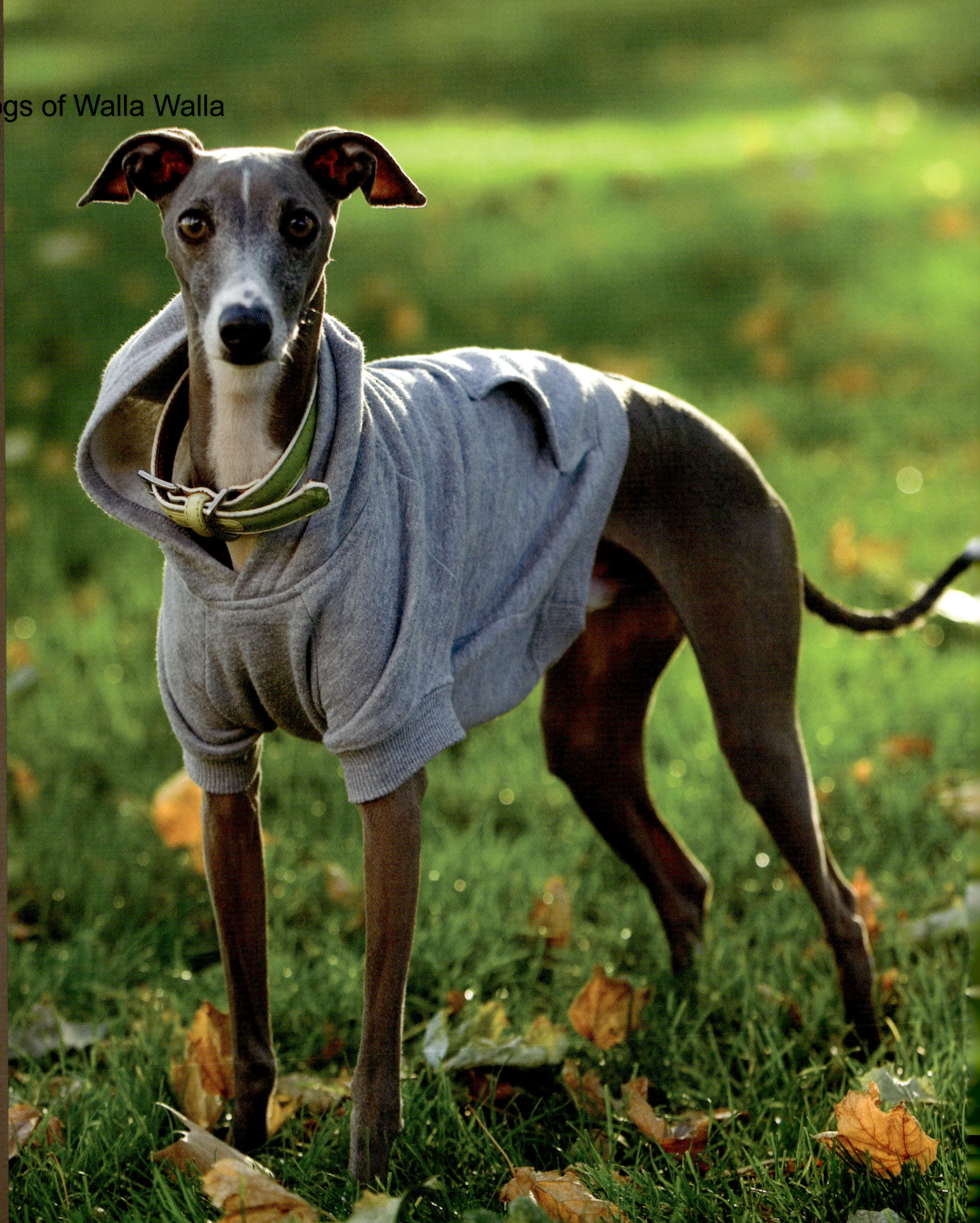

Forward

For as long as I can remember my life has been enhanced by the unconditional love of a dog.

TAFFY, when I was a toddler, tried to engage me in play by grabbing me by the seat of my diaper and pulling me around the yard.

HANNIBAL was my companion through the grade school years. A Chihuahua mix that was always there to assist with gardening, house chores and fetch.

My first dog, when I moved out on my own, I appropriately named DOZER to fit in with my new ambition of building and construction. The big yellow Labrador Retriever was my loyal friend through all the changes life brought my way for the next dozen years. He moved with me over 12 times and adapted perfectly. Some homes provided pool privileges, some he could curl up in front of the fireplace on cold winter nights, others he was tied up with a chain outside or kenneled. DOZER never complained and always had a friendly greeting and tail thrashing for me. DOZER had two wild nights in his life where his expertise in stud duties were called upon. He successfully fathered two litters of 10 and 12 all-yellow pups. I got DOZER a girl playmate - DAISY - although it soon became clear that they brought out the worst in each other. DAISY was adopted by a local couple that has given her the life she deserves and she never looked back. I still get pictures of her sent my way at Christmas time. DOZER fell asleep one night and peacefully slipped away. I've kept his ashes with me.

Then the day arrived that my life would be changed forever.

For my birthday, I was given this sleek, skinny, lightening fast, Italian Greyhound. All lungs and legs, he had to be named STYX. STYX and I, lets just say, are inseparable. If I am working in my office he climbs up and sits behind me in my chair. If I am driving to town, he has to be squarely on my lap as if he is literally in the drivers seat. My friends know it's me when they see this little nose on the dash driving down the street. When I sit or sleep at home he has to be draped over me like a blanket. His favorite things are back rubs, noisy kisses, treats, my cat Nelli and of course running at forty miles per hour.

Okay, I have to say how smart he is too. At obedience training; he would sit and intently observe the instructor's demonstration and when his turn came he would just show off the new command he learned perfectly. STYX will let you know what he wants at any given time. If he needs some lovin', he will sit up next to me or on me and just pull my hand towards him. If it's meal time, he takes me to his dish. If it's time to rise and shine in the morning he nibbles on toes and fingers until I have to get up.

I have to remember this in not a book about me or my dogs, but a picture book full of the images and stories of our valley's wine and vineyard owners' dogs. The experience of sharing my love of dogs by bringing to you this publication has been the most exciting and rewarding of projects to date. You will find that the dogs featured here each have a beautiful and touching story to tell. They are an integral part of each of their owners worlds. I'm sure they must have a role in the magical outcome of the wines produced in our valley.

Dog people are good people. They bring us peace, joy, love, balance and overall fulfillment. Toast a great glass of wine from Walla Walla, "TO THE DOGS" and enjoy this book.

I am very proud and happy to share that a percentage of the proceeds from the sale of this book will be contributed to the completion and maintanance of the Walla Walla Dog Park and provide support for our Blue Mountain Humane Society.

Barbara Whatley

Dixie

Tim Hall Photography

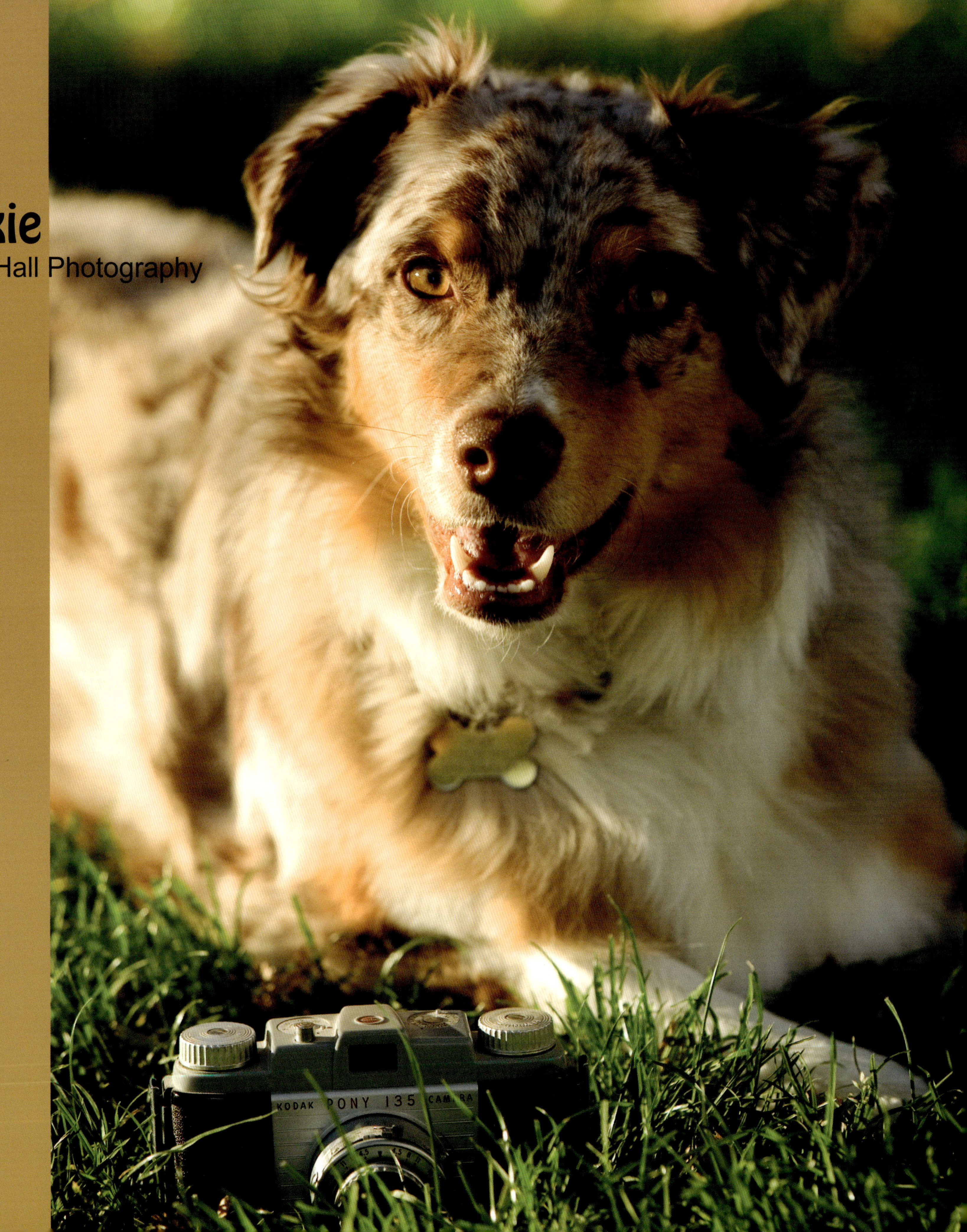

Introduction

I have always used photography as a way to show people the everyday things they don't see because they're busy looking at other things. That's what I loved most about working on this project. This collection of photos is all about introducing us to another winery denizen that visitors may not notice – the dog.

A mysterious phone call from Barb started the whole thing. She wanted to talk about "a photo project," but wouldn't go into detail over the phone. When we met, she grilled me with questions: Did I have allergies? Phobias? Had I ever been bitten by a dog? I must have said all the right things, because she invited me to be the photographer for this book.

I was nervous at first. I have photographed wind turbines while roped in high above the ground. I have photographed explosions for the U.S. Army. I have photographed Fortune 500 CEOs, software boxes for Microsoft, irrigation systems, and an author for Oprah Magazine. But I have never photographed dogs.

The next three weeks were crazy, racing from one winery to another, fueled by McDonald's and Starbucks. Not knowing what weather, light and scenery conditions would be at each location, I had to be prepared for anything. For some reason, sessions with the most high-contrast dogs – black or white – often were scheduled at noon, when the light is brightest and nuanced photography is most difficult.

Before every shoot I prowled the winery looking for the best place to set up the photo, and then spent some time tussling with each dog down at their level so they'd feel comfortable with me before I aimed a camera at them. It was a lot like photographing people, except my subjects were much less self-conscious. Barb had pockets full of doggie treats, squeaky toys, rope chews and tennis balls to make the "getting-to-know-you" process fun.

I kept clicking the shutter until I knew I had captured the one shot in which the dog was motionless and making eye contact with me for a nanosecond. Sometimes I snapped several hundred photos of one dog and sometimes I only needed a dozen to get the right pose.

All the photos were taken with a Canon D5 12-megapixel digital SLR, and cropped and color-corrected on a Mac. We took over 4000 raw images – 15 GB of data – which made editing and organizing a real challenge.

That said, Barb and I are very pleased with how these photos turned out and I hope you enjoy meeting the delightful dogs pictured in this book. They say that dogs mirror the emotions of the people they're around and if the many contented canines I met during this journey are any indication, the wineries of the Walla Walla Valley are happy places indeed.

Tim Hall

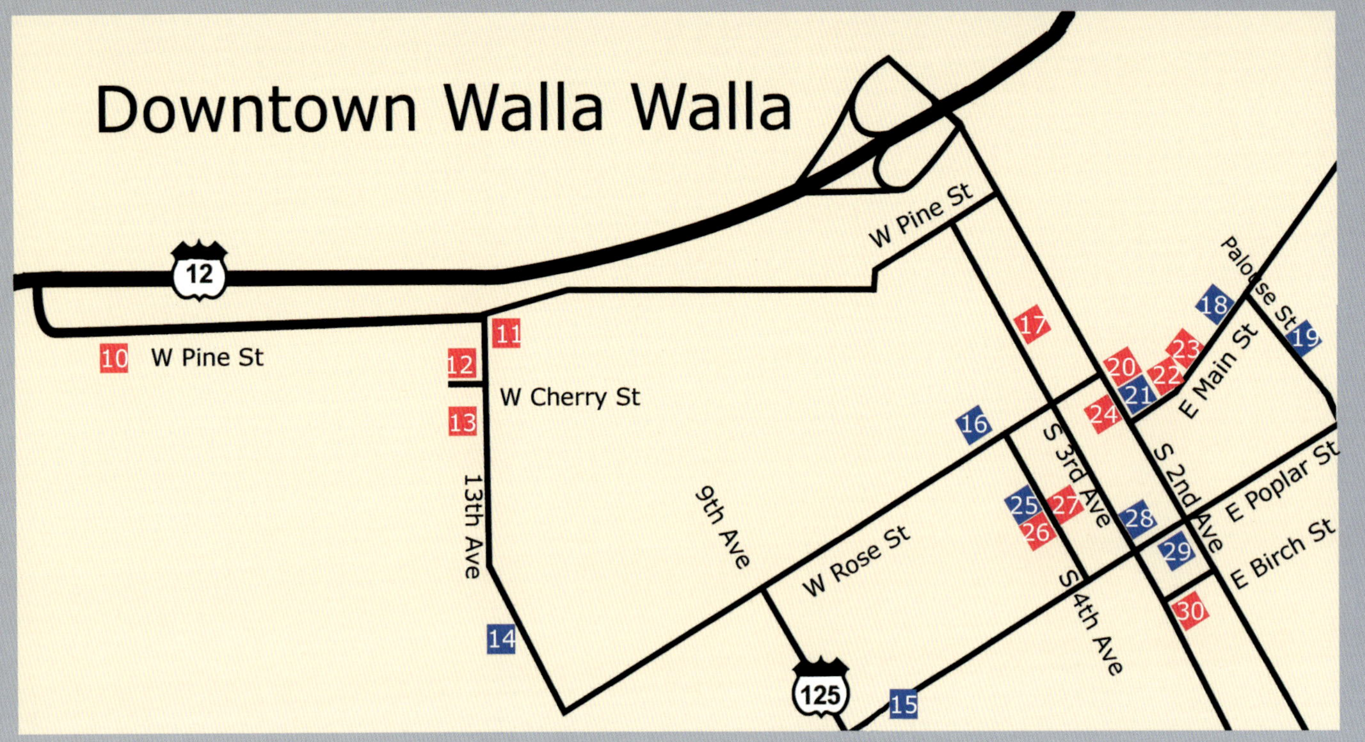

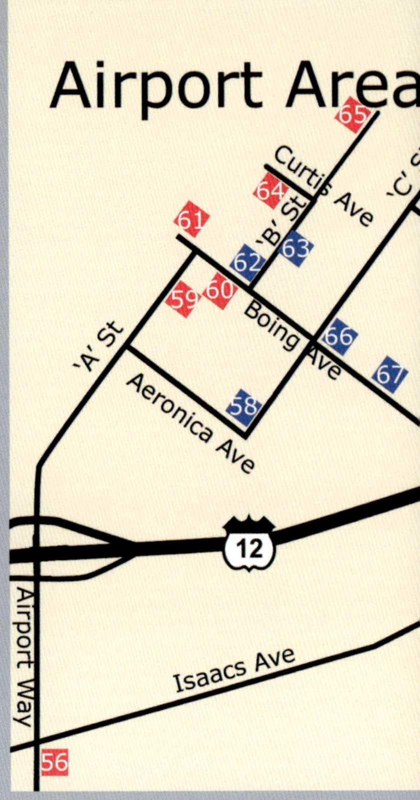

Lower Dry Creek Rd
3 4
Frenchtowne Rd
5
12
Lowden Rd
Barney Rd
Detour Rd
1 2
6
7
8
Last Chance Rd
Campbell Rd
9
Wallula Ave
E. Rose St
W. Poplar St
31
Main St
2nd Ave
9th Ave
3rd Ave
Damson St
College Ave
125
Taumarson
Plaza Wy
Old Milton Hwy
46
45
44
43
Pranger
Braden Rd
32
Old Milton Hwy
Peppers Bridge Rd
40
34 35 36
41
Lyday Ln
37 38 39
42
Washington
Stateline Rd
Oregon
33
49 50 51 52

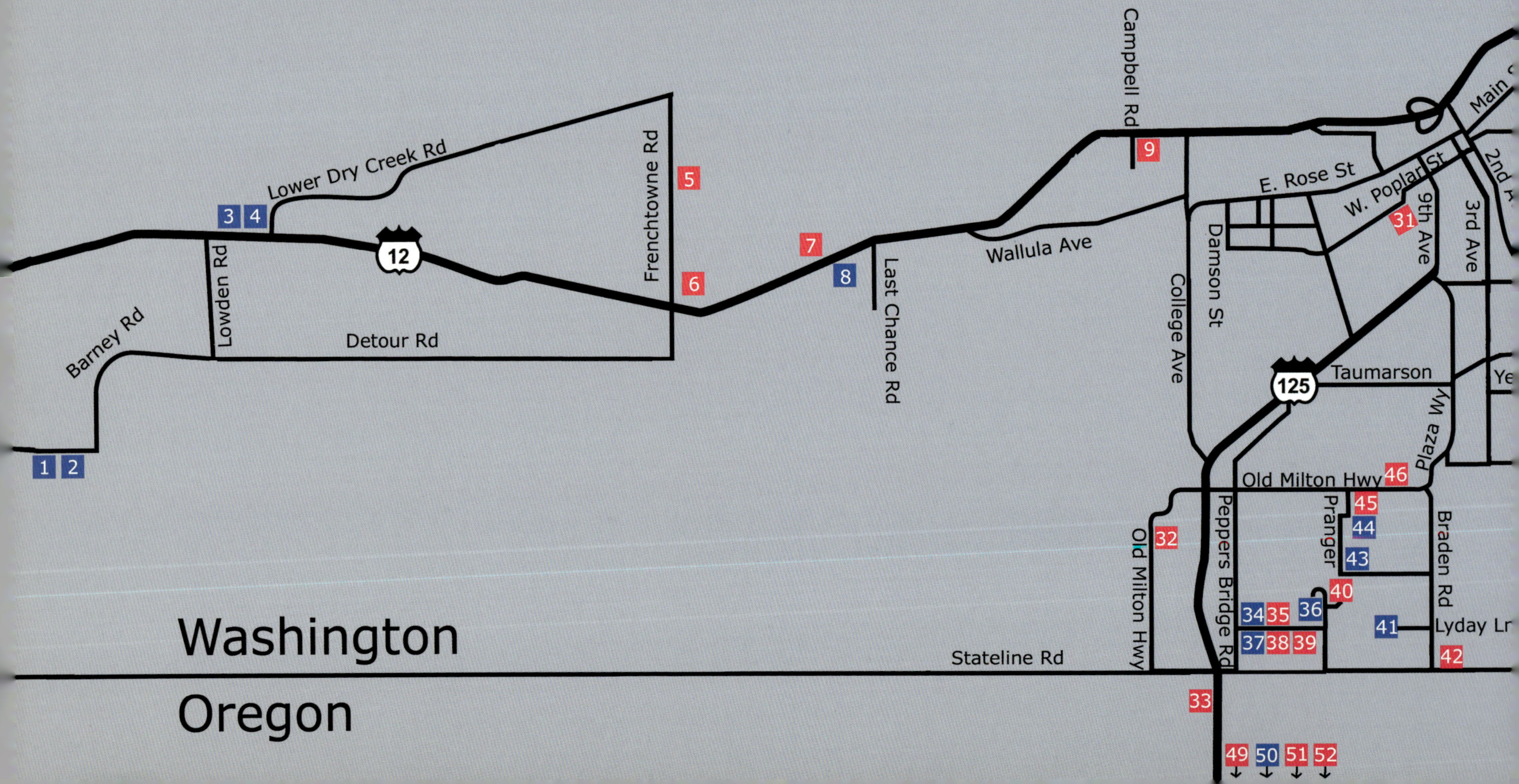

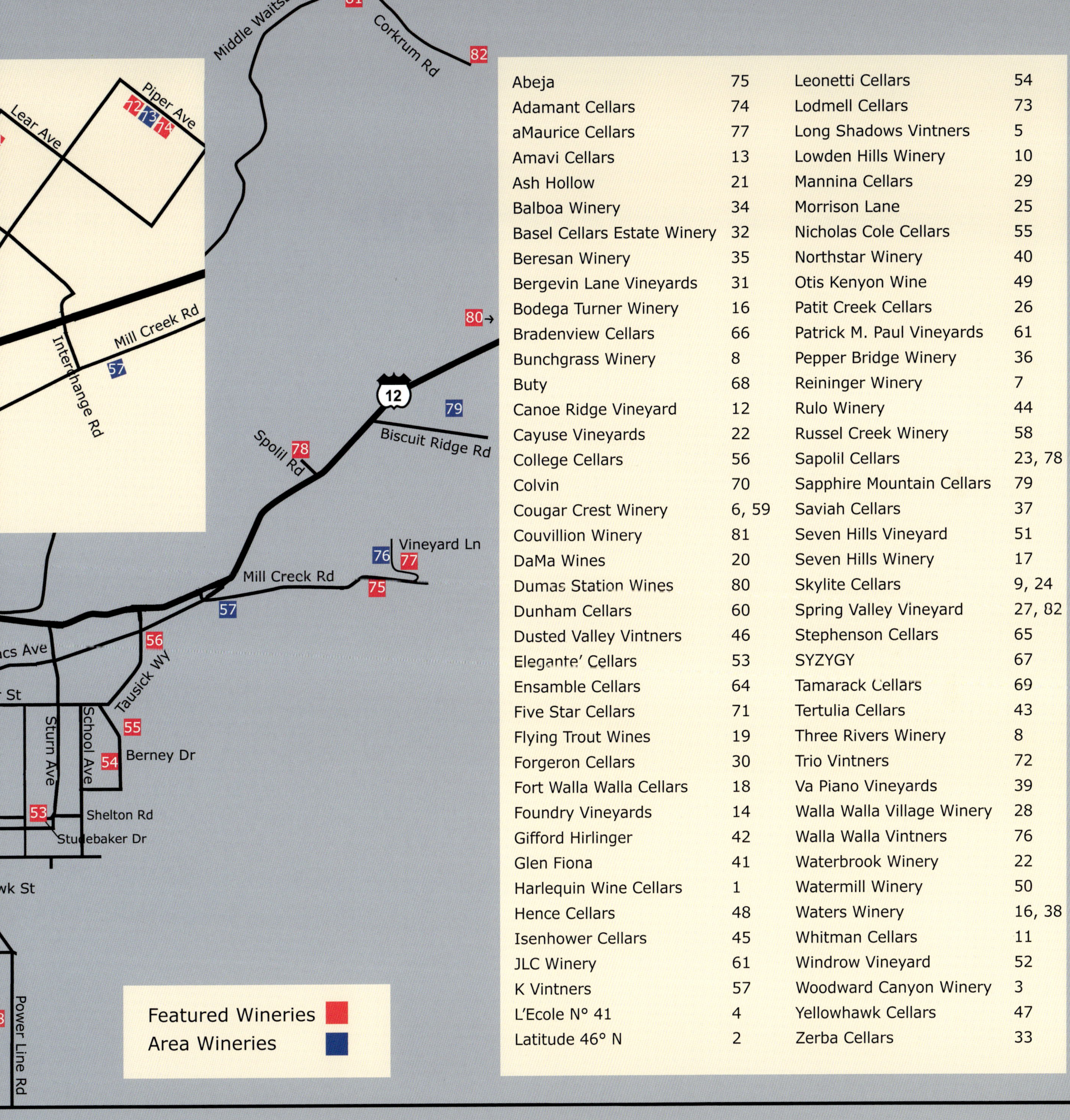

Winery	No.
Abeja	75
Adamant Cellars	74
aMaurice Cellars	77
Amavi Cellars	13
Ash Hollow	21
Balboa Winery	34
Basel Cellars Estate Winery	32
Beresan Winery	35
Bergevin Lane Vineyards	31
Bodega Turner Winery	16
Bradenview Cellars	66
Bunchgrass Winery	8
Buty	68
Canoe Ridge Vineyard	12
Cayuse Vineyards	22
College Cellars	56
Colvin	70
Cougar Crest Winery	6, 59
Couvillion Winery	81
DaMa Wines	20
Dumas Station Wines	80
Dunham Cellars	60
Dusted Valley Vintners	46
Elegante' Cellars	53
Ensamble Cellars	64
Five Star Cellars	71
Flying Trout Wines	19
Forgeron Cellars	30
Fort Walla Walla Cellars	18
Foundry Vineyards	14
Gifford Hirlinger	42
Glen Fiona	41
Harlequin Wine Cellars	1
Hence Cellars	48
Isenhower Cellars	45
JLC Winery	61
K Vintners	57
L'Ecole N° 41	4
Latitude 46° N	2
Leonetti Cellars	54
Lodmell Cellars	73
Long Shadows Vintners	5
Lowden Hills Winery	10
Mannina Cellars	29
Morrison Lane	25
Nicholas Cole Cellars	55
Northstar Winery	40
Otis Kenyon Wine	49
Patit Creek Cellars	26
Patrick M. Paul Vineyards	61
Pepper Bridge Winery	36
Reininger Winery	7
Rulo Winery	44
Russel Creek Winery	58
Sapolil Cellars	23, 78
Sapphire Mountain Cellars	79
Saviah Cellars	37
Seven Hills Vineyard	51
Seven Hills Winery	17
Skylite Cellars	9, 24
Spring Valley Vineyard	27, 82
Stephenson Cellars	65
SYZYGY	67
Tamarack Cellars	69
Tertulia Cellars	43
Three Rivers Winery	8
Trio Vintners	72
Va Piano Vineyards	39
Walla Walla Village Winery	28
Walla Walla Vintners	76
Waterbrook Winery	22
Watermill Winery	50
Waters Winery	16, 38
Whitman Cellars	11
Windrow Vineyard	52
Woodward Canyon Winery	3
Yellowhawk Cellars	47
Zerba Cellars	33

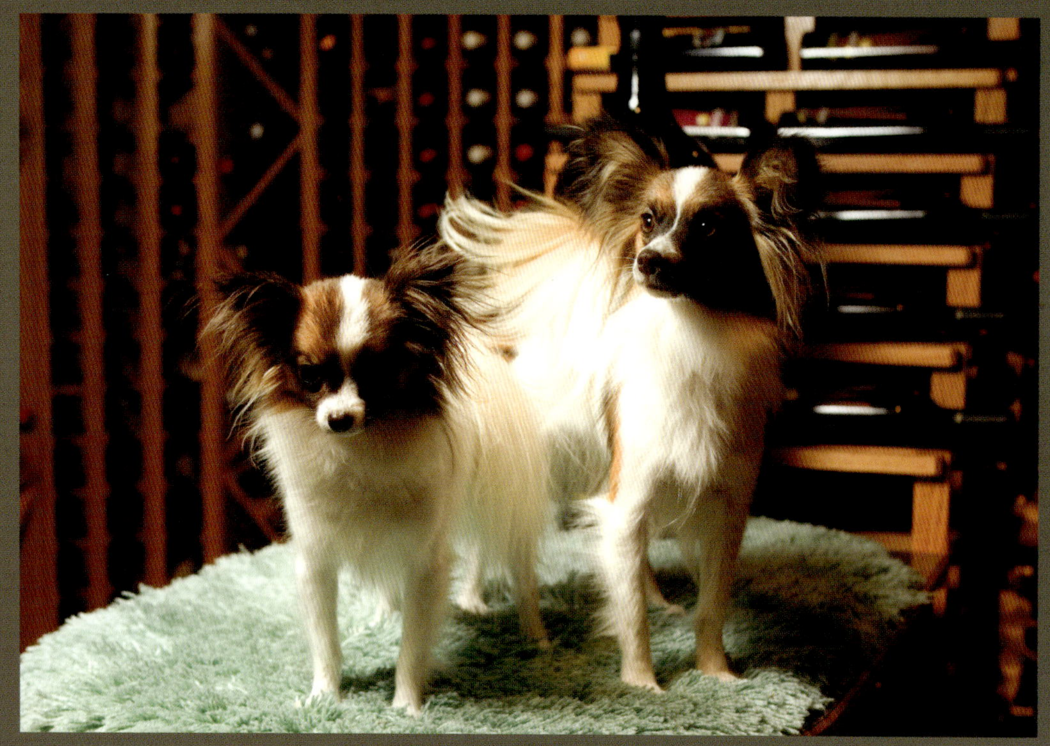

Lovi, Paris, Bailey

Whitman Cellars

We are Paris (yes, named after that one) and Luvi Darlin - a pair from the Papillon family that we fell in love with when we were first introduced to the breed by a wine club member from Tri-Cities.

Paris is the oldest, but the smallest weighing in at three pounds. She was born in Texas and flown to Walla Walla in February, 2006. Paris is smooth, refined, classy - a Merlot dog all the way.

Luvi is four months younger, but weighs in at five pounds. She hails from South Carolina and also made the flight to Walla Walla. Her favorite pastime is hunting gophers and sitting on your lap. She is full bodied, long on finish and stands up to anything spicy - a Cabernet dog all the way.

Larry and Sally Thomason

Bailey was born on July 15, 2004 in Vancouver, Washington, as one of a 10 puppy litter. Her parents, Goldi and Skip, are my nephew's dogs so she was already "one of the family" so to speak. We went that day to meet them and visited every week until Bailey was ready to come home with us.

We chose Bailey because she was the smallest female, lightest in color and her "first one out the gate" personality. For being the runt, she ended up an 80-pound girl.

Bailey loves people, tennis balls, chewies and playing with her sister Kona. Walks and going "bye bye" in the car are among her favorites. She likes being next to "her people" at all times, is a snuggler and bed hog. When she visits the winery, Bailey is great with guests.

Tonya Woodley

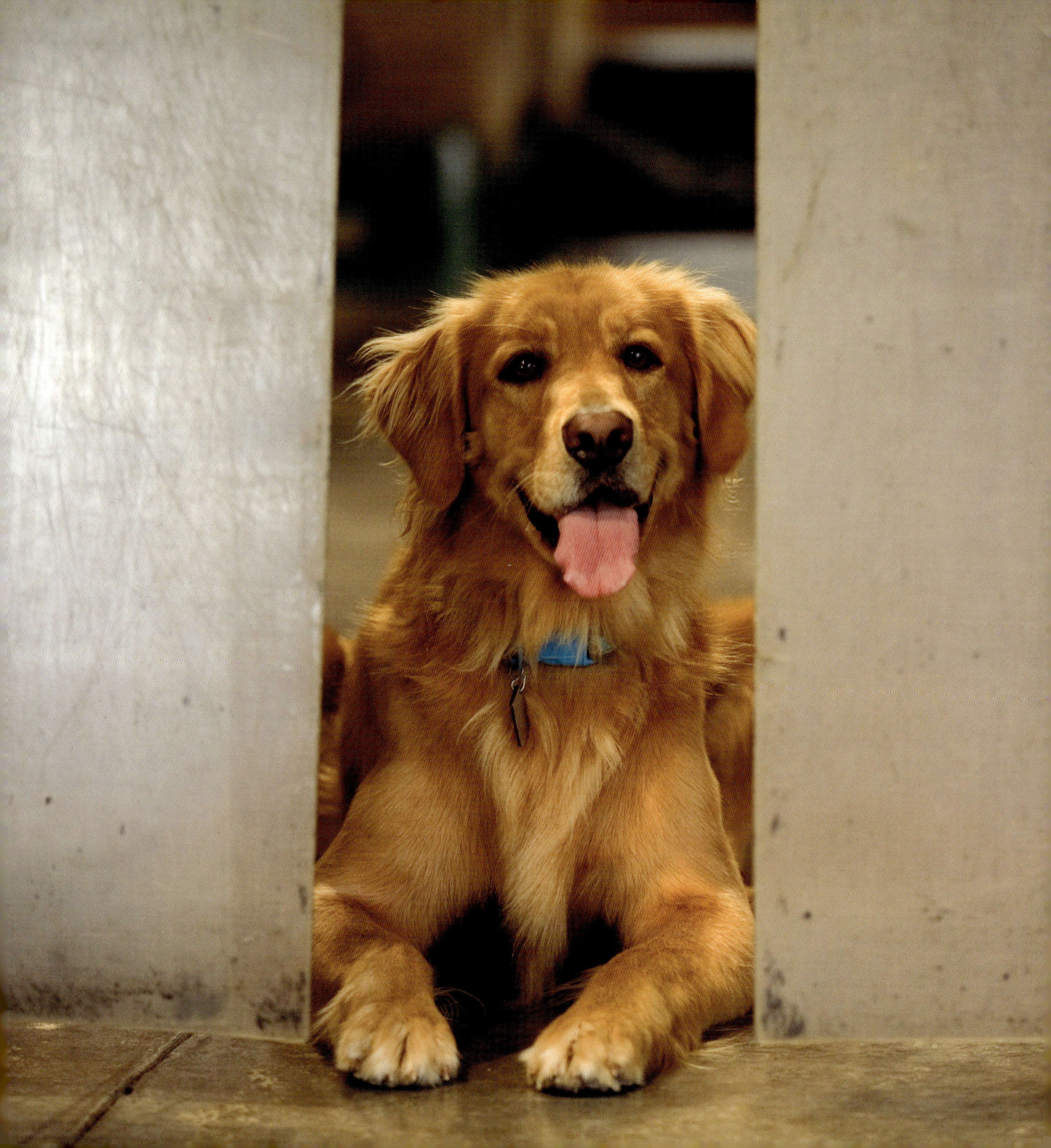

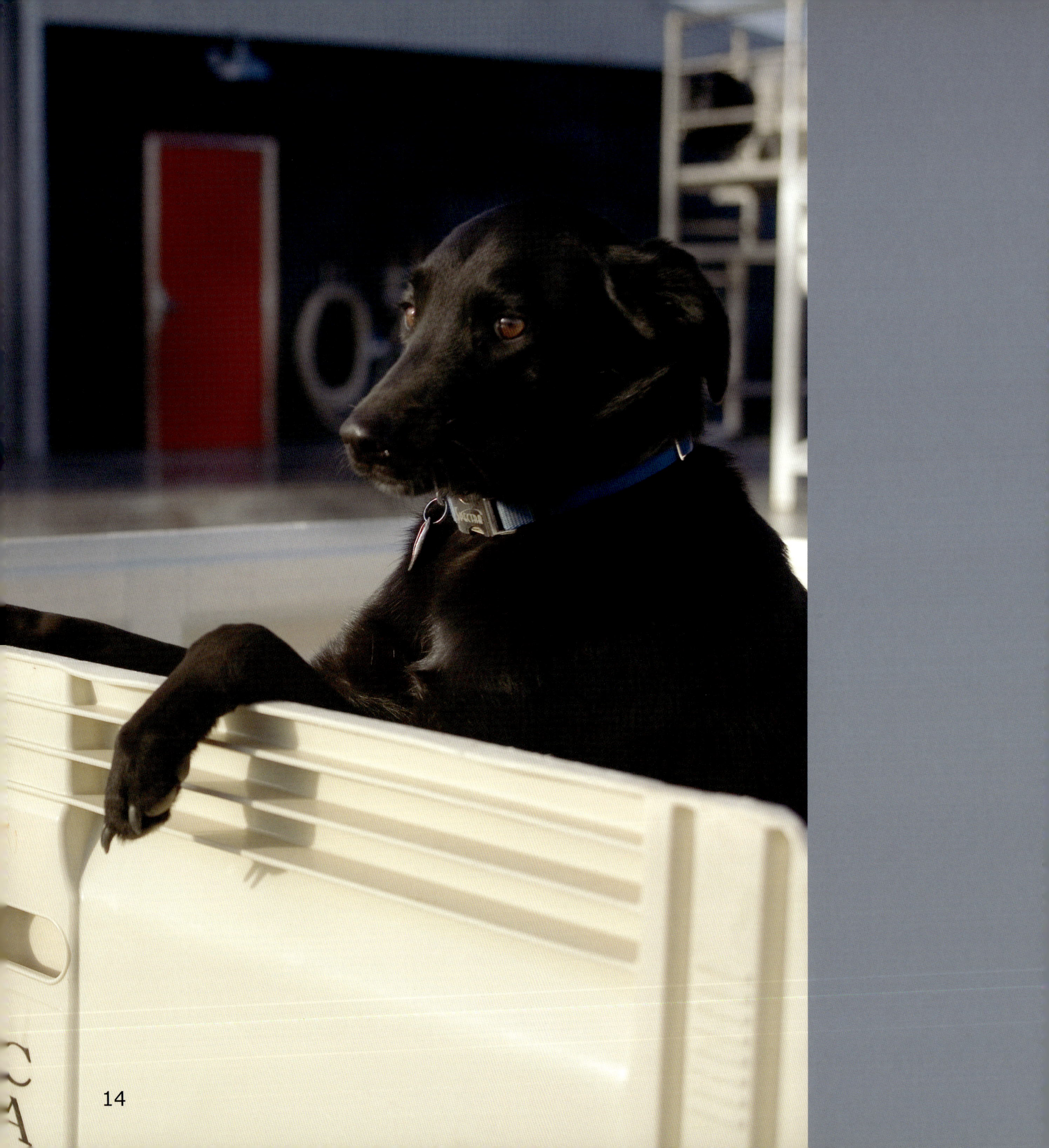

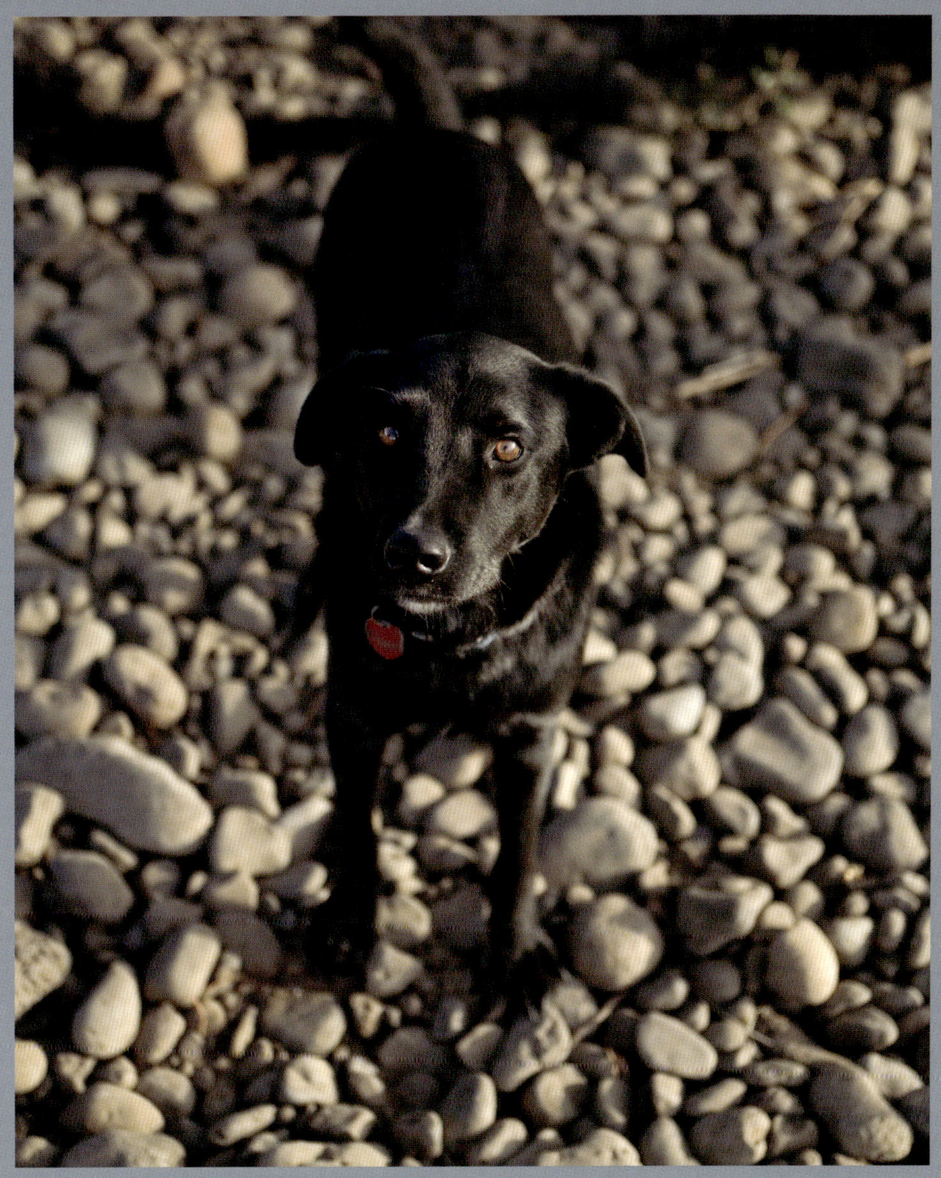

Arnie

Cayuse Vineyards

Ever since his humble beginning as a Blue Mountain Humane Society adoptee, Arnold Kennedy has won over the hearts of man and beast alike. The humans who know and love Arnie (and there are many) find that his gentle spirit exudes from his thoughtful eyes & vigorously wagging tail. He is dubbed, Petit Monsieur, for his human-like qualities which include: dancing, cuddling, deep tissue massage, sleeping in, hygiene, and fine dining. Possessing pure joy of life, Arnie can be found playing with dogs, cats, gophers, chipmunks, and a variety of birds. A cheerful part of the Cayuse Vineyards team, Arnie is happiest strolling among the vines with his loving owners.

Christophe and Jenna

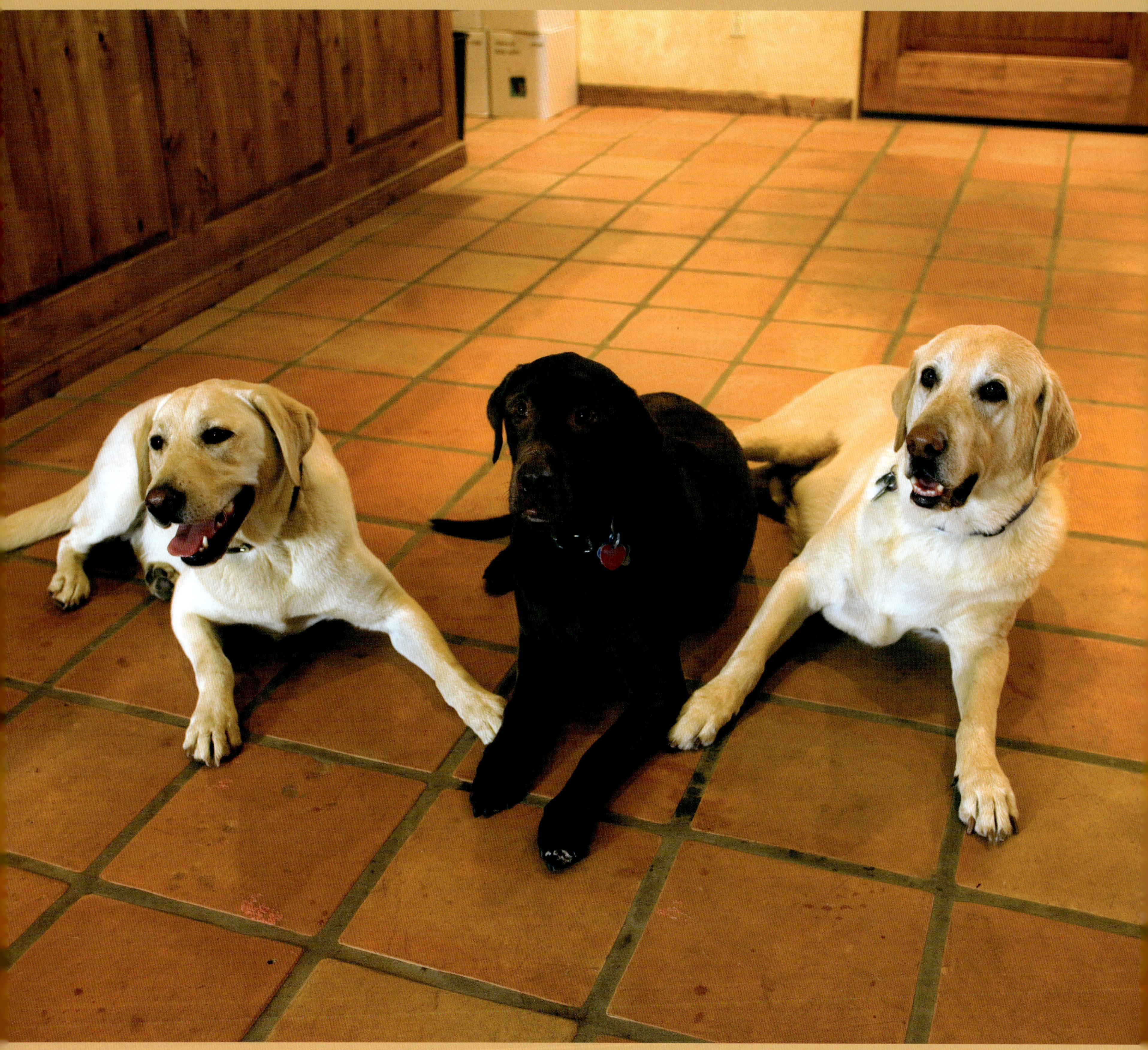

Rigs, Rex, Bruno

Va Piano Vineyards

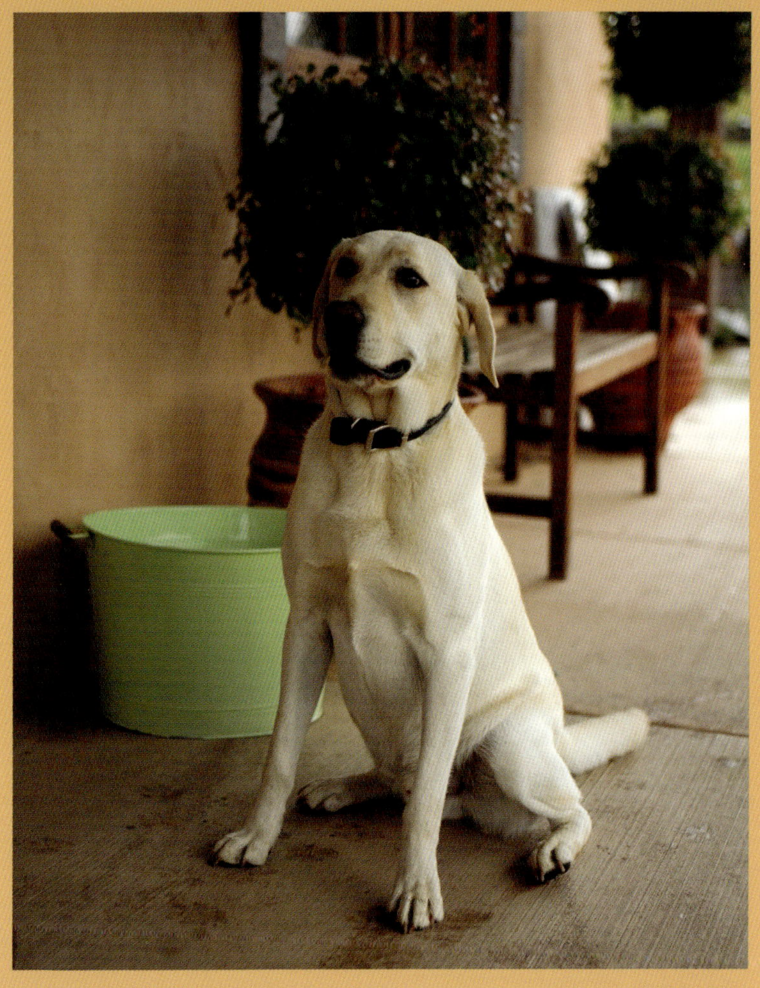

Rigley is a happy, joyful and sometimes mischievous 4 year old yellow Lab. Much like the winemakers at Va Piano, Rigley likes to sample grapes and make guests feel welcome. He is likely to share kisses while you are in the tasting room. His hobbies include a mean game of fetch, swimming, and chasing the four-wheeler through the vineyard.

Ryan Crane

Bruno, our 8-year-old Yellow Lab, is a big dog from a big family. At birth, he was the largest of a large litter - 14 puppies. We named him after Fr. Bruno Segatta, Justin's friend when he studied in Florence, Italy.

Our two children have grown up with Bruno. Many times they've tried to ride him like a horse, an activity his gentleness allowed. He even gets along with our winery cat, Shadow and we've found them napping together on the dog bed.

Bruno is a loving lab who lives to fetch, go on walks and greet with a happy wag of his tail every person who visits the winery.

Rex, owned by Justin's parents, Rick & Patty Wylie, is a Lab of another color. Chocolate.

A frequent Va Piano visitor, Rex loves to chase pheasants in the vineyard and occasionally sneaks off for a swim in the irrigation pond.

Rex and Bruno play together like best friends will, even carrying one stick together when they play fetch.

Liz and Justin Wylie

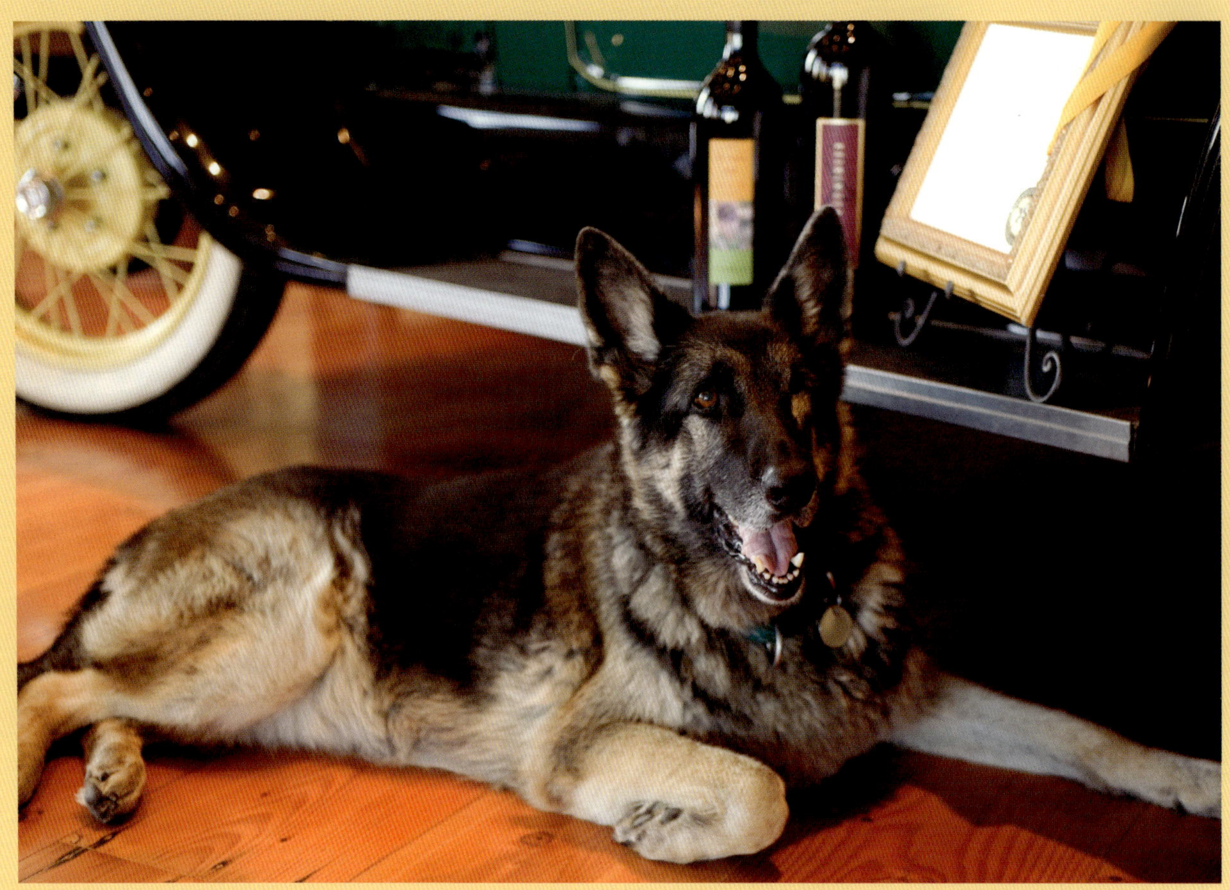

Nika

Reininger Winery

Nika is a 9-year-old German Shepherd, half American and half European. She weighs 110 pounds, is black and brown spotted.

After long walks, Nika enjoys sneaking away to the nearby creek and plunging in, no matter how hot or cold. When it snows, she begs you to chuck snowballs at her so she can catch them and eat them up. Whenever people walk by our house, Nika always lunges at them, but only to greet them and lick them. She is always loud and obnoxious, but always friendly. She especially likes when other dogs and cats walk by so she can bark at them.. Every once in awhile Nika loves to tag along with Jay and terrorize people at the winery.

Because of numerous health problems like cancer, she is missing an eye and she is very spastic due to epilepsy, but Nika is easily loved.

Jay Tucker, Written By My Daughter, Katherine Tucker

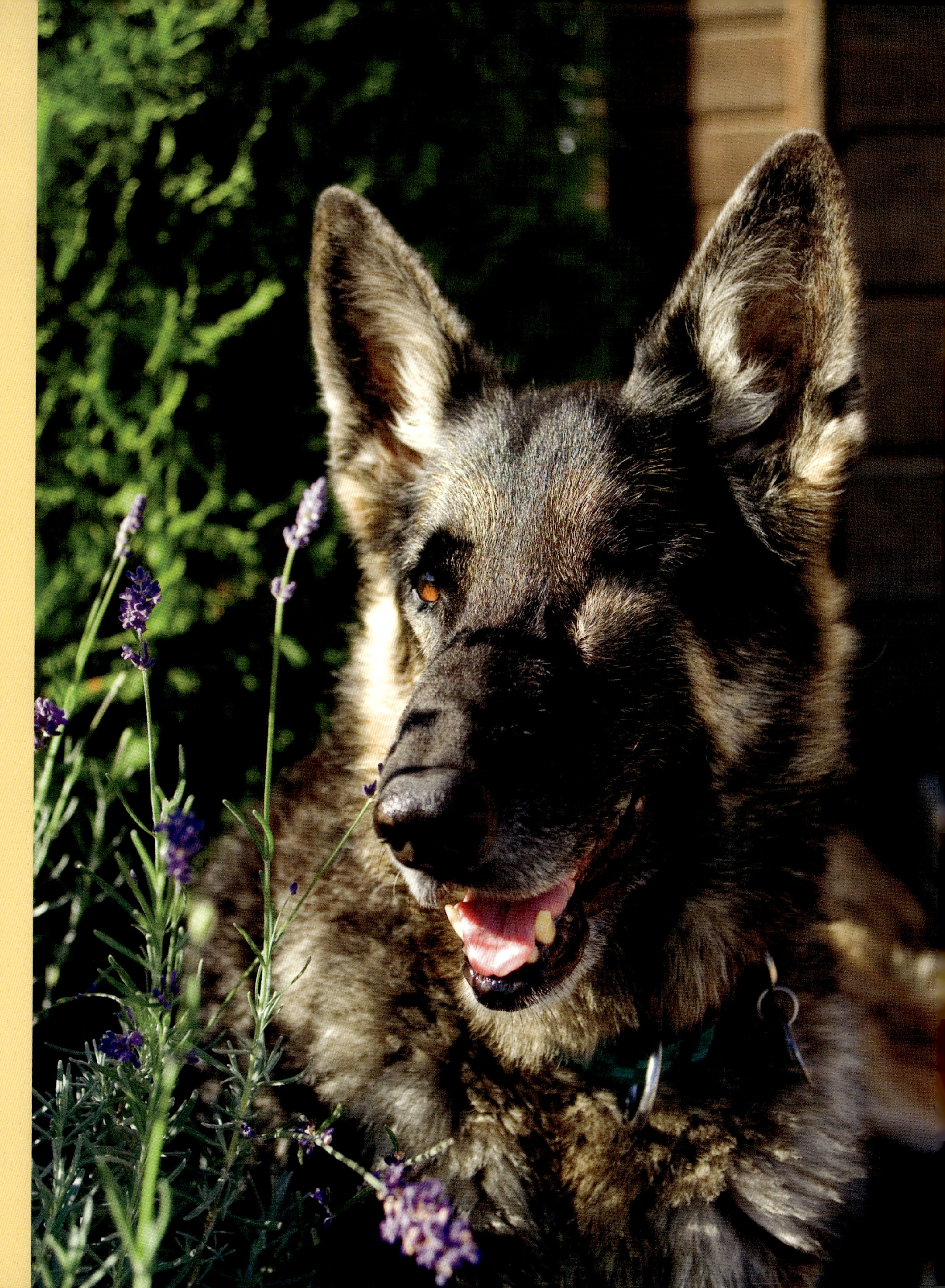

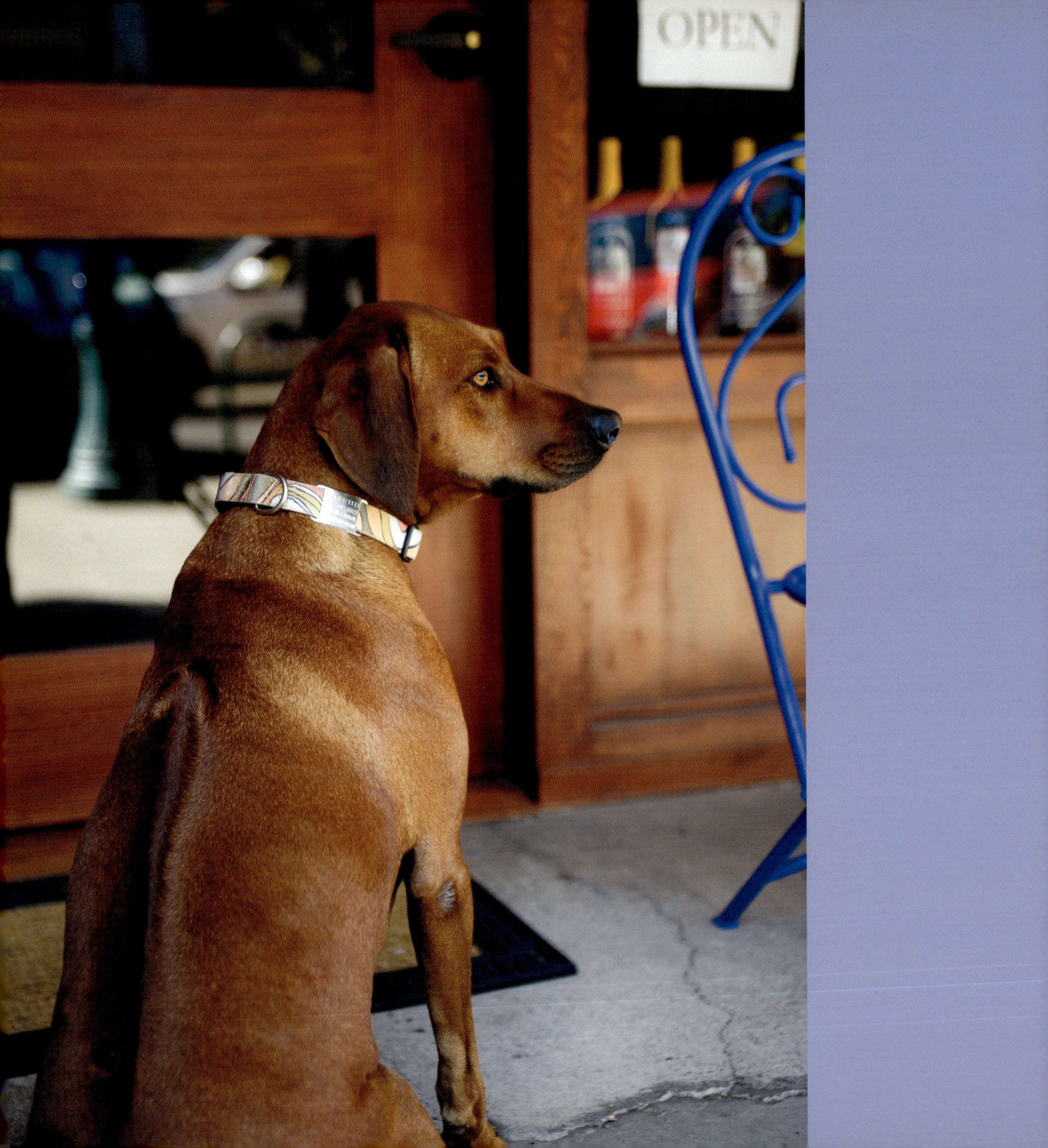
OPEN

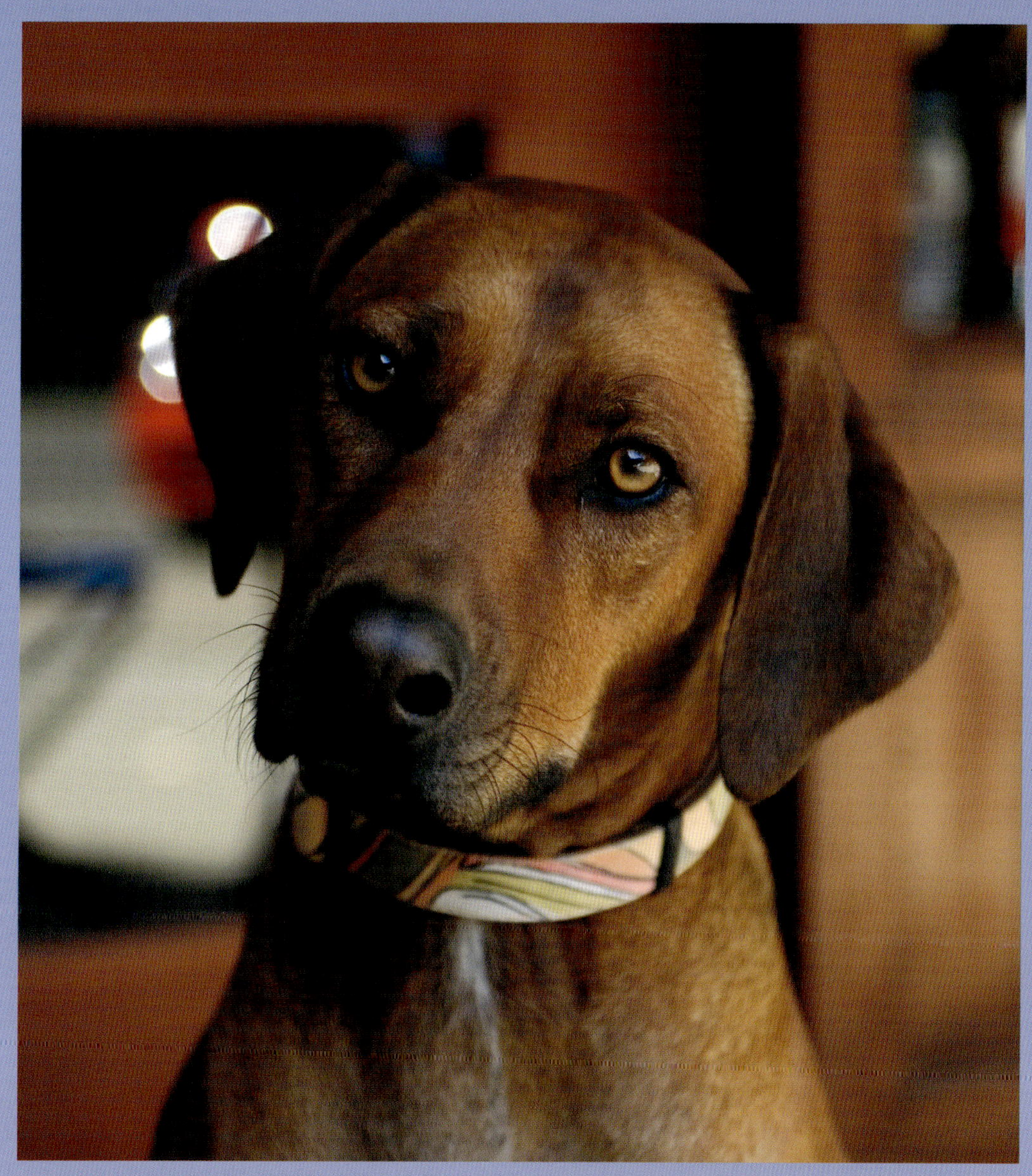

Nefertiti

Sapolil Cellars

Sapolil Cellars' first release in 2003 was a Syrah, primarily sold in Southern California. This is where Nefertiti was born and raised. Her first job with the winery, you might say, was in outside sales.

Now in Walla Walla a great deal of the time, Nefertiti primarily splits her time between the winery and the tasting room. In season she also takes on the task of a soon-to-be-patented process of 'scavage and sprint' in the vineyards – basically scavaging whole bundles of fruit on the vineyard grounds then sprinting to find a private place for consumption of the grapes. All in all, very busy and integral indeed.

Abigail Schwerin

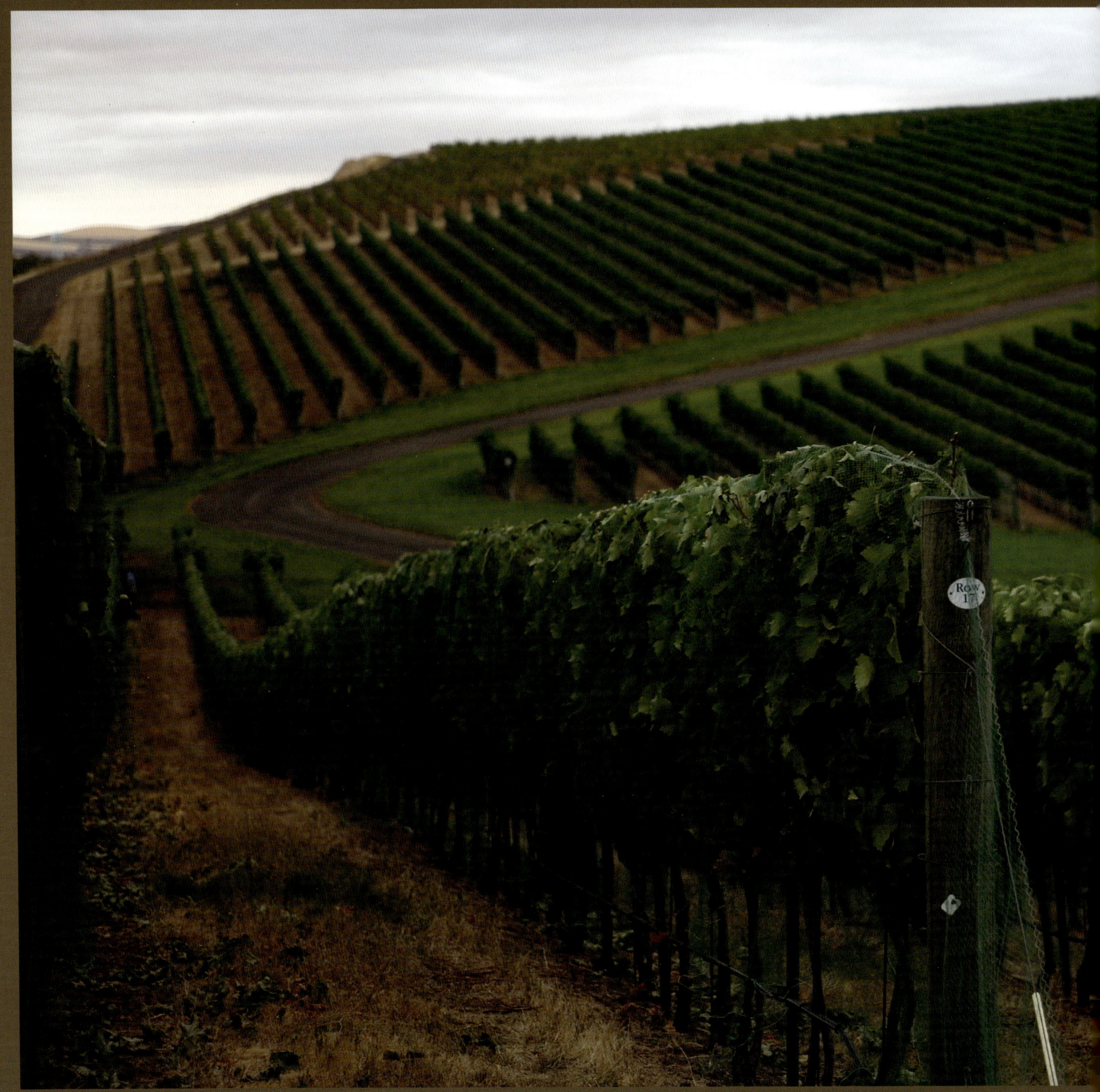
Row
17

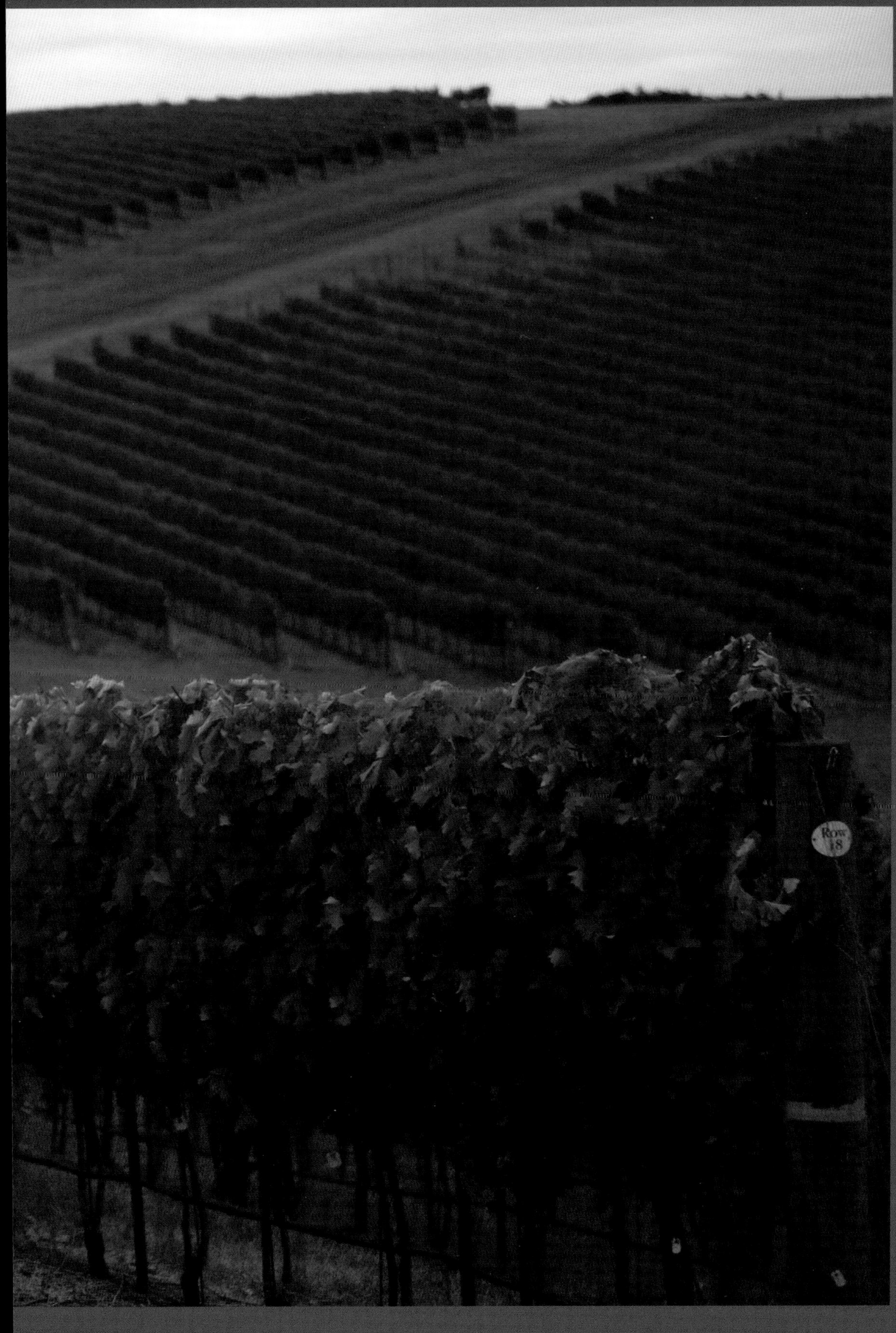

Nicholas Cole Estate Vineyard

Shadow and Bella

Walla Walla Vintners

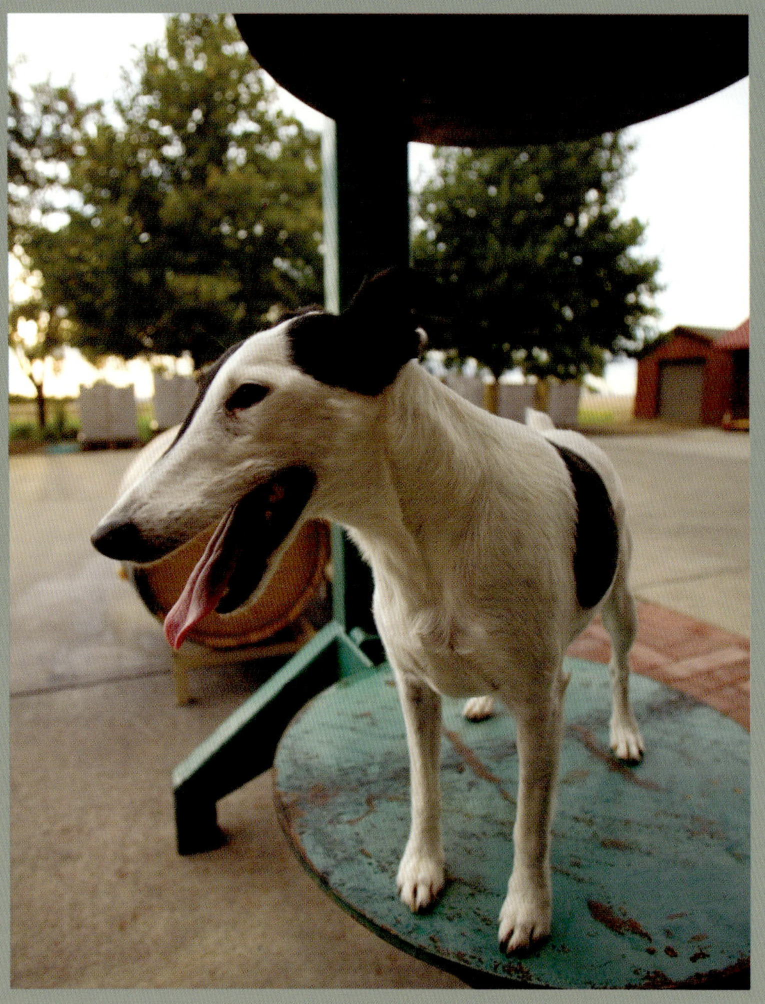

Shadow is a 7-year-old smooth Fox Terrier with two speeds – "on" and "off". Her favorite "on" activity is to fetch and fetch and fetch and fetch and fetch. Shadow's favorite "off" activity is to snuggle when you are lying in bed or reading a book.

When Shadow visits her Walla Walla Vintners space, the first thing she does is run upstairs to find Gordy Venneri and Myles Anderson, owners and winemakers. Gordy calls her "shadow dancer" or "crazy pooch."

She loves to visit the tasting room and greet the guests. Even the most serious of wine tasters are known to raise their voices a few octaves and reward her with an "Oh my! What a cute little dog."

So when you're wine tasting at Walla Walla Vintners and see a little black and white dog wagging her tail, it's Shadow and she is waiting for you to throw something so she can fetch.

Tom and Barbara Commare

Von Stocker's Isabella aka Bella came to us with more than little fame. She is the daughter of Von Stocker's The Jig Is Up, winner of the Best of Breed award at the 2007 Westminster Dog Show in New York City and winner of the Doggy Poster Contest for the Walla Walla Little Theatre's production of Silvia.

Because the Standard Schnauzer is considered a working dog, Bella displays boundless energy and considers it her job to take Kate for a walk, go jogging with Gordy and greet all the workers and visitors at the winery at every possible opportunity.

Even if she weren't so "famous," Bella is more than successful as our affectionate, stubborn, playful and athletic companion.

Gordy and Kate Venneri

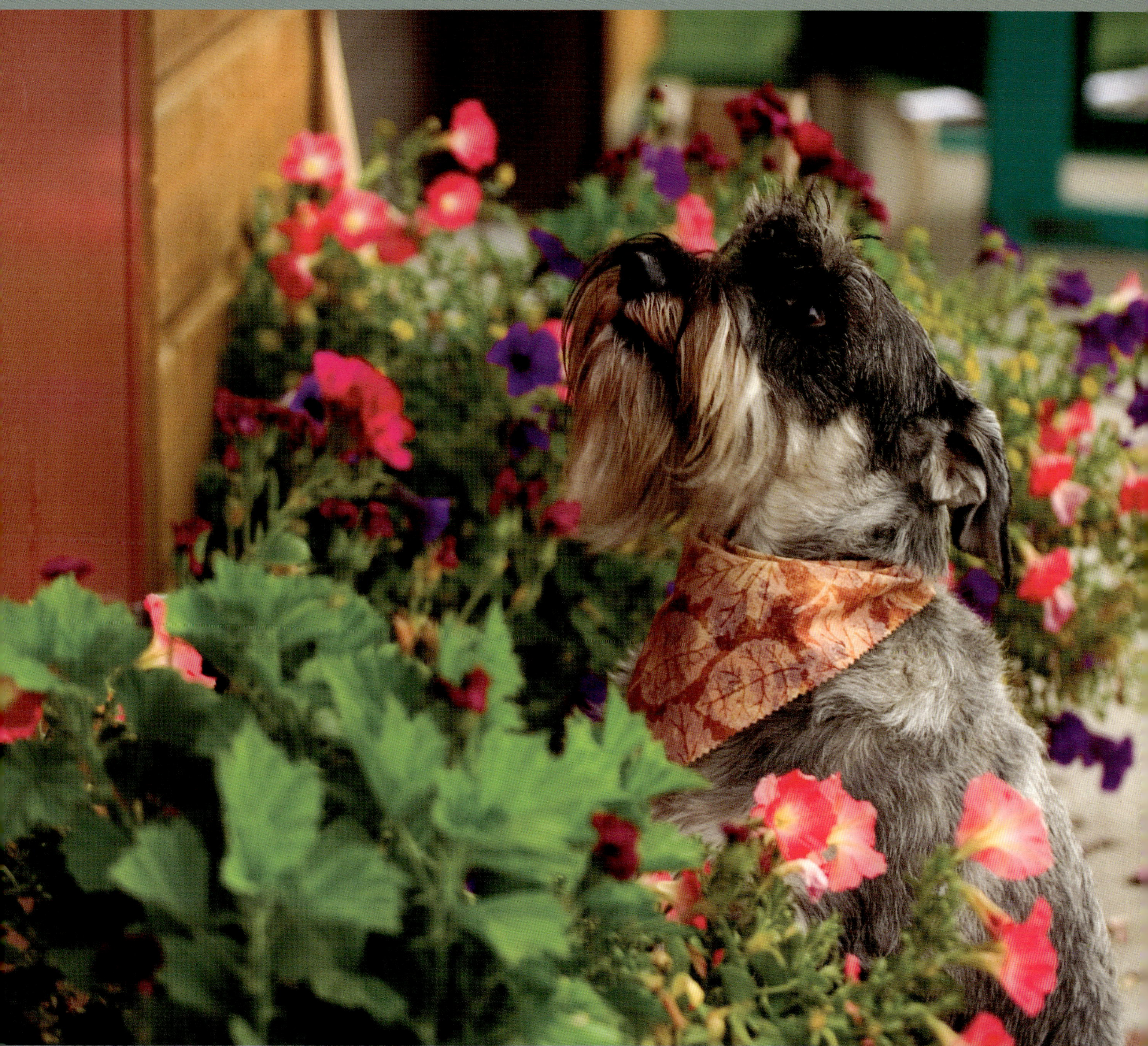

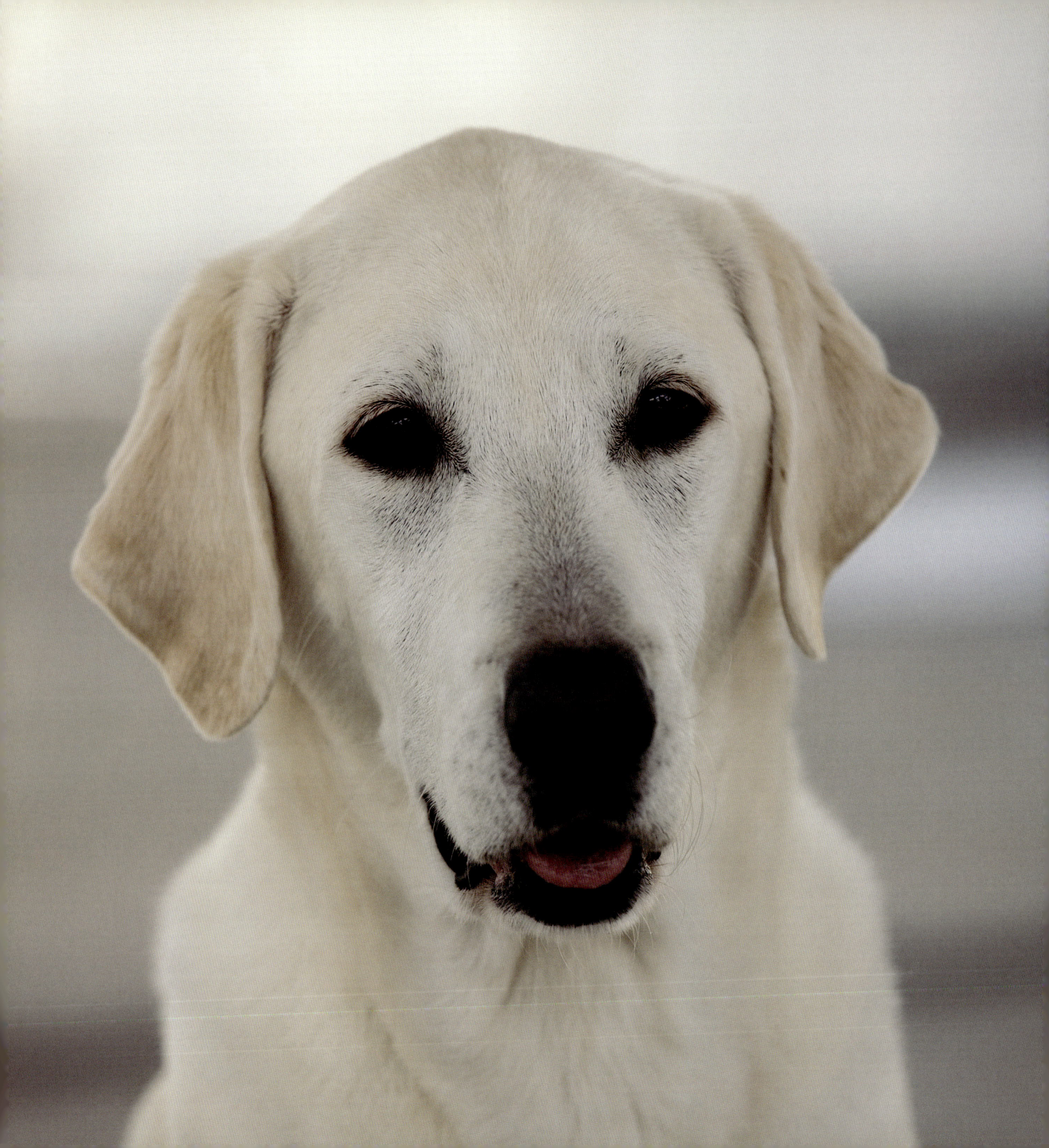

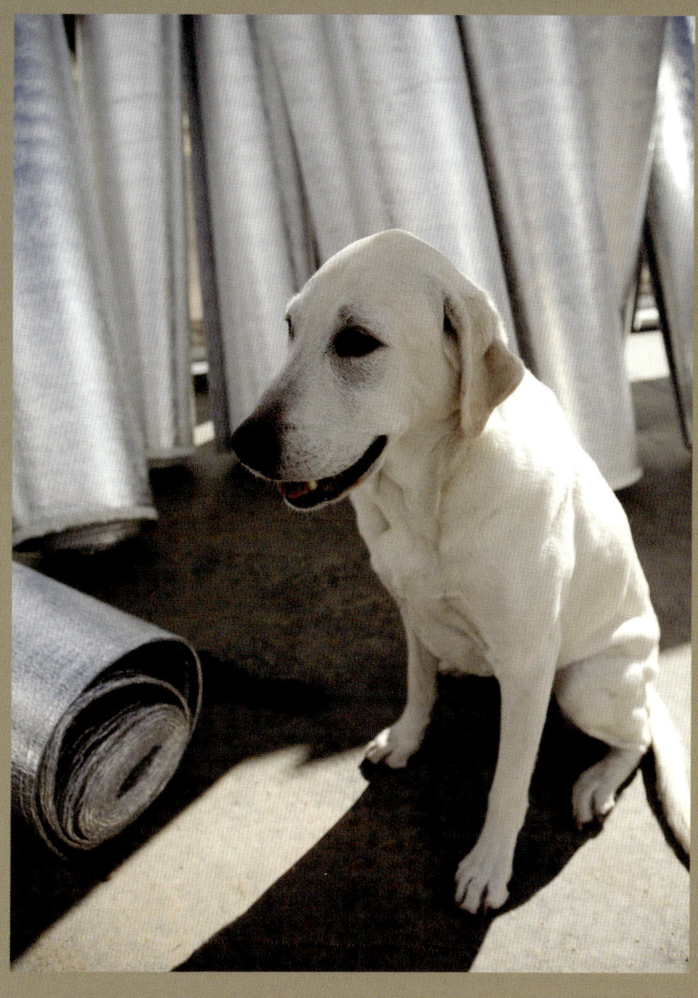

Roux

Patit Creek Cellars

When I first saw her, it was love at first site. At eight-weeks old she was this puffy ball of golden-blonde fuzzy fur – the exact color of a French roux which every cook knows is the foundation for all those yummy sauces you enjoy in delicious French cuisine. As the daughter of a Frenchman, I felt that name was perfect for her based on her color and appearance.

While Roux loves swimming, duck hunting, hiking and all the great outdoors, at the winery she is happy being part of the scene, whether it's during the chaos of crush or racking and topping barrels. She is very affectionate and welcomes every visitor as a long lost friend!

At the end of the day when we pause to enjoy a glass of "the fruit of our labor," Roux lays gently by our feet as if to endorse the fact we've had a wonderfully productive time together. She truly is the best four-legged companion and the consummate winery dog!

Karen La Bonte and Edward Dudley

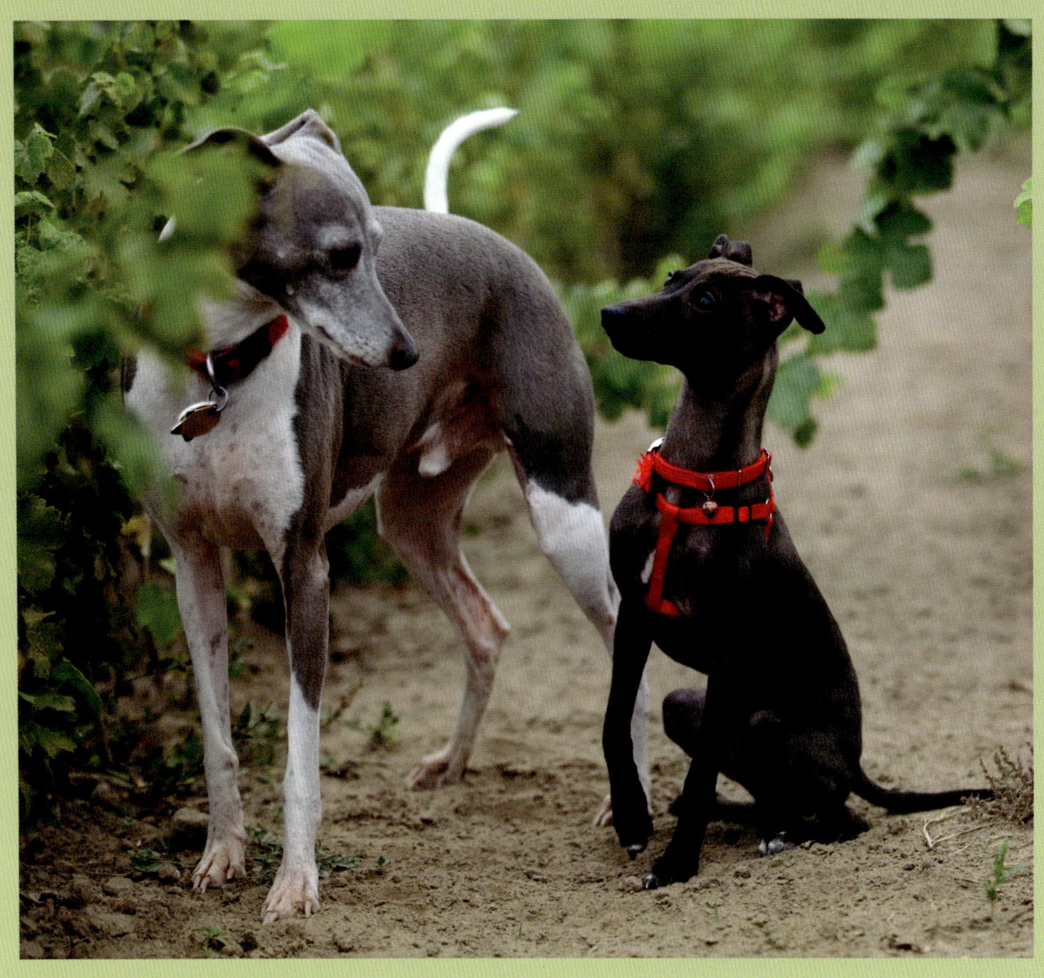

Merlin, Hono, Lulu

Lowden Hills Winery

Merlin, a 7-year-old Italian Greyhound, was a first year wedding anniversary gift to ourselves.

Since we married in Honolulu we were going to name him Hono and later get a second dog and name her Lulu. But we got very busy and figured that we would never have two dogs. So we named our pup "Merlin." After all, everybody needs a little magic in their lives.

The next year I saw an advertisement for Yorkshire Terrier puppies for sale and they just happened to be born on my birthday. We went just to look and came home with our "Lulu' girl.

This year we added a rescue Italian Greyhound puppy to the mix and named him "Hono". He is a charmer and never fails to make us laugh and take time to play.

Both Merlin & Lulu have their own Lowden Hills Winery label: Merlin Winemaker's Reserve 2003, and Lulu Red 2004 which is soon to be released.

Sonja and Jim Henderson

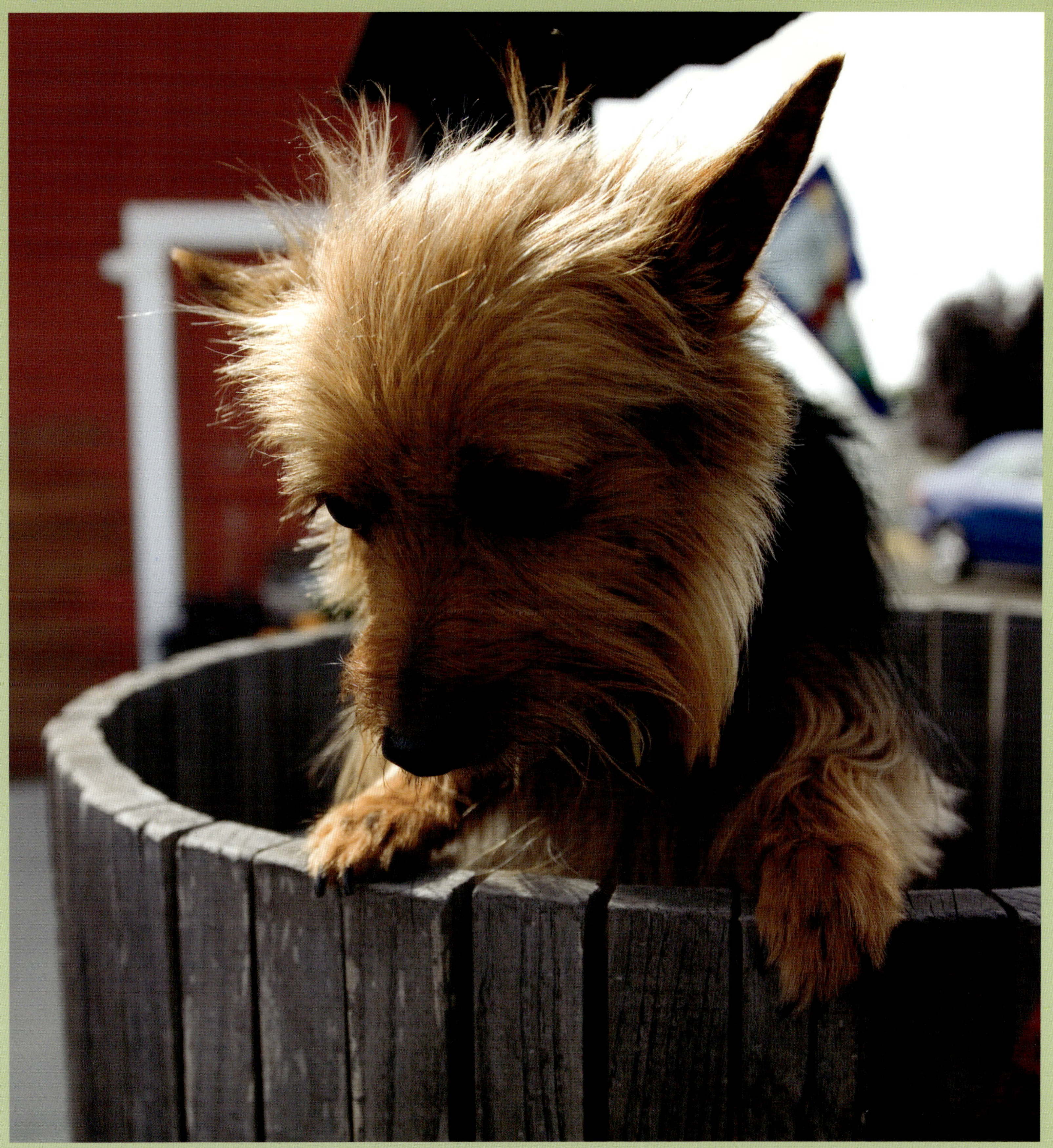

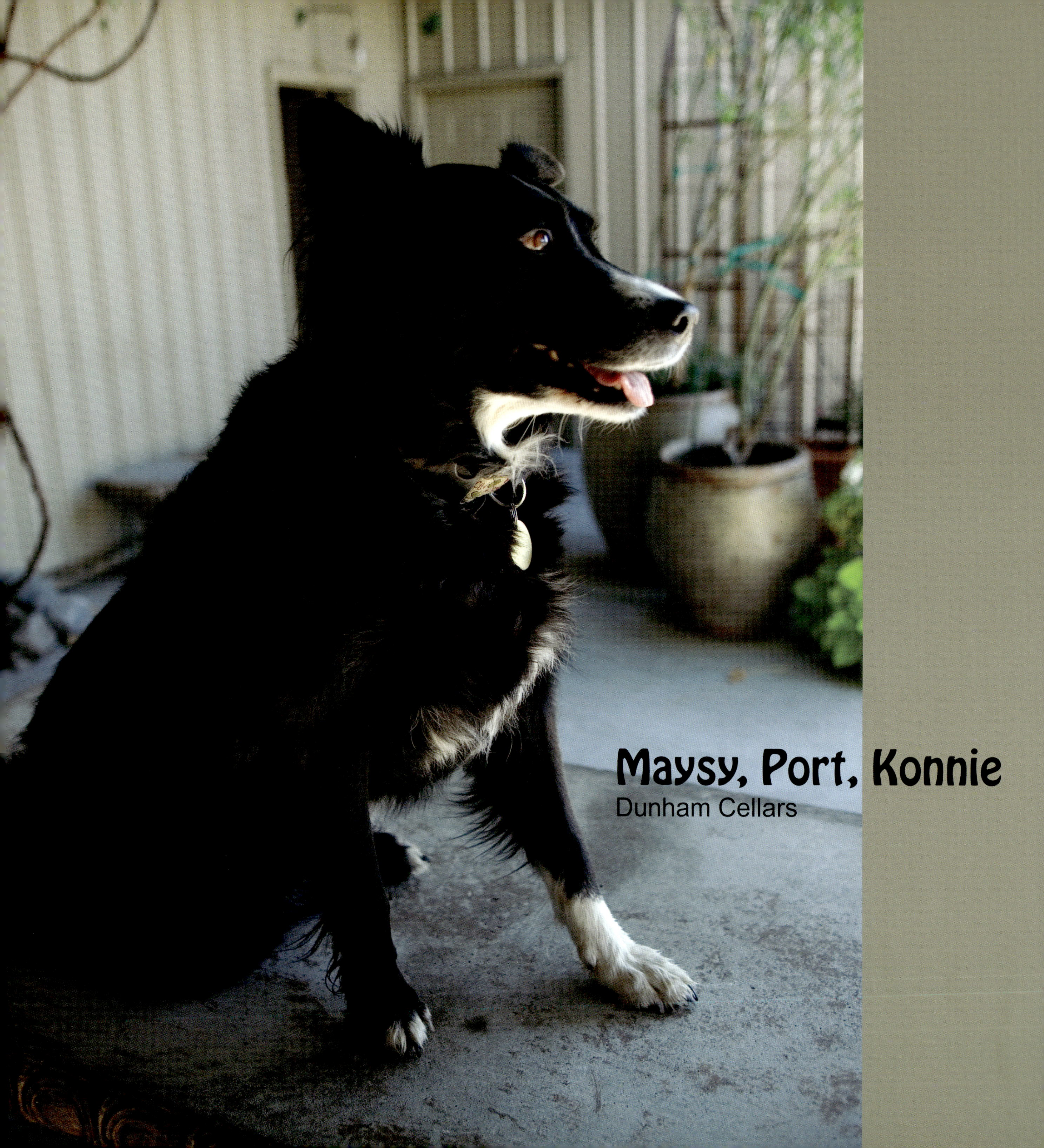

Maysy, Port, Konnie

Dunham Cellars

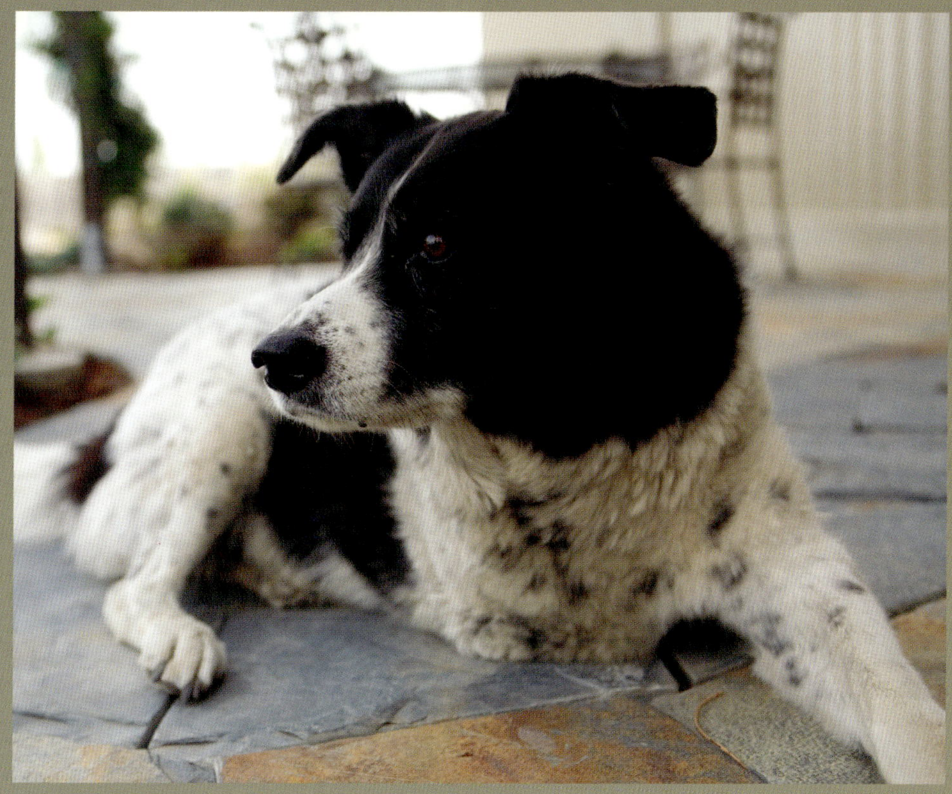

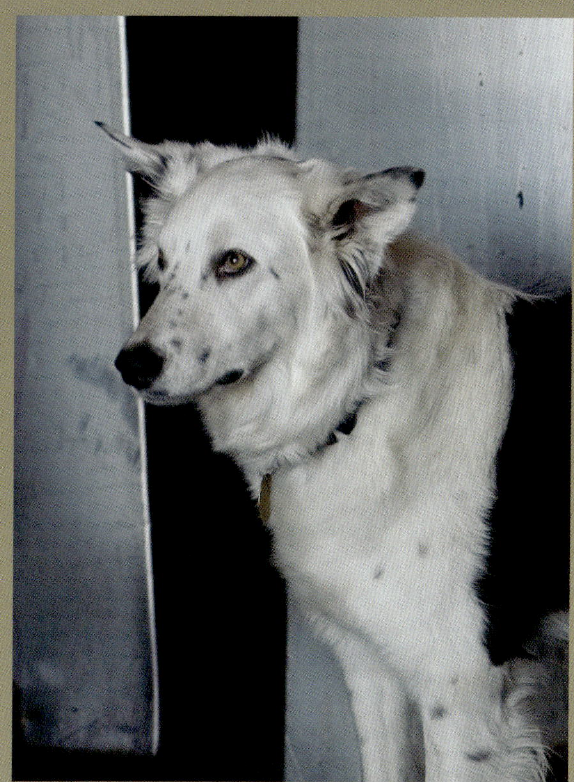

Dunham Cellars is home to a trio of Border Collies.
Port is the most famous. Rescued from a dog fight by Eric when he was a puppy, Port came away from the battle with just three legs. He was the first to have a vintage named in his honor – the 2002 Three Legged Red. Port has refined begging for treats into a fine art. Visitors are good about the "no treats rule" until Port perches on his back legs, lets his one front leg kind of dangle, and wiggles his stump. People melt!
In 1999, Konnie, a Border Collie mix, just turned up. Port growled at something under the deck and it turned out to be a skinny, dirty puppy that had obviously been on her own for a while. Konnie adopted Joanne and soon discovered the joy of tennis balls. She brings the balls to winery visitors and she never stops until we intervene. Konnie is featured on the winery brochure, but the right wine for "her" hasn't yet been discovered.
Maysy became a Dunham dog in March 2005. Discovered on the Border Collie Rescue Web site, her coloring is striking, nearly pure white on her front half. She has a really "girly" face with penetrating yellow eyes. Maysy is the winery concierge, meeting every car, escorting everyone inside. She's also Mike's special partner and has her own wine, too, Four Legged White.

Eric, Joanne and Mike Dunhan

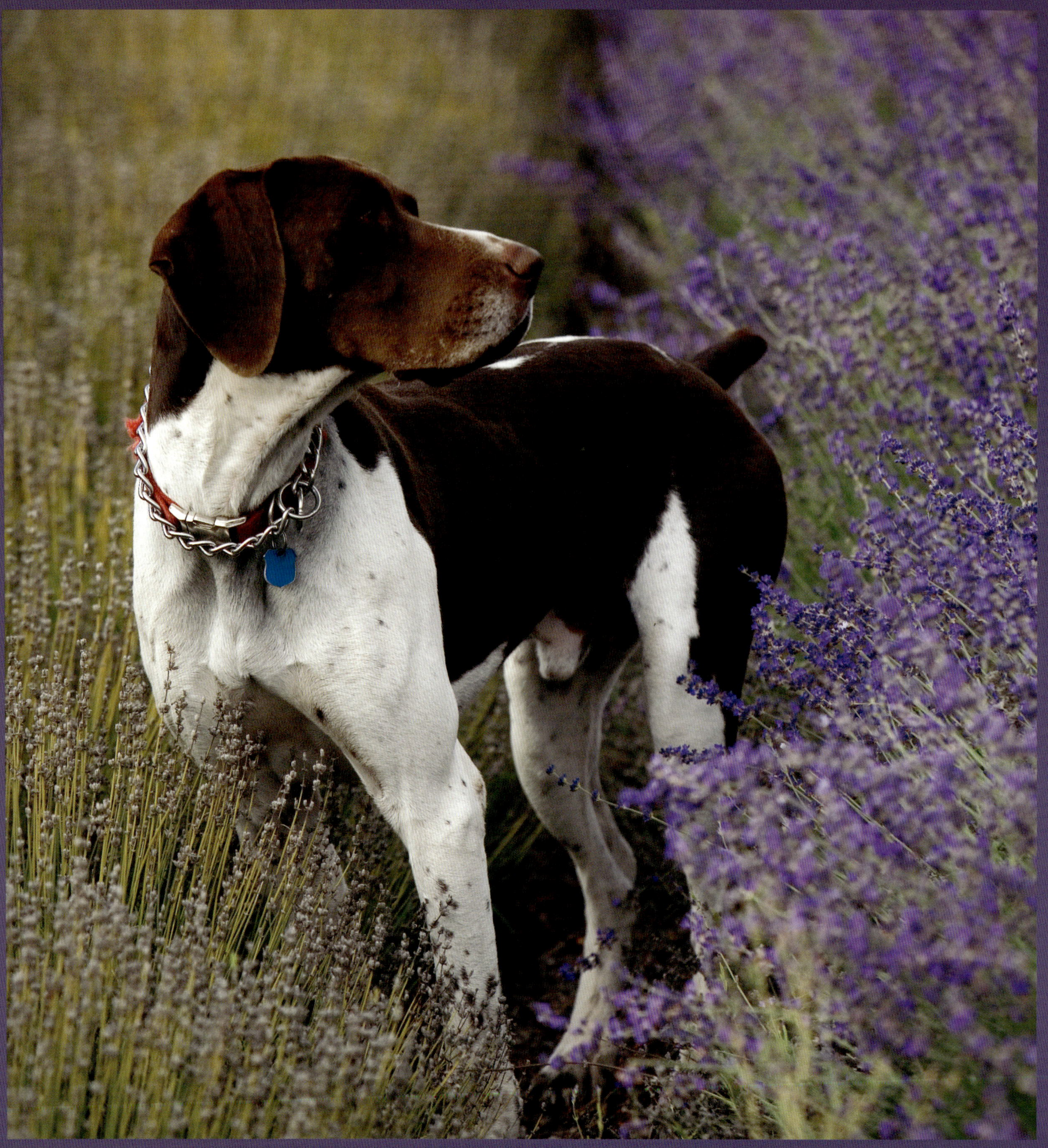

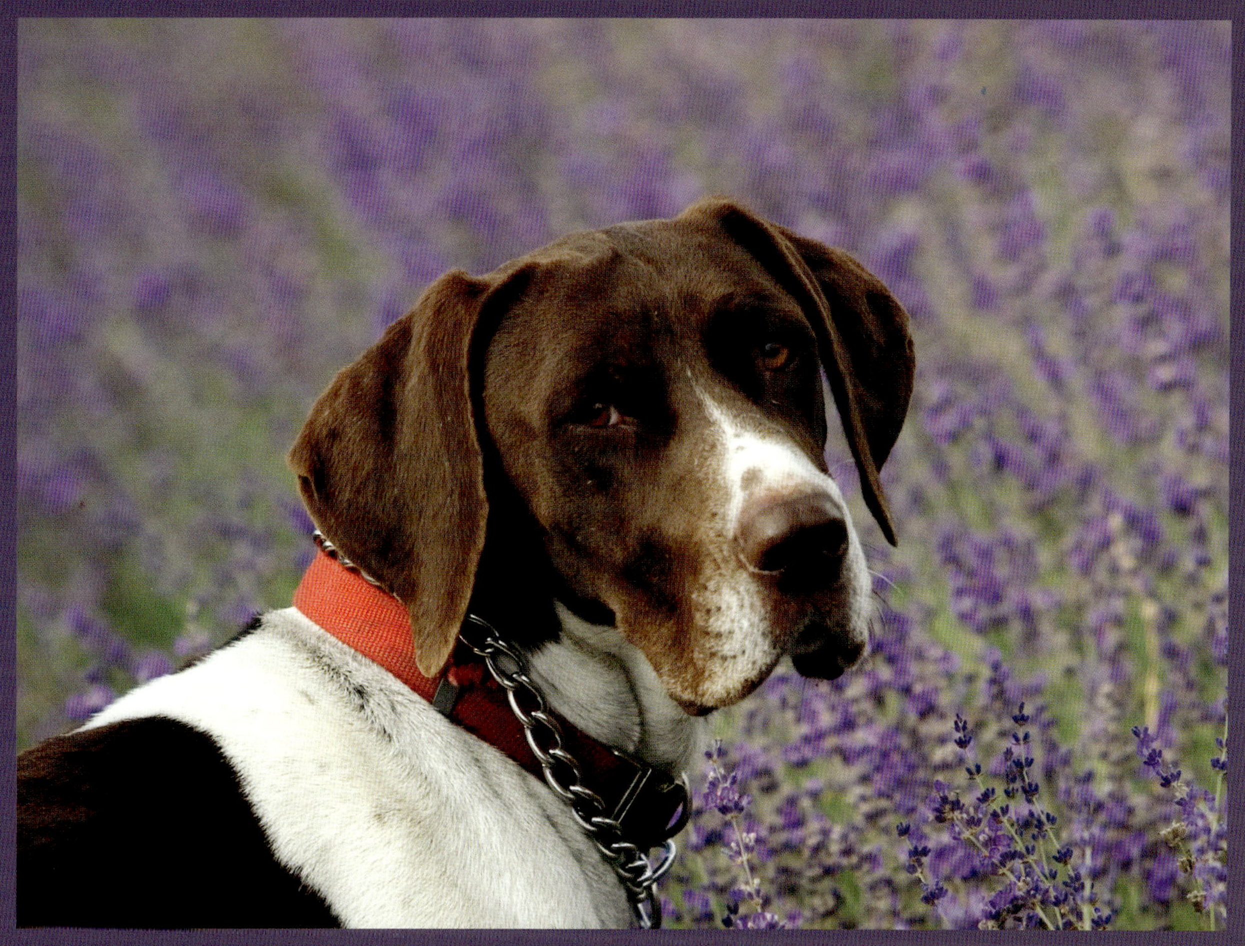

Shotgun

Leonetti Cellars

I recently rescued Shotgun, a 3-year-old AKC registered German Shorthair, from a "bad situation."

While I've had him for little more than six months, Shotgun has become my constant companion. He shares much of what I do – hunting pheasants, rounding up cattle, and hanging out at Elk Camp where he helps us take care of "left overs."

Shotgun is the perfect winery dog. He's loves to ride in a pickup...and eat grapes.

Chris Figgins

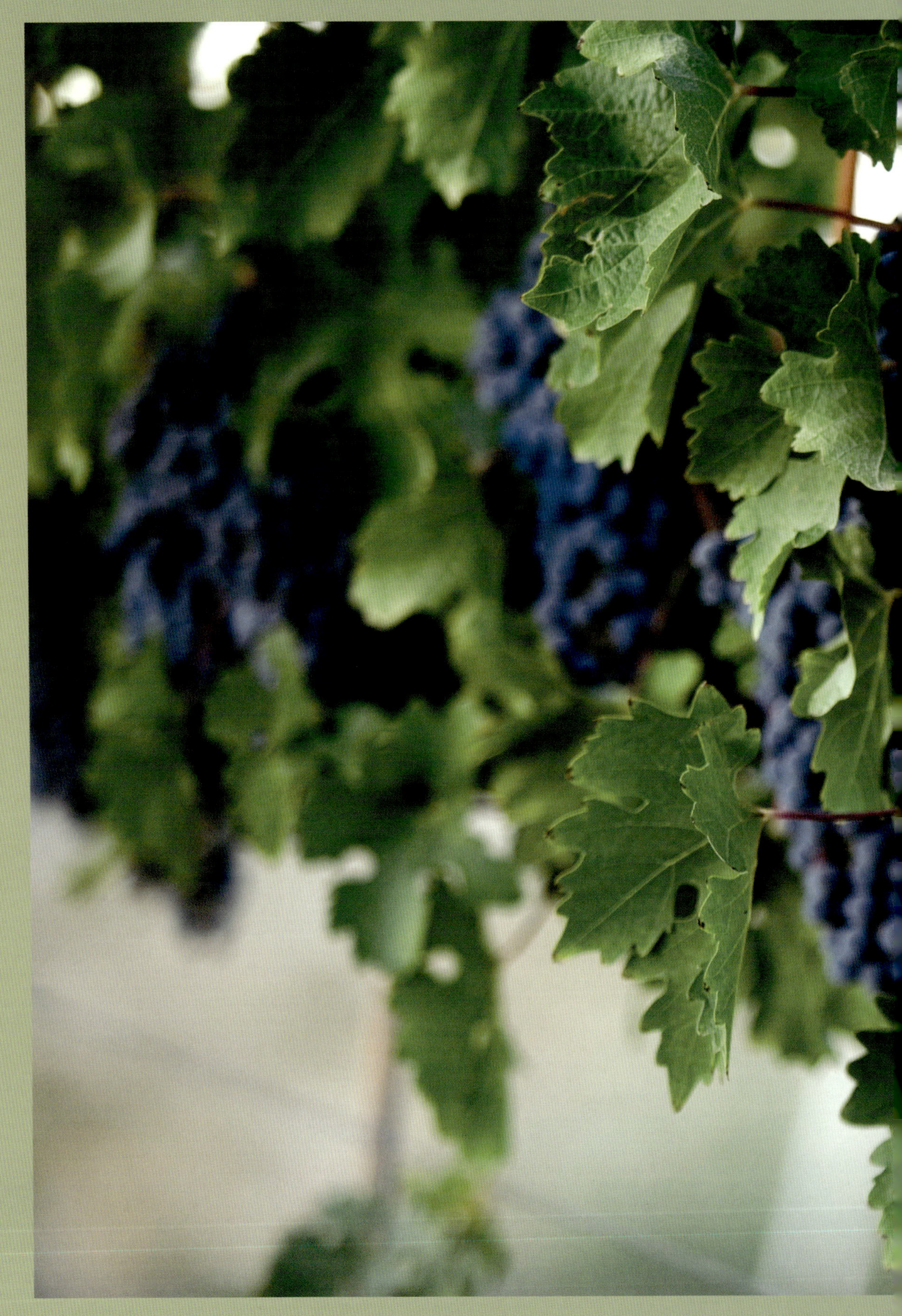

Va Piano Fruit

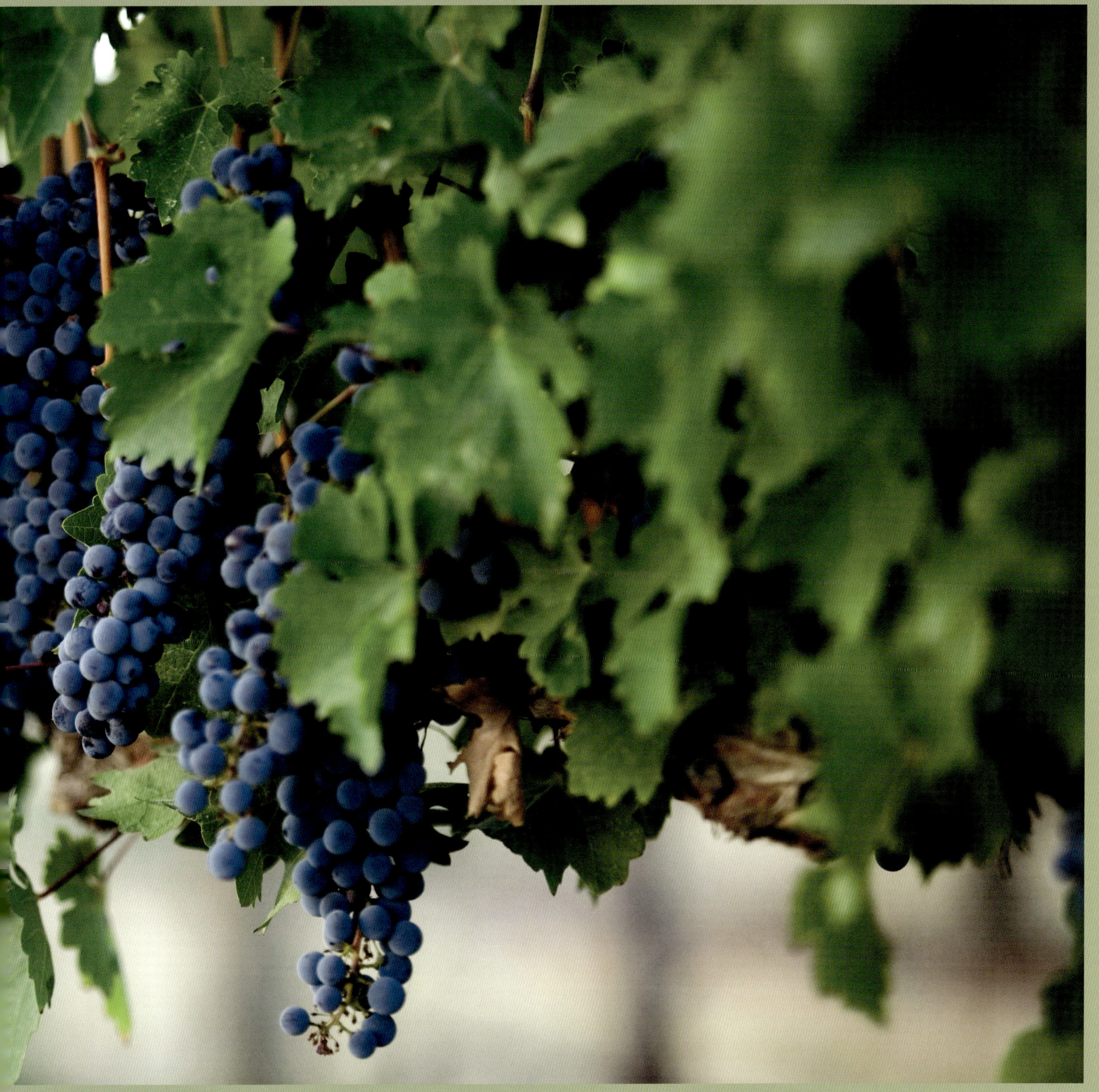

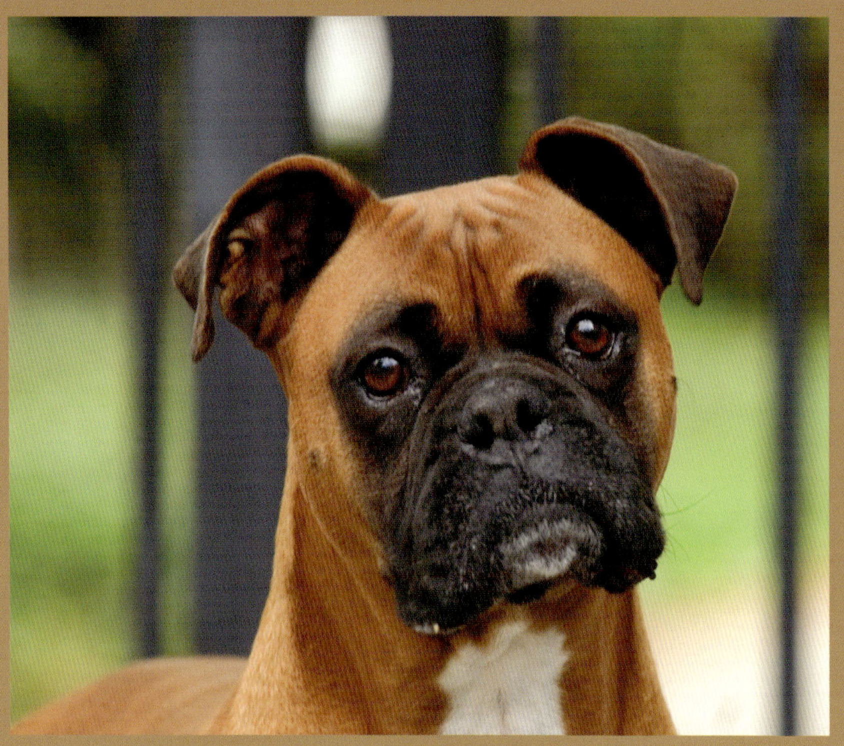

When we rescued Oscar, he was on his way back to the shelter...again. Fact is, we're Oscar's fourth home and he's happy to be here. While he experiences the "wanderlust," he knows where his bread is buttered and he always finds his way home.
Among Oscar's dislikes are cats. He hates 'em – chases and corners them, then sits on them. What he likes are grapes. We use the pumas from wine grapes to fertilize the yard and he loves to roll in it. It's the aroma he relishes...or maybe the alcohol residue. Whatever, Oscar is here to stay!

Jack and Dawn Kammer

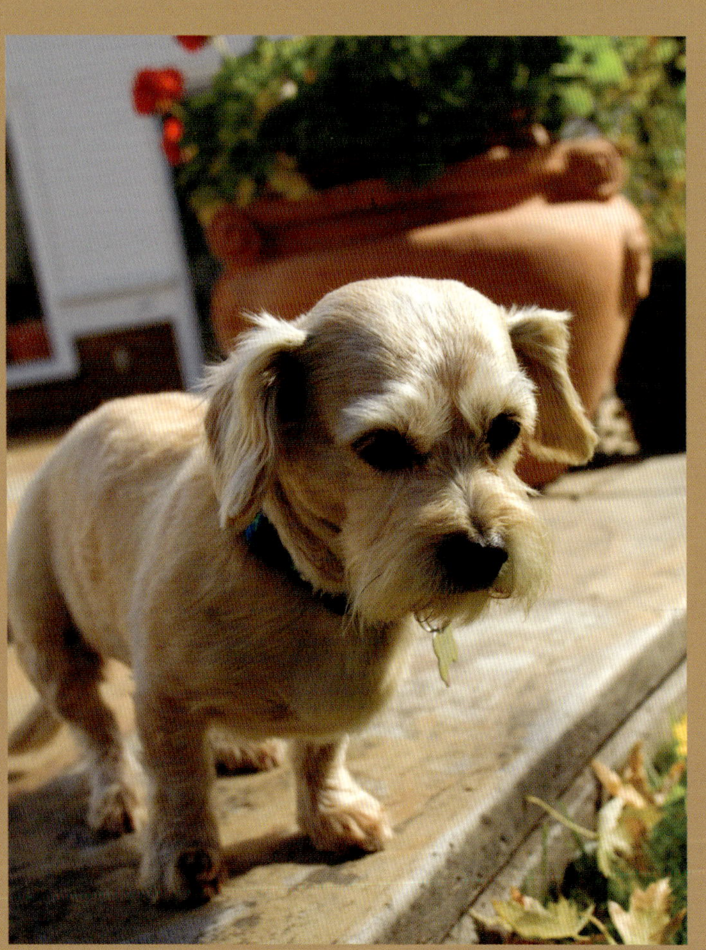

My name is Brandy. It is said I am Terrier, Dachshund and Chihuahua. I think I'm special, but of course I am female. My age is very young. I love to look very fierce while chasing the mailman across my property, making a lot of noise. So far I'm ignored. While on watch, I may appear to be napping. I like red wine but not so much syrah.
Sometimes my teeth are red.

Roger and Julia Russel

Lulu, our strawberry-blond Labradoodle, joined us on a whim. When you go to look at puppies, you never come home empty handed. My son, Simon, chose the name Lou, but when the him turned out to be a her, she became LuLu. Even as a 1-year-old, she's a proven romantic sipping our golden chardonnay at sunset.

Mary Derby

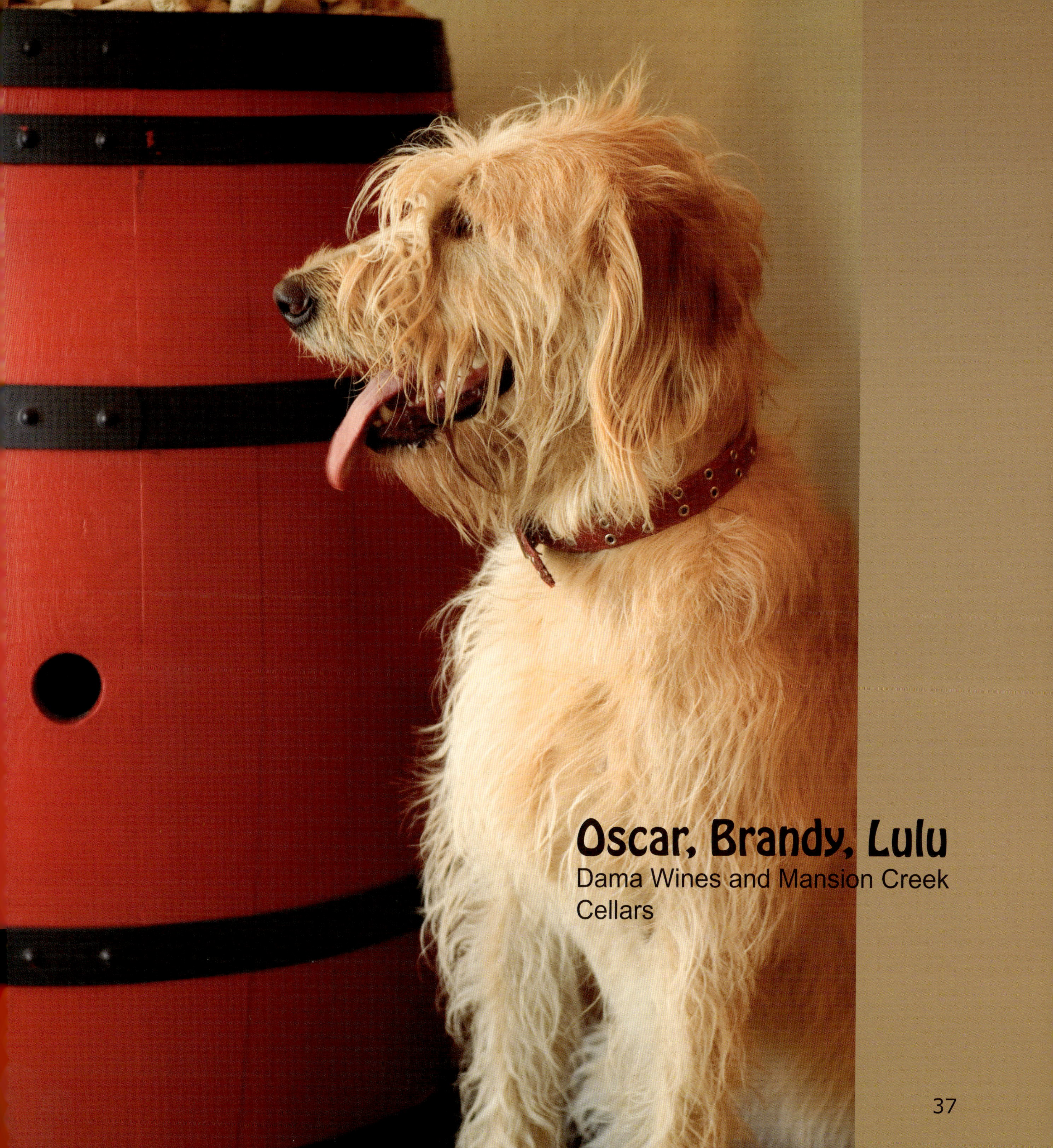

Oscar, Brandy, Lulu

Dama Wines and Mansion Creek Cellars

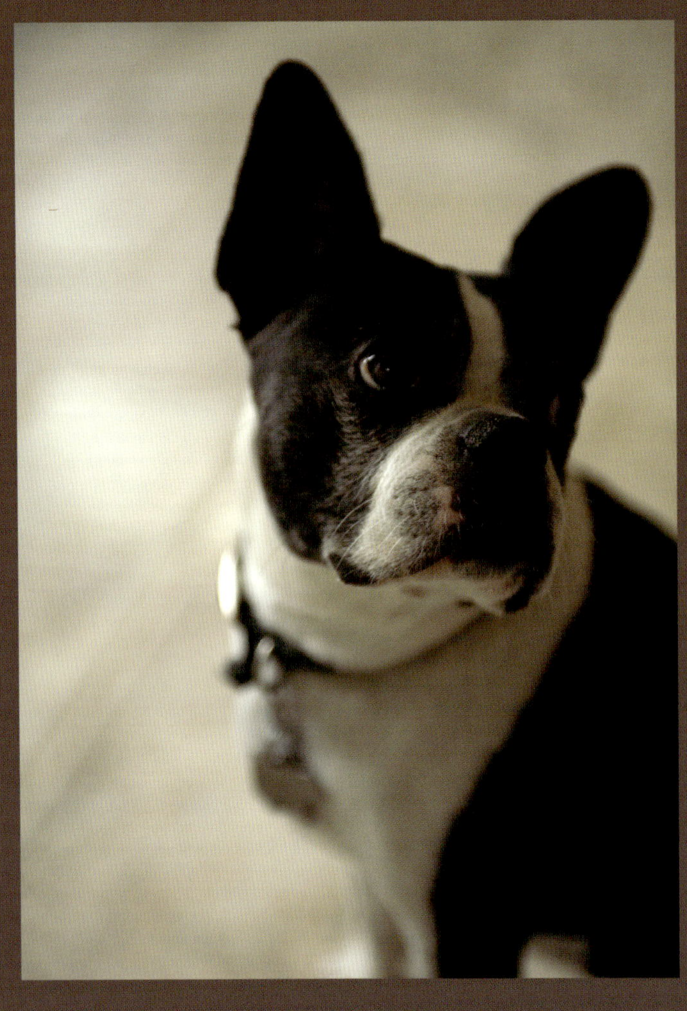

Ring

Elegante' Cellars

When Doug Simmons, at Eleganté Cellars, "inherited" Ring he knew the gregarious Boston Terrier would be a great companion for his wine ambitions.

Since he was a puppy, Ring had proven himself a loyal companion for Doug's mother, Abbie Simmons. For seven years, Ring and Abbie were inseparable – building a lasting friendship, taking daily walks, sharing their lives with neighborhood kids – until 2006 when Abbie died at age 87.

In his new role, Ring quickly got comfortable with Doug's career in wine making. Doug was helping Five Star Cellars and planning his own winery. He completed Eleganté Cellars at the Walla Walla Airport in 2007 and Ring was part of the project from the beginning. He loved the construction site, often "conned" builders for bites of their lunches and now loves to greet visitors to the tasting room.

When he's not "at work," Ring still enjoys the regular walks he started with Abbie and a frequent French vanilla ice cream snack to end another wonderful day.

Doug Simmons

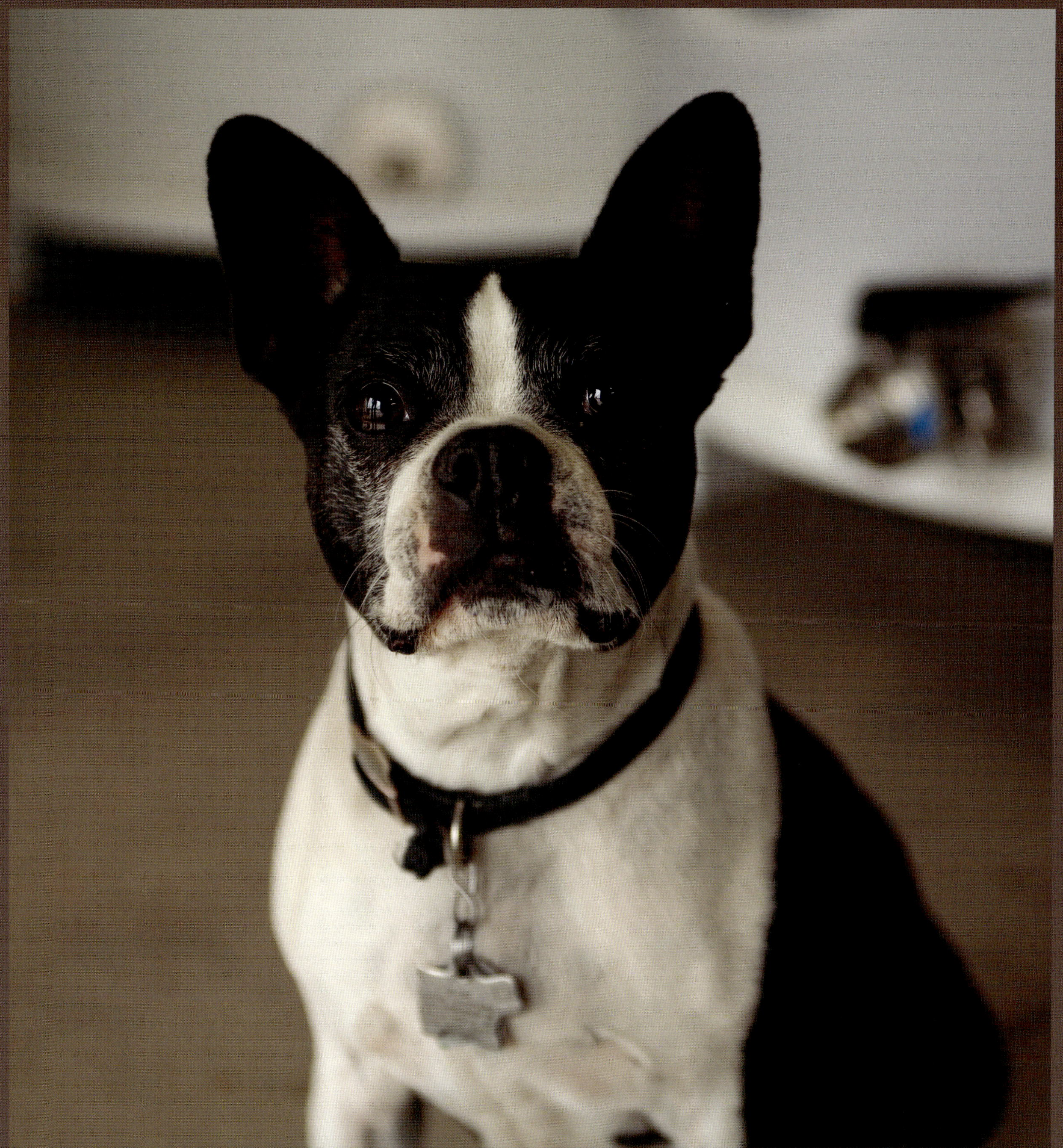

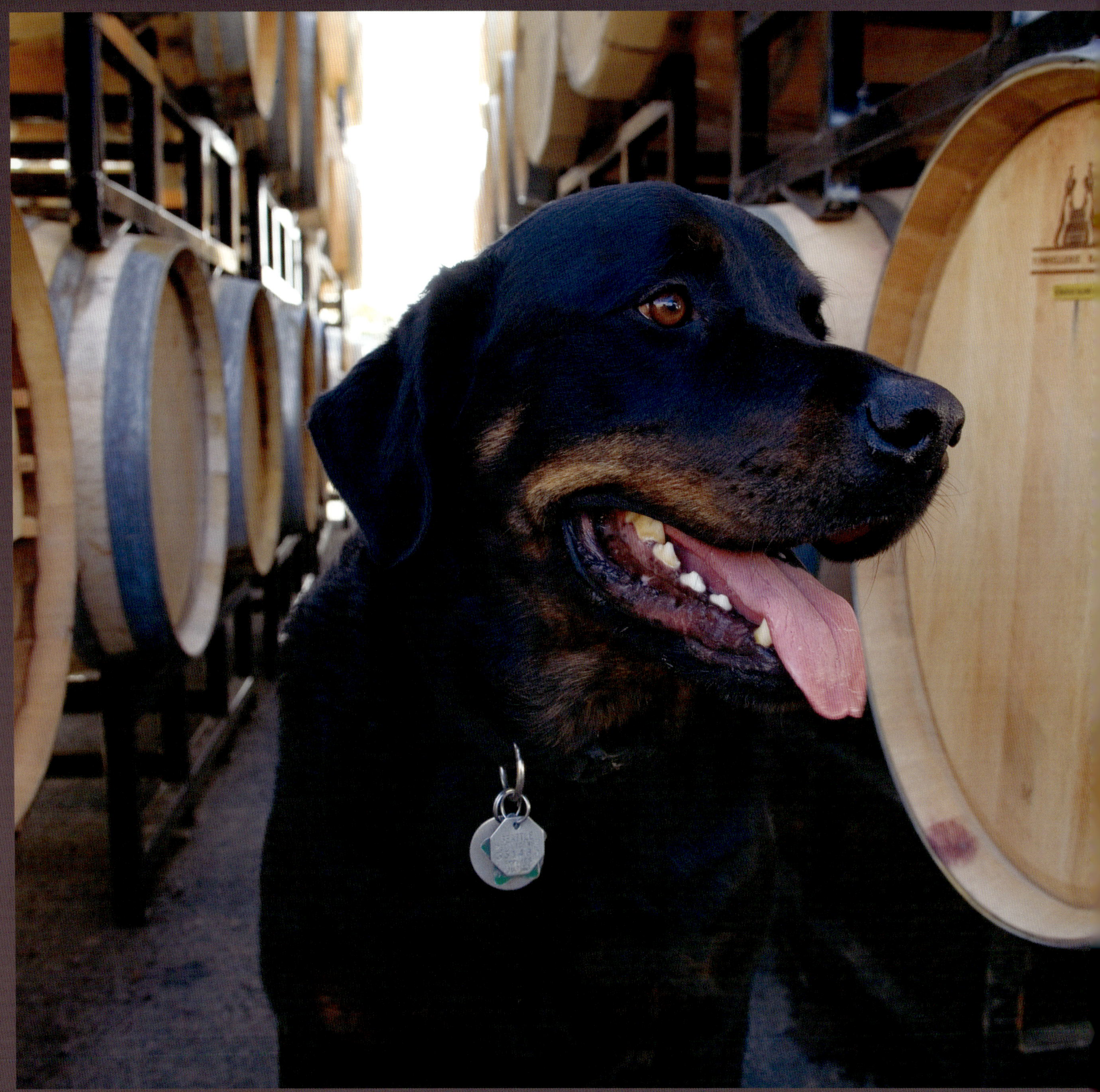

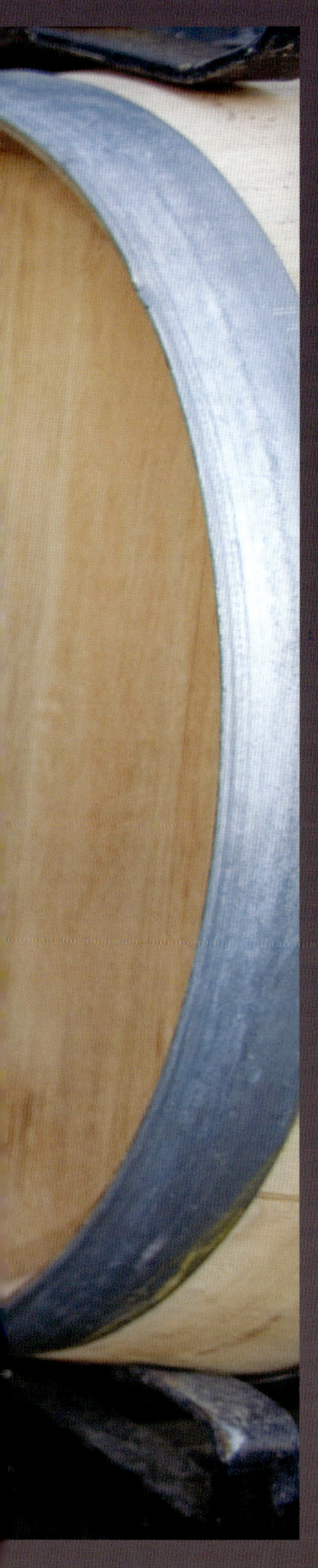

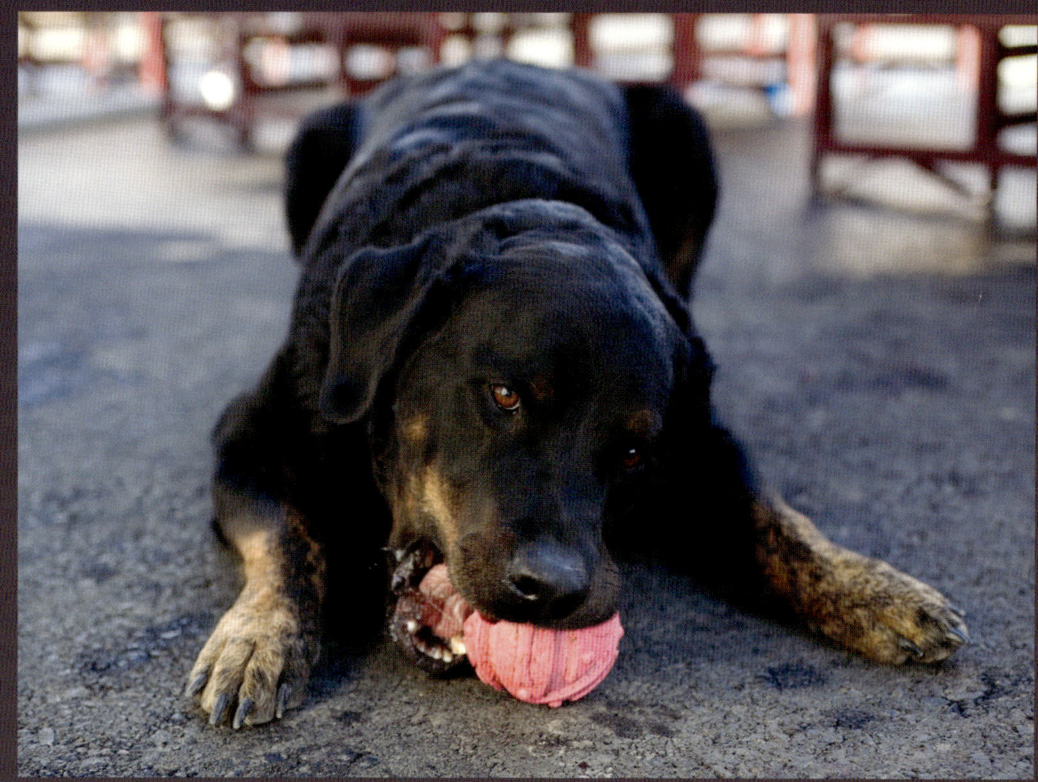

Caine

Waters Winery

While Caine lives the lifestyle of a Walla Walla winery dog, his beginnings with us were much more challenging. He joined our family when Annie and I lived in a West Seattle neighborhood where crime was a factor. Since my work then required travel, I worried about Annie's safety and decided a big dog that looked mean would be a good idea. I found Caine locked up in a Yakima shelter. He looked tough. The handlers loved him. He was perfect.

Back home, Caine looked the part, barked loud and discouraged passing punks who migrated to the other side of the street and eventually just went away. There was no crime on Caine's watch.

Now that we're in Walla Walla, where crime is limited, Caine enjoys barking from behind his fence at every passing dog, swimming, chasing his ball, protecting Annie and Marlee, and hanging out at the winery.

Sean and Annie Boyd

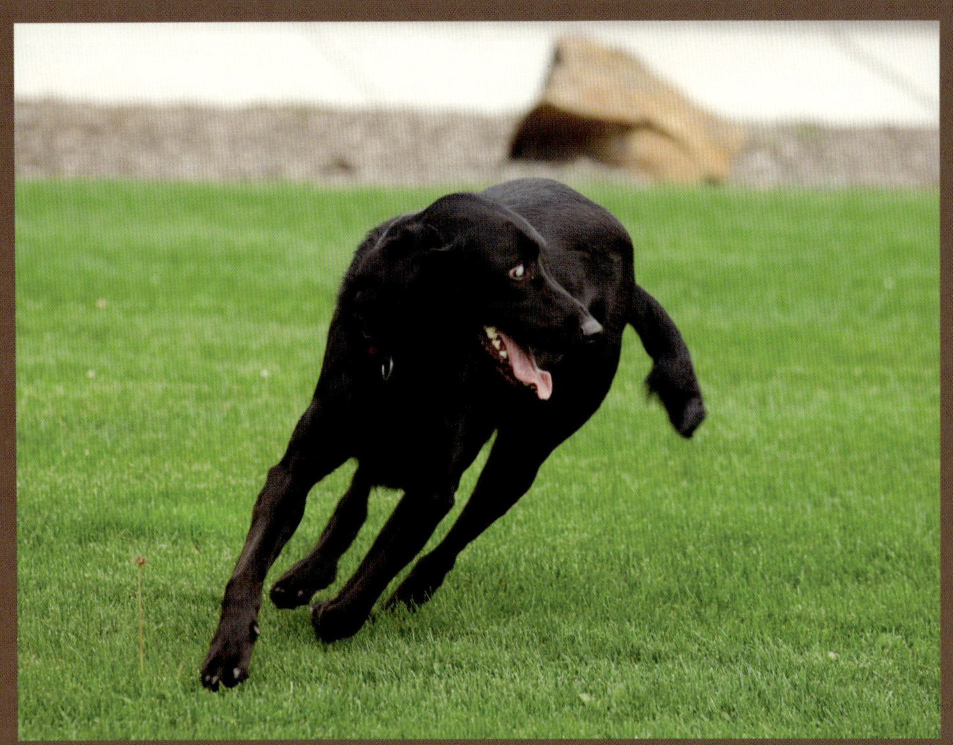

Strummer

College Cellars of Walla Walla

I obtained Strummer, who was "free to a good home," as a birthday present to myself while living in Corvallis, Oregon. While still a puppy, Strummer traveled with me and waited in the car while I interviewed for my current position at Walla Walla Community College.

During the 2003 vintage, Strummer would join me for weekend punch-downs and pumpovers until we noticed that he was blind. Unable to see, but quite energetic, Strummer frequently runs into objects in his path, especially when engaged in his favorite activity, chasing the cat. While his blindness has contributed to more than a few bumps and bruises, it has also greatly sharpened Strummer's sense of smell, which every winemaker knows is his or her most powerful analytical tool.

Michael and Erica Moyer

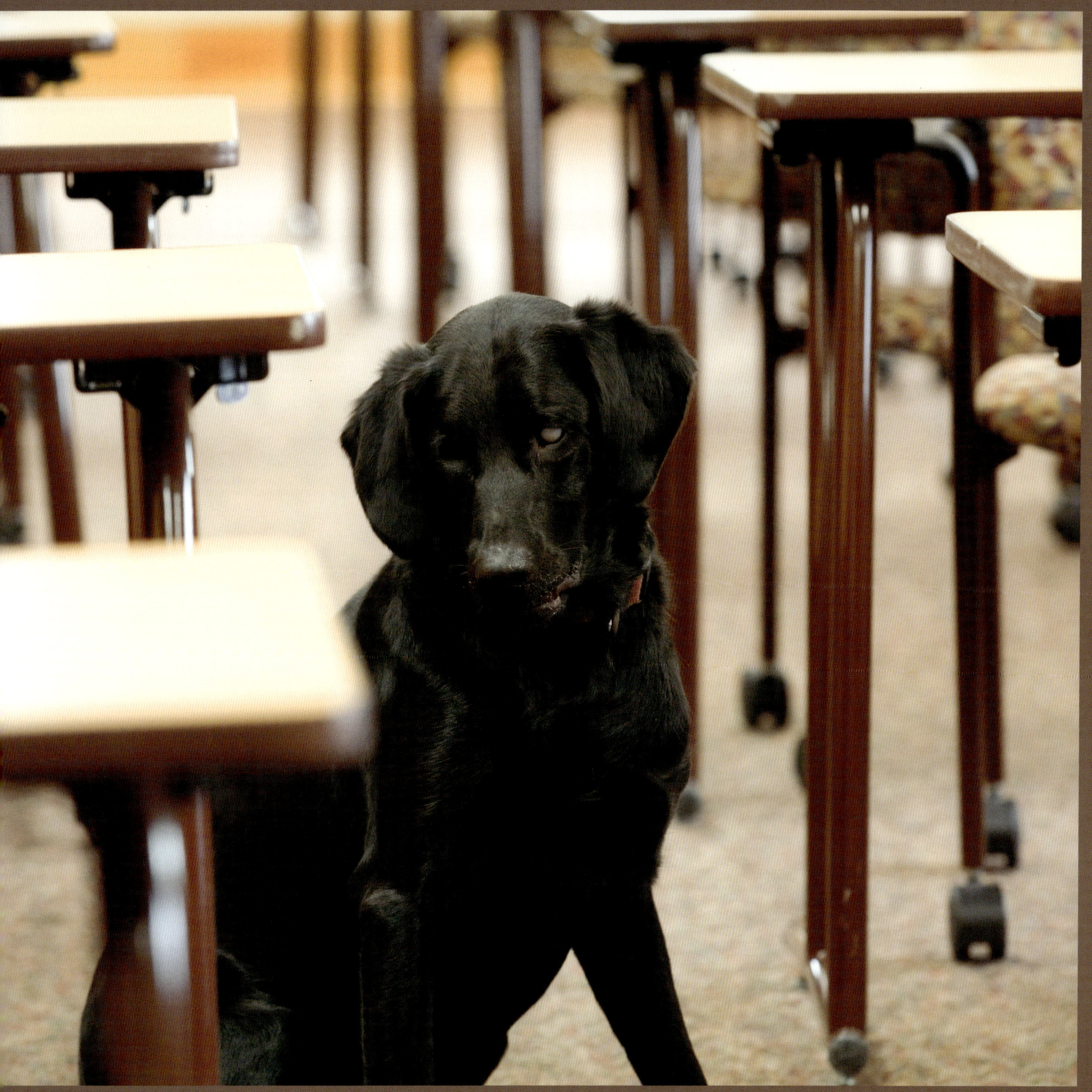

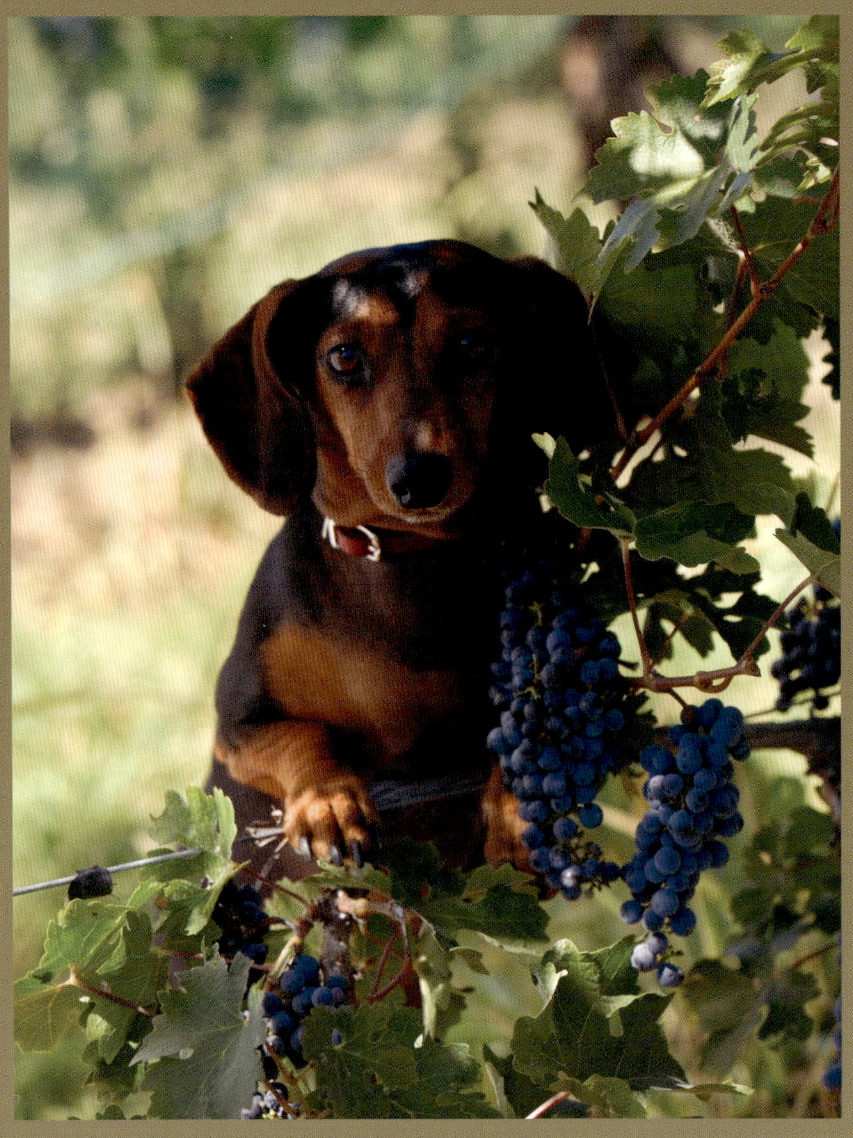

Joey

Otis Kenyon Wine

Joey Otis Kenyon is a miniature Dachshund. While he's no bigger than a magnum of Otis Kenyon Cabernet, there is nothing small about Joey's heart or attitude. He races his big dog pals through the Syrah at Stellar, winning only by ducking under the rows. His snout is often pointed down snake holes and grass, or up into the grape vines and clusters. He chases varmints around Otis House like he really intends to catch them, and herds his bright red ball around the winery like it's an errant heifer.

More lover than fighter, Joey greets every Otis Kenyon guest with affection and a marvelously happy and quiet countenance. It's impossible not to smile upon meeting Joey and when he undulates over the cobblestones at top speed, it's hard to stop laughing. Joey's "vintage" is 2003 and he will tell you it was a very good year.

Debra Dunbar

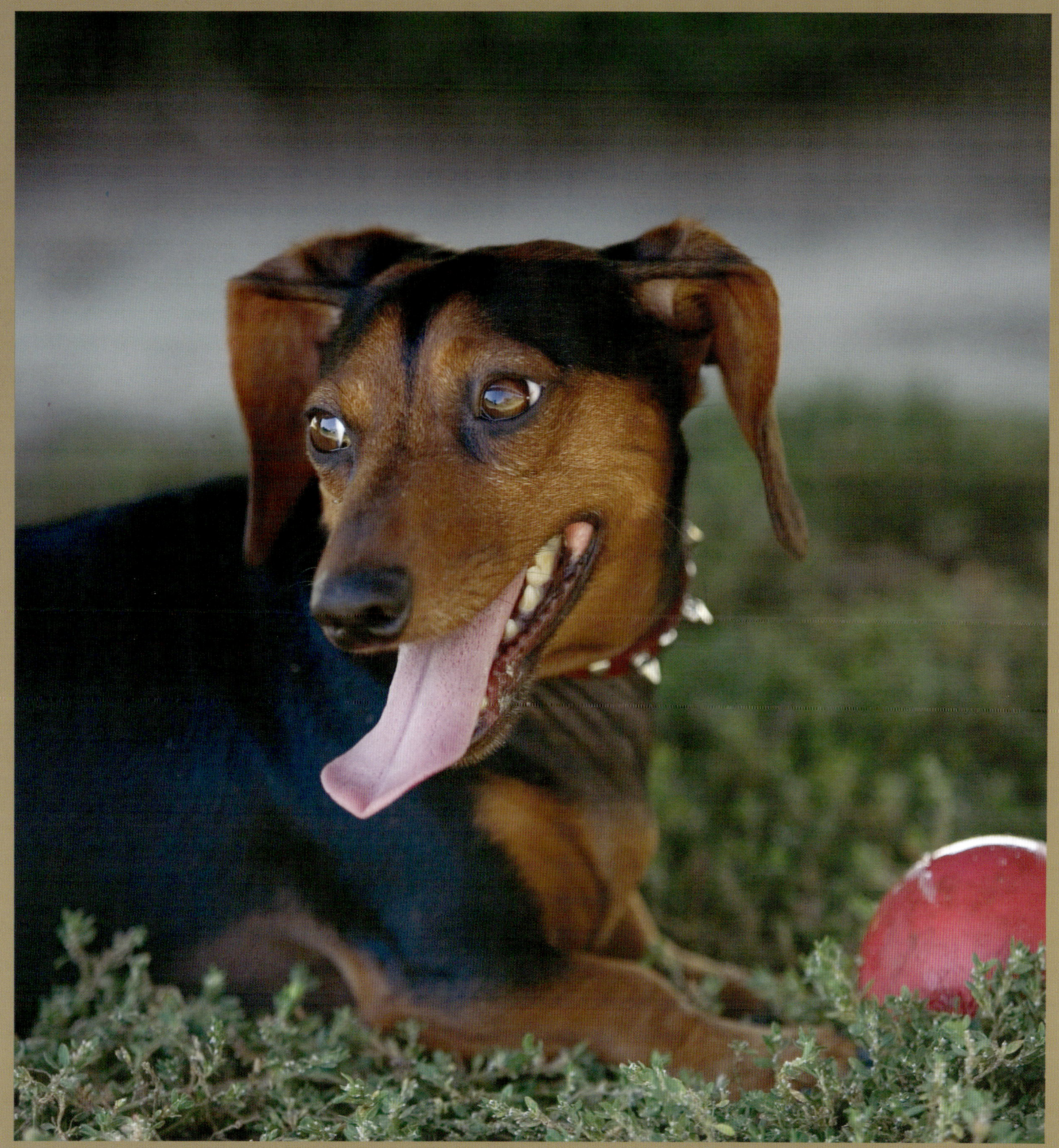

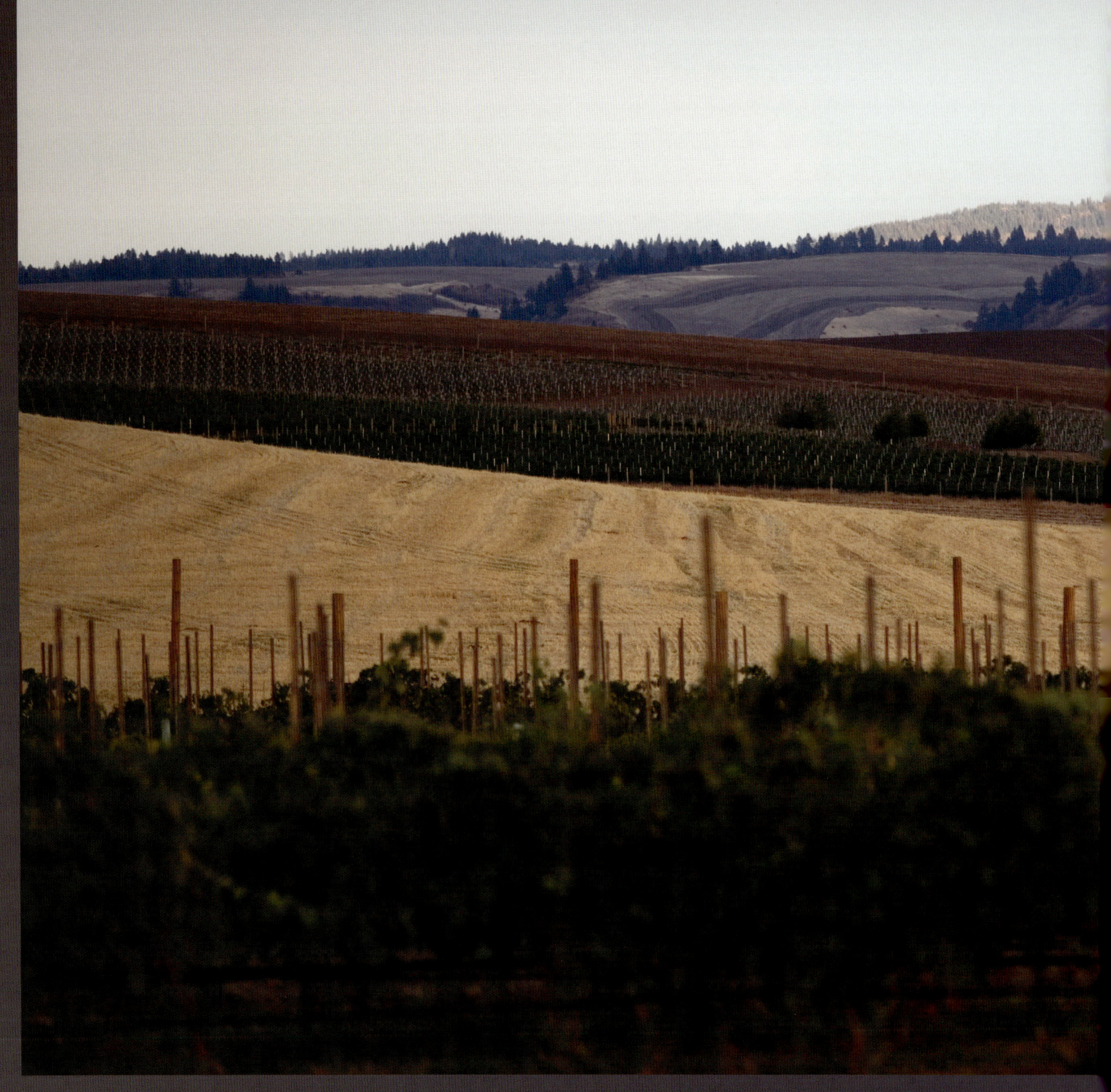

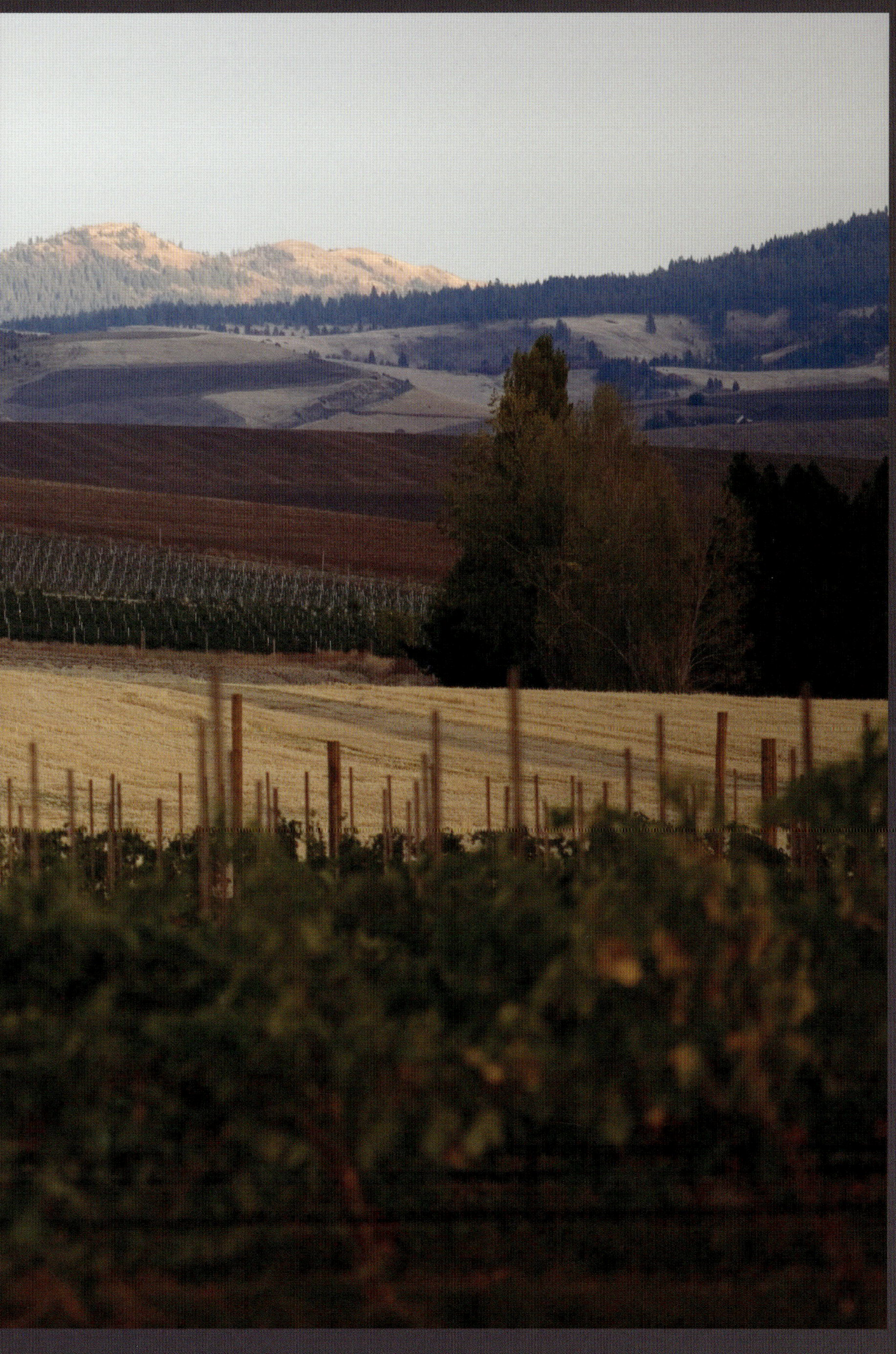

View East to Blue Mountains

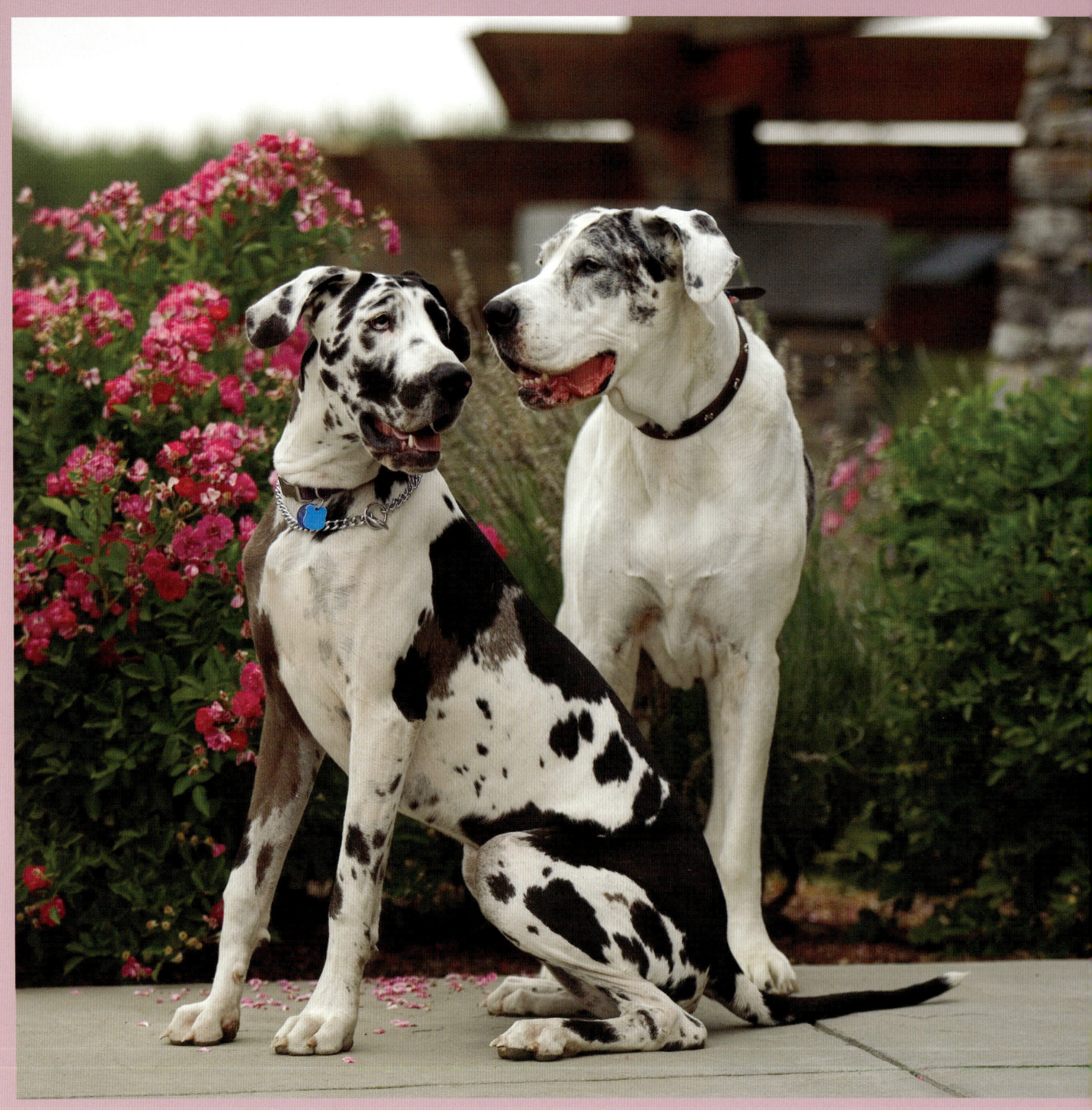

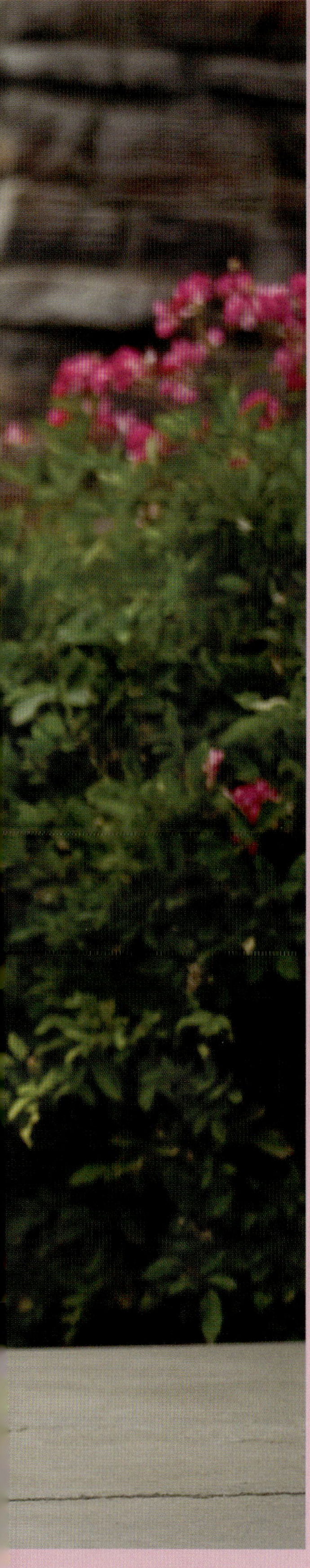

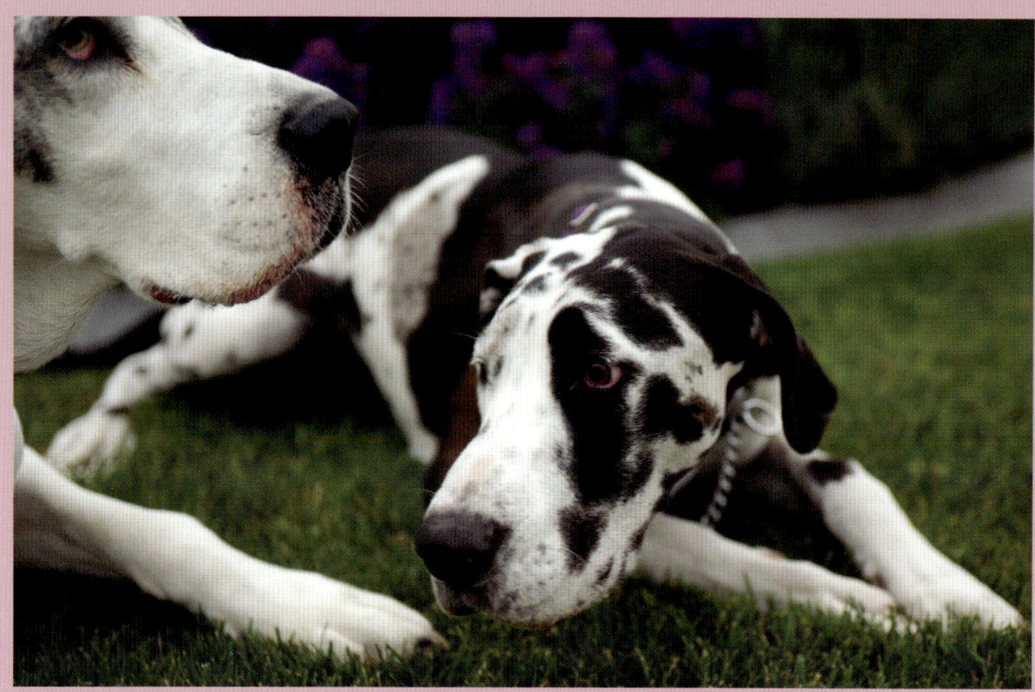

Izzy and Pearl

Northstar Winery

A Christmas puppy is the gift that keeps on giving.
That's how Issabella came into our lives. Her full name is Issabella Wears Big Girl Shoes, like the little girl trying on her mom's shoes. That's how she looked as a puppy – as if she were trying on a big dog's feet. Izzy has two gears - sweet and snuggly or pure terror. She changes gears in a split second. Around the winery, Izzy is not likely to sit quietly. She runs everywhere and loves chasing "anything that moves" through the vineyard.
We had been watching the Great Dane rescue Web site before we got Izzy and that's where we found Pearl. Our first thought when we saw her was "She's a shetland pony!" Pearl immediately took on the role of mentor and guardian for Izzy. She is sweet and gracious with the patience of an angel. Pearl loves to greet people at the winery, but most of all she likes to sit quietly, leaning against you and getting pets.

Lynne Anderson and David "Merf" Merfeld

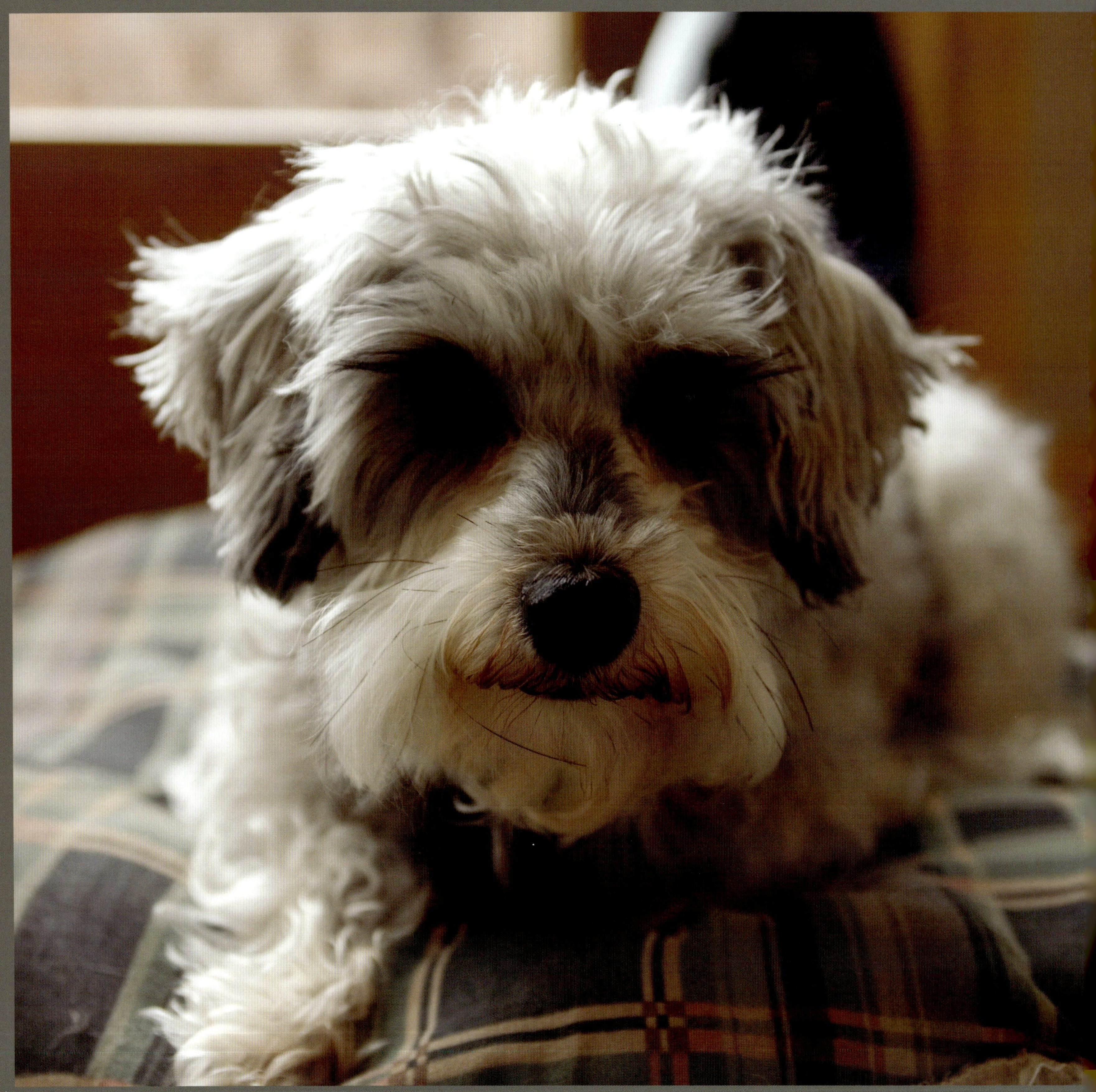

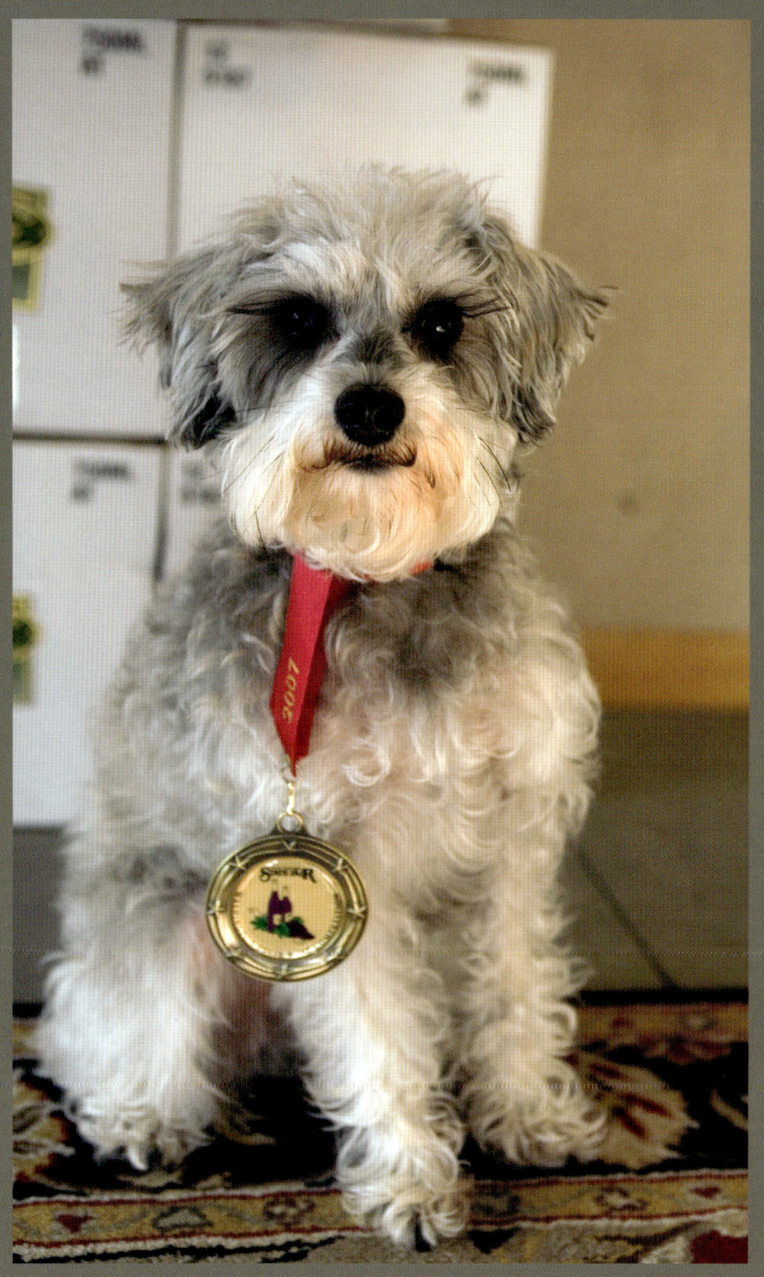

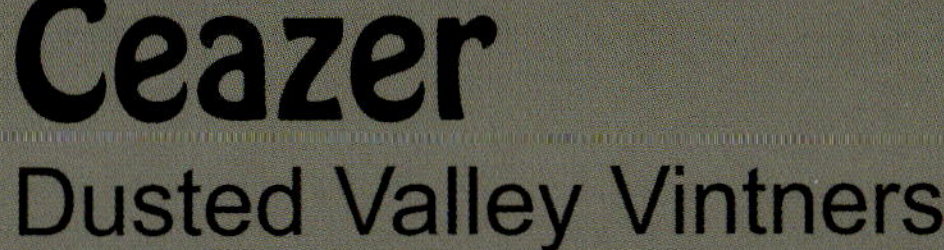

Ceazer

Dusted Valley Vintners

Ceaser is a dog that refuses to be ignored. Any visitor to Dusted Valley knows that. He sits back and howls until a proper greeting is shared. A beautiful silver-grey Schnoodle (Schnauzer/Poodle), Ceaser flashes eyelashes that "go on forever." Fact is, many a female taster has left Dusted Valley envious of those eyes.

Janet Johnson

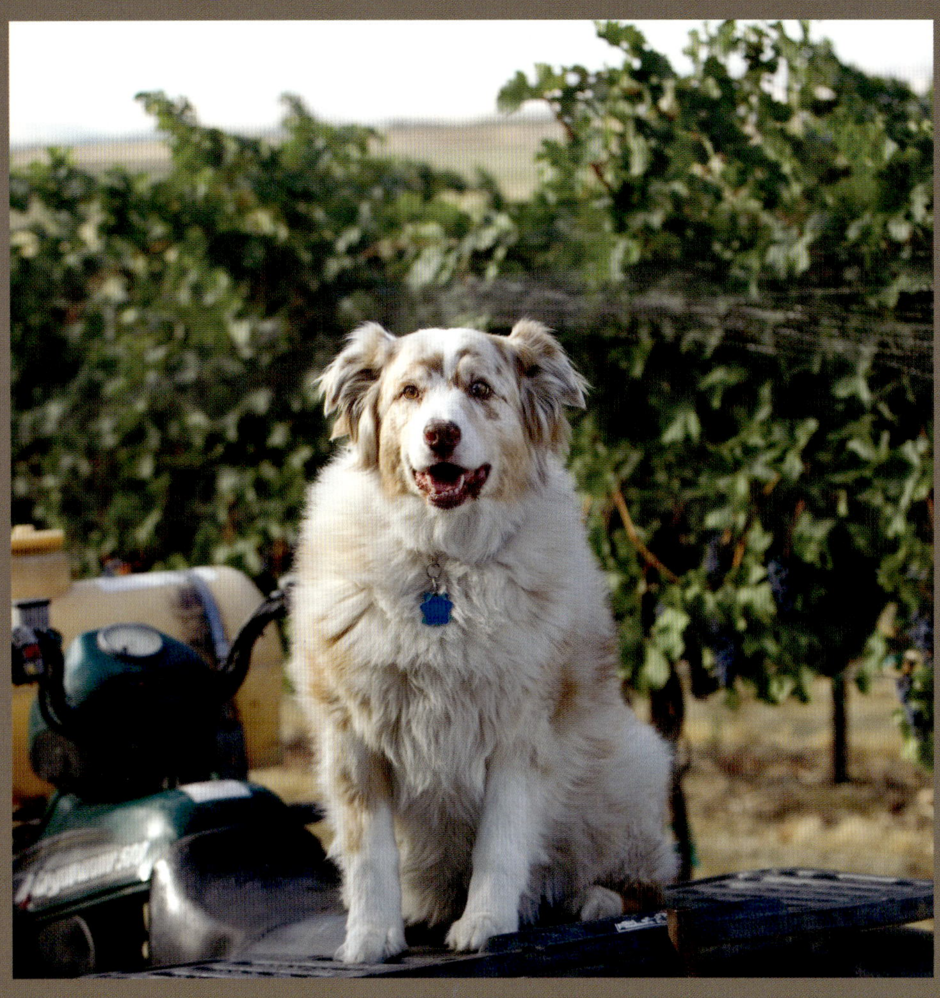

Chase

Bergevin Lane

Chase, an 8-year-old Australian Shepherd, was born with seven brothers and sisters. We've enjoyed his company since he was 11-weeks-old.

His first fame came as a puppy being photographed in a Christmas stocking, hanging on the fireplace. Chase has since posed for many photos, always with a huge smile on his face.

Chase feels his strengths are in the vineyard helping us select fruit to determine ripeness and readiness for picking. He takes pride in protecting us as we walk each row. Chase has tried administrative work, however he has said that his skills are being under utilized.

He particularly enjoys Cabernet Sauvignon, but is eager to sample all varietals.

Recently, when I was scratching his tummy to thank him for all his help and he looked at me with his beautiful gentle eyes and told me he truly believes Washington State is the perfect climate for wine AND for vineyard/winery dogs.

Annette Bergevin and Amber Lane

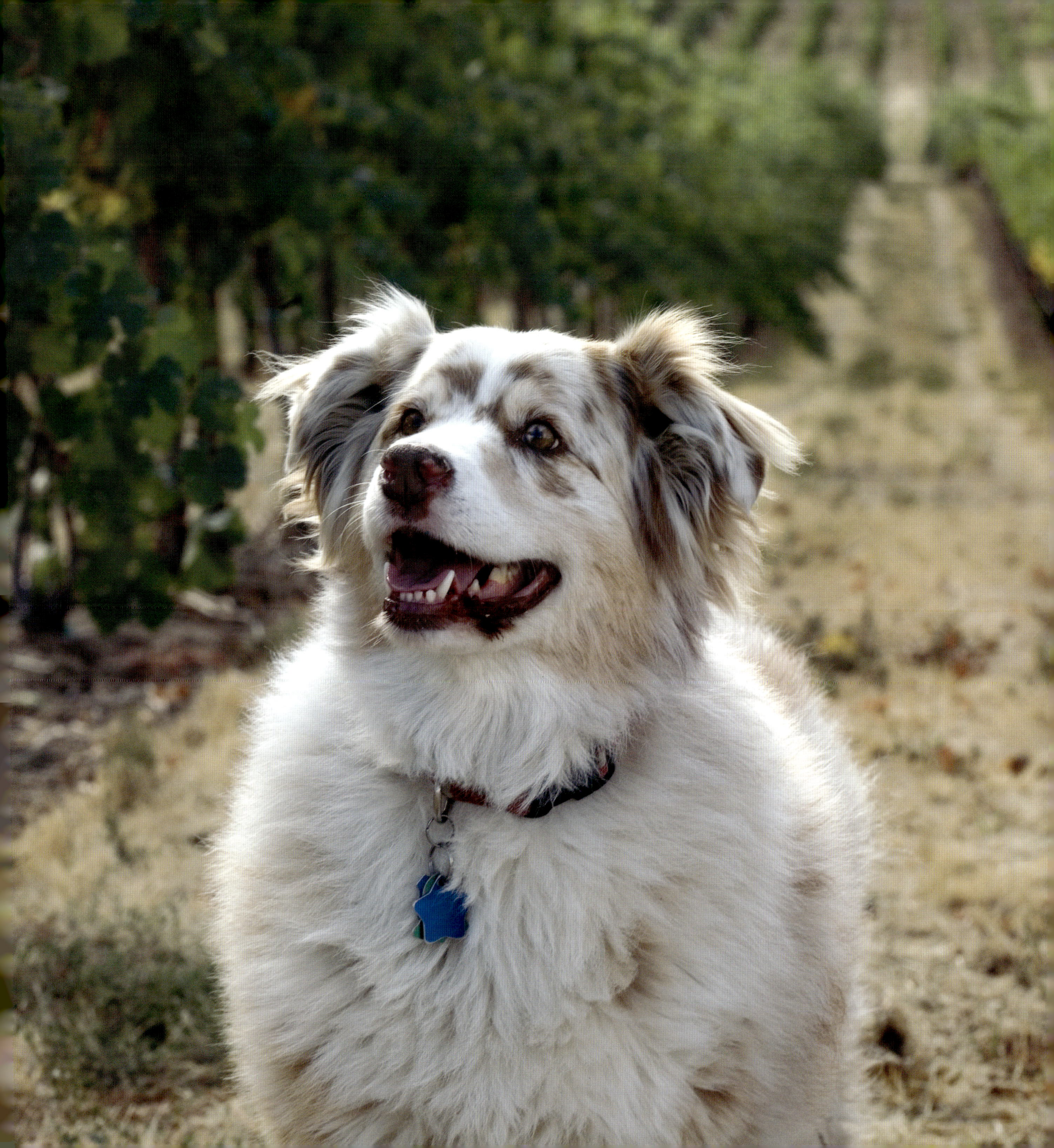

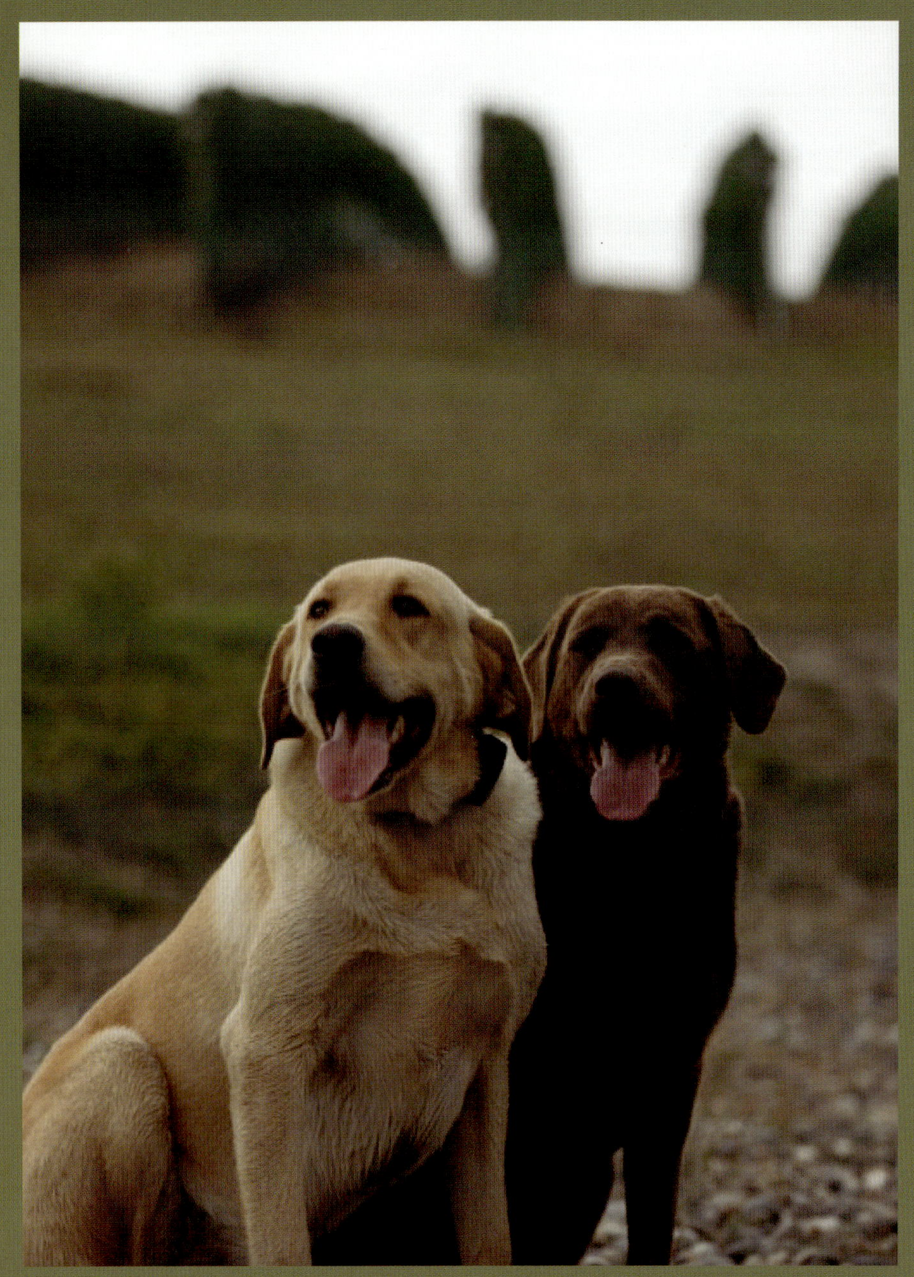

Bullit and Bear

Nicholas Cole Cellars

Bullit, (the Chocolate) and Bear (the Yellow), are "Lab litter mates" that could be described as the "Holiday hounds." They were born on Halloween – they've been trick or treating ever since. Santa delivered the pups to Michele and Nick on Christmas Eve 2001. Now just six years old, the "boys" do their best to contribute to our rural environment. Bullit and Bear share an interest in deer pellets (savored like caviar) and dead creatures. But in spite of their unique favorites, both have surprisingly sweet temperaments and are ready to share their personalities with all who come to visit.

Mike Neuffer

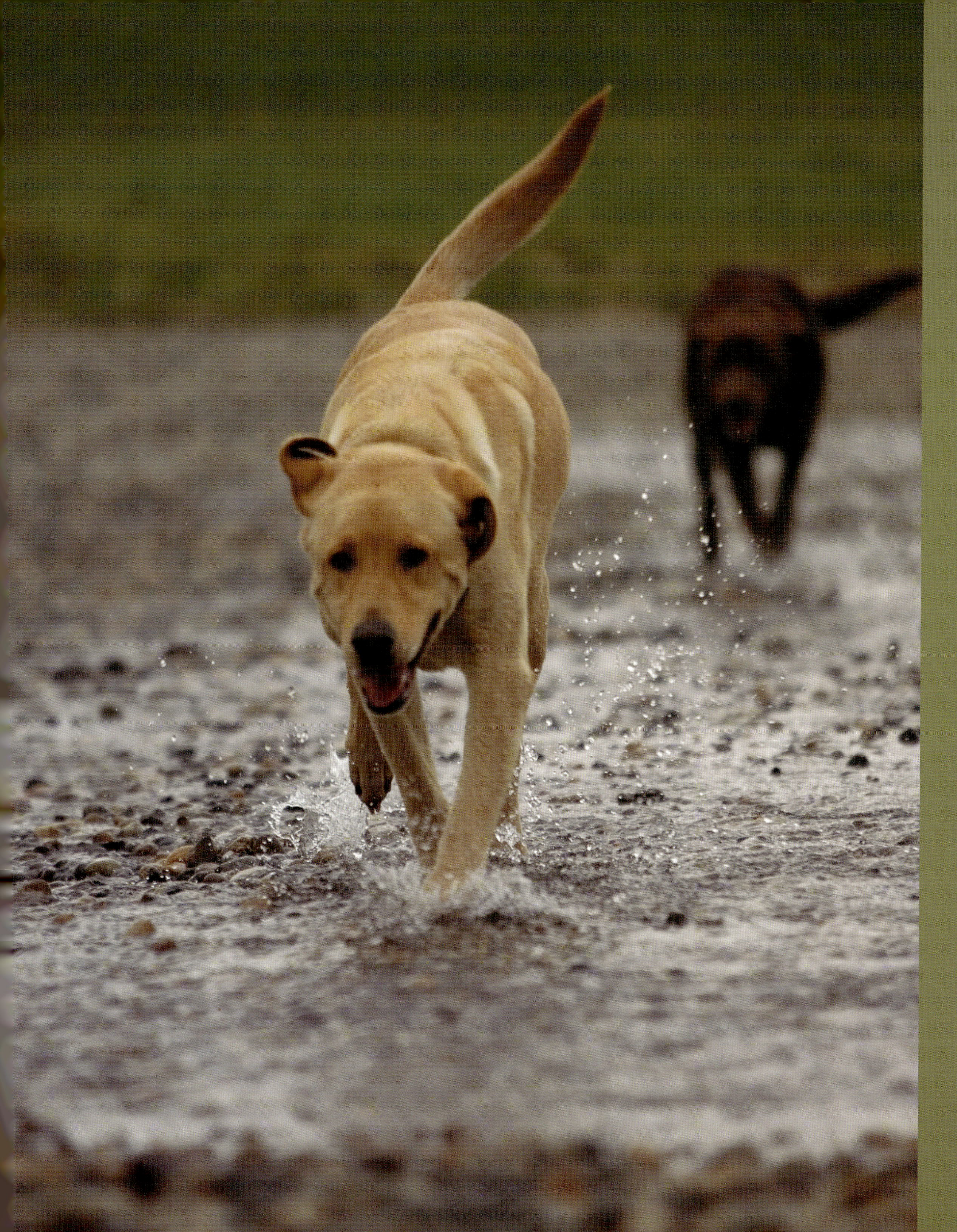

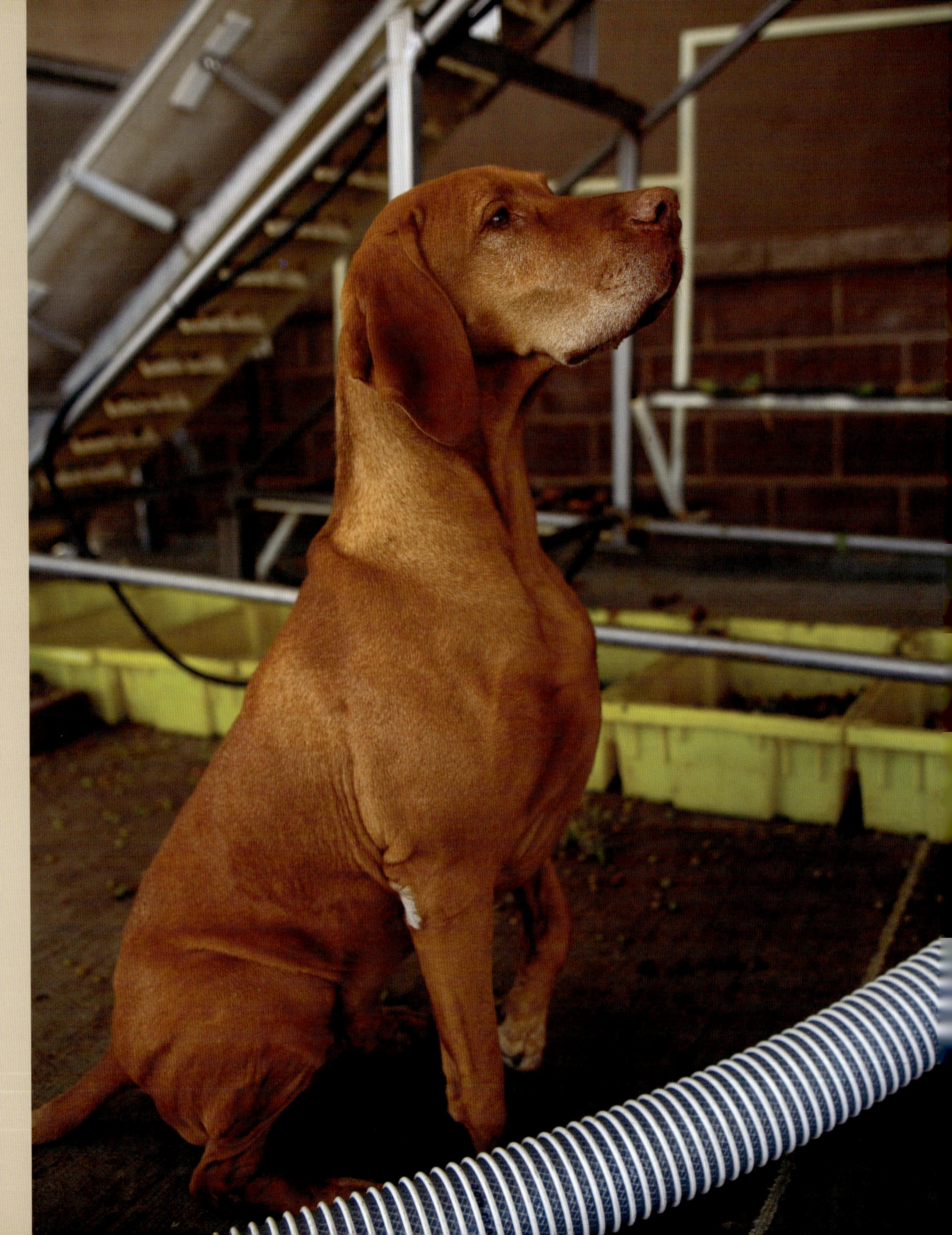

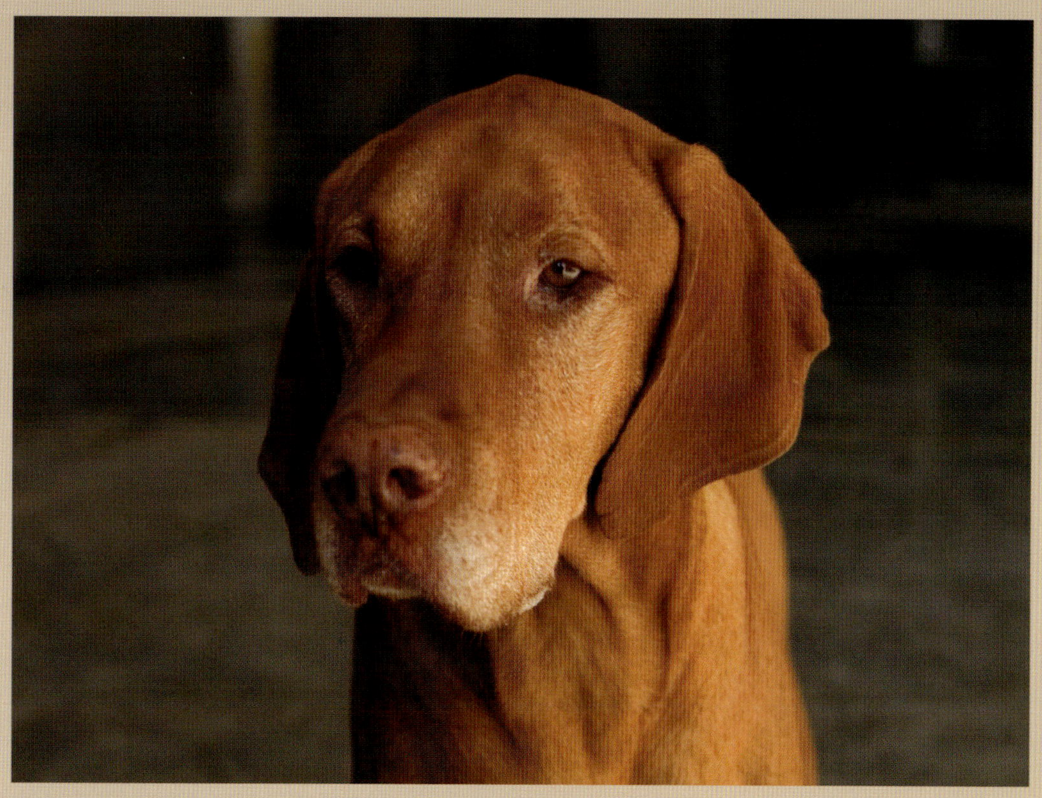

Rufous

Cougar Crest Winery

Rufous is an 8-year-old Vizsla, a short-haired pointer type bird dog originally from Hungary. He has a few quirks.
Rufous is large for his breed and at first, with new people, he tends to be a bit gruff. He thinks it's important to bark and let us know that someone is on the premises. However, when one of the Cougar Crest crew give the okay, Rufous is "lovey-dovey" and wants to be petted. At that point, watch out because he can practically knock you over when he leans in to be close to you.
Of course Rufous loves to fetch, but being run over twice has left him with a "bum" shoulder so we limited some activity.
I have given him the nickname of "The Doginator".
One other thing, he loves eating grapes when we are crushing.

Brian Carlson

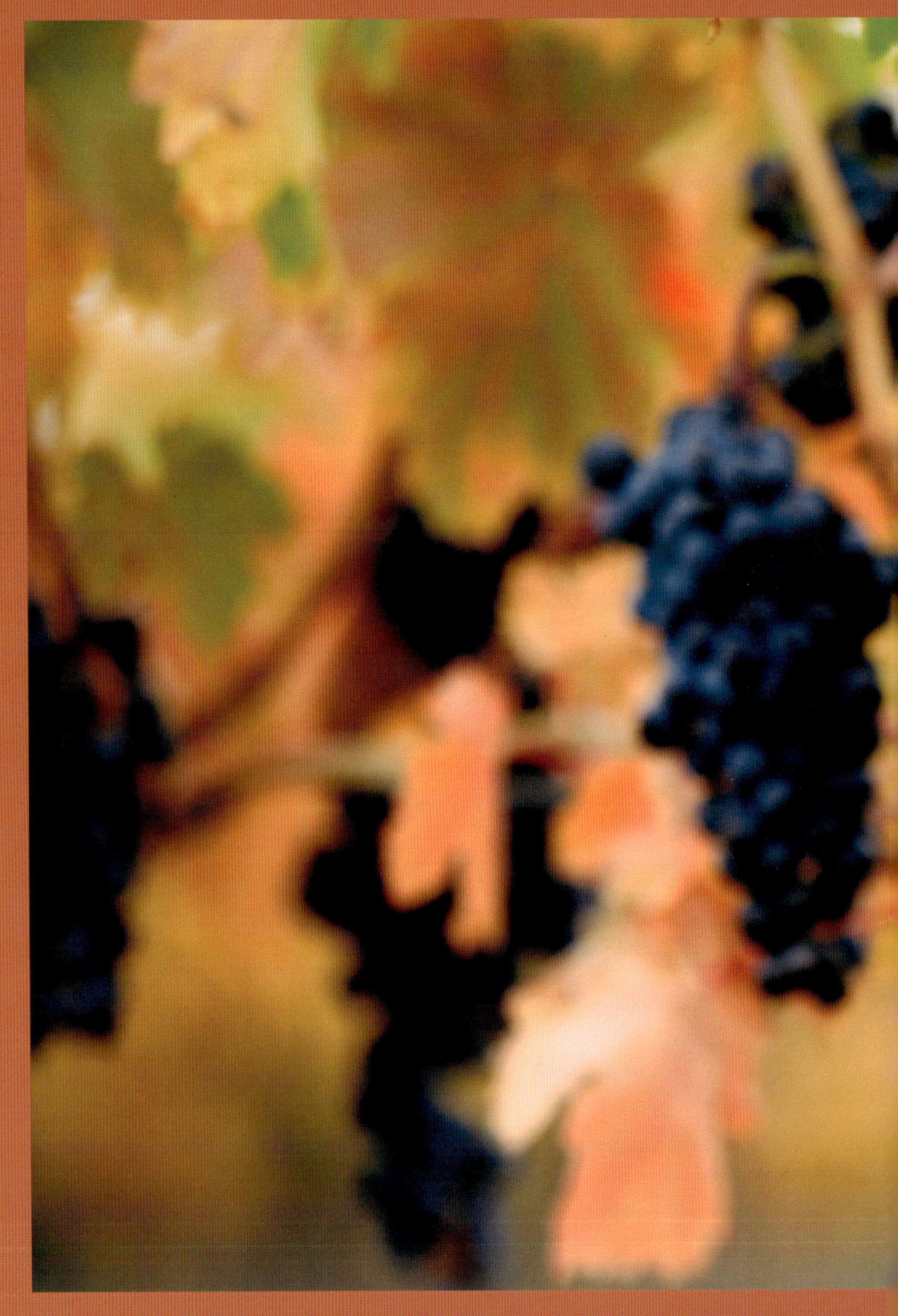

Fall Fruit Harvest

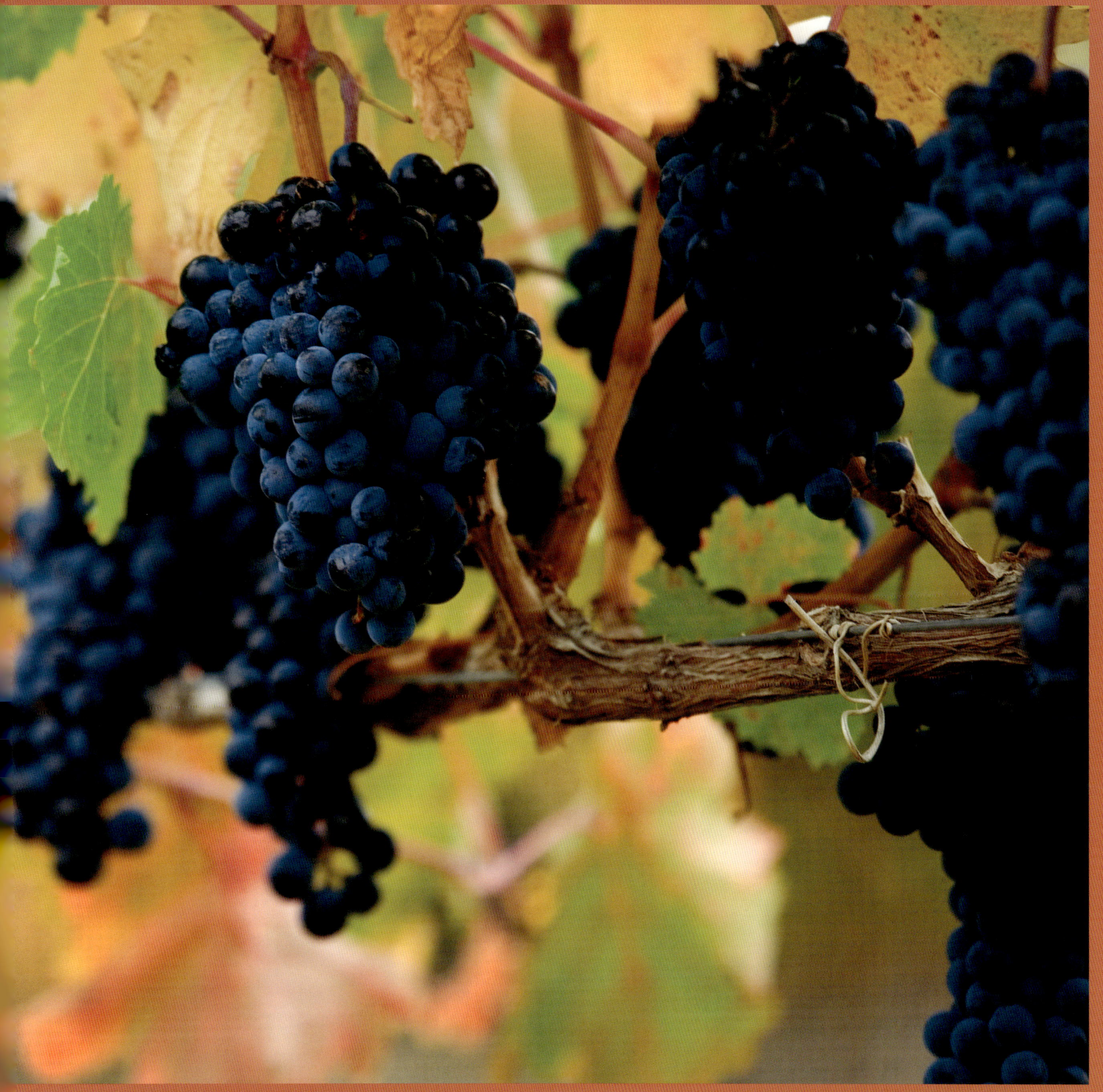

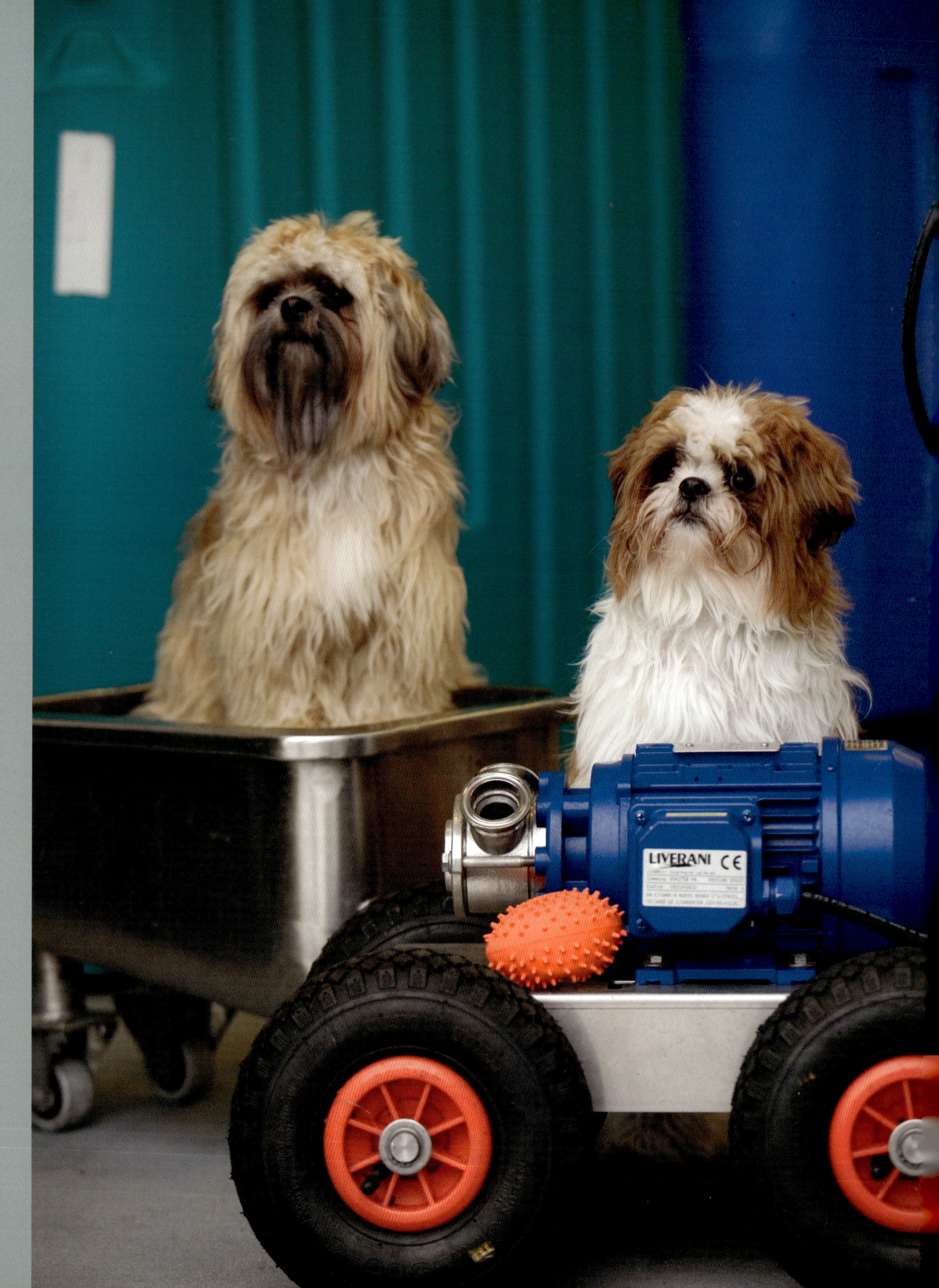
LIVERANI CE

Devin & Debra for Isra & Zazu

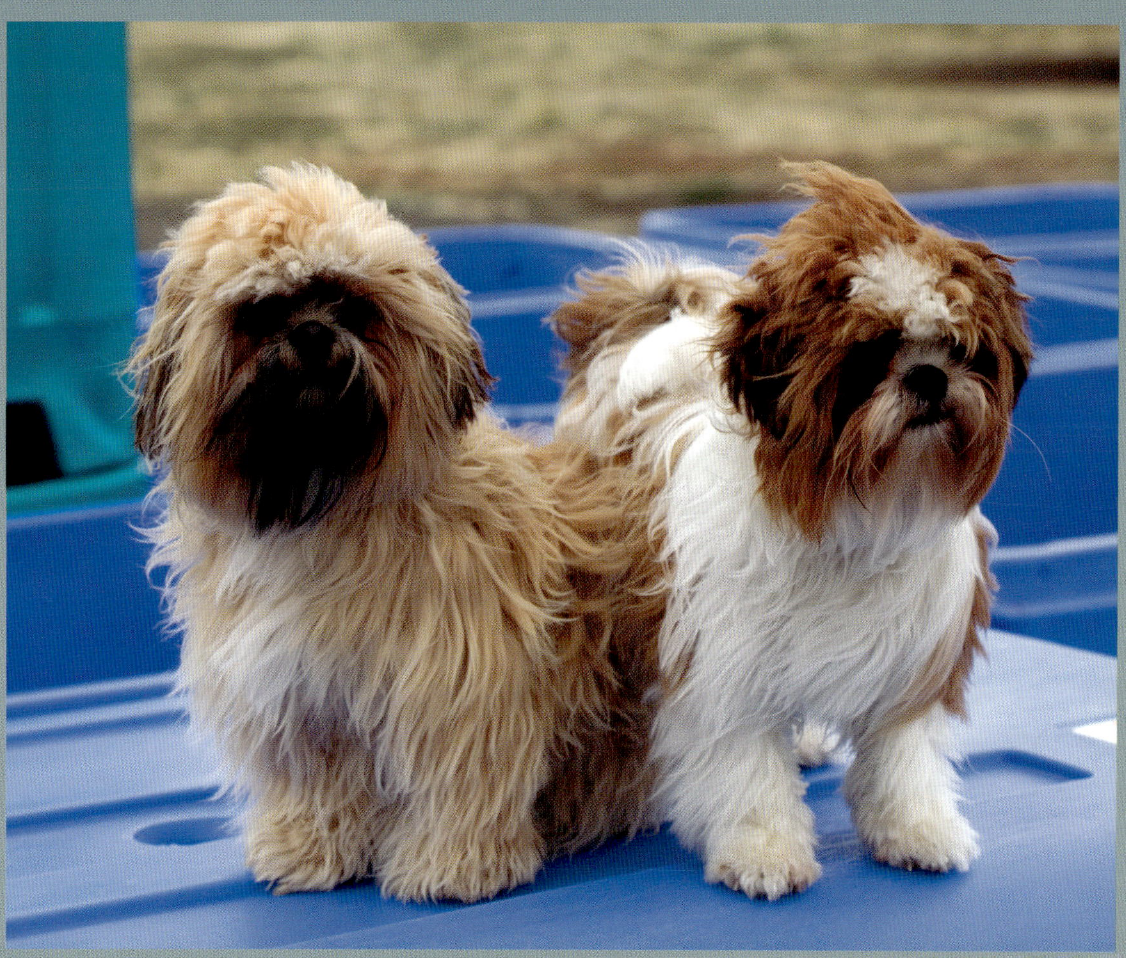

Isra and Zazu

Adamant Cellars

"Honey, are you sure you only want one dog?" I asked.
"Well, what are you thinking?" he responded.
"This little guy is mighty sweet, couldn't we get him, too?" I said.
The breeder offers a discount if we take the two and informs us that the brown and white color combination signifies good luck. How can you deny bringing good luck to your life?
That's how Devin and I ended up with Isra and Zasu – two Shih Tzu brothers who are an integral part of our lives and winery.
While we envision them becoming our eight-paw custom crush crew, as puppies Isra and Zasu have an active role as vacuum cleaners, sucking up every little bug, grape, stem, and scrap within their reach.
At the winery they are the official welcoming committee, although we are working on mellowing their animated responses.
Isra and Zasu have taught us to be patient and kind, and have brought joy and utter silliness to our lives.

Devin and Debra Stinger

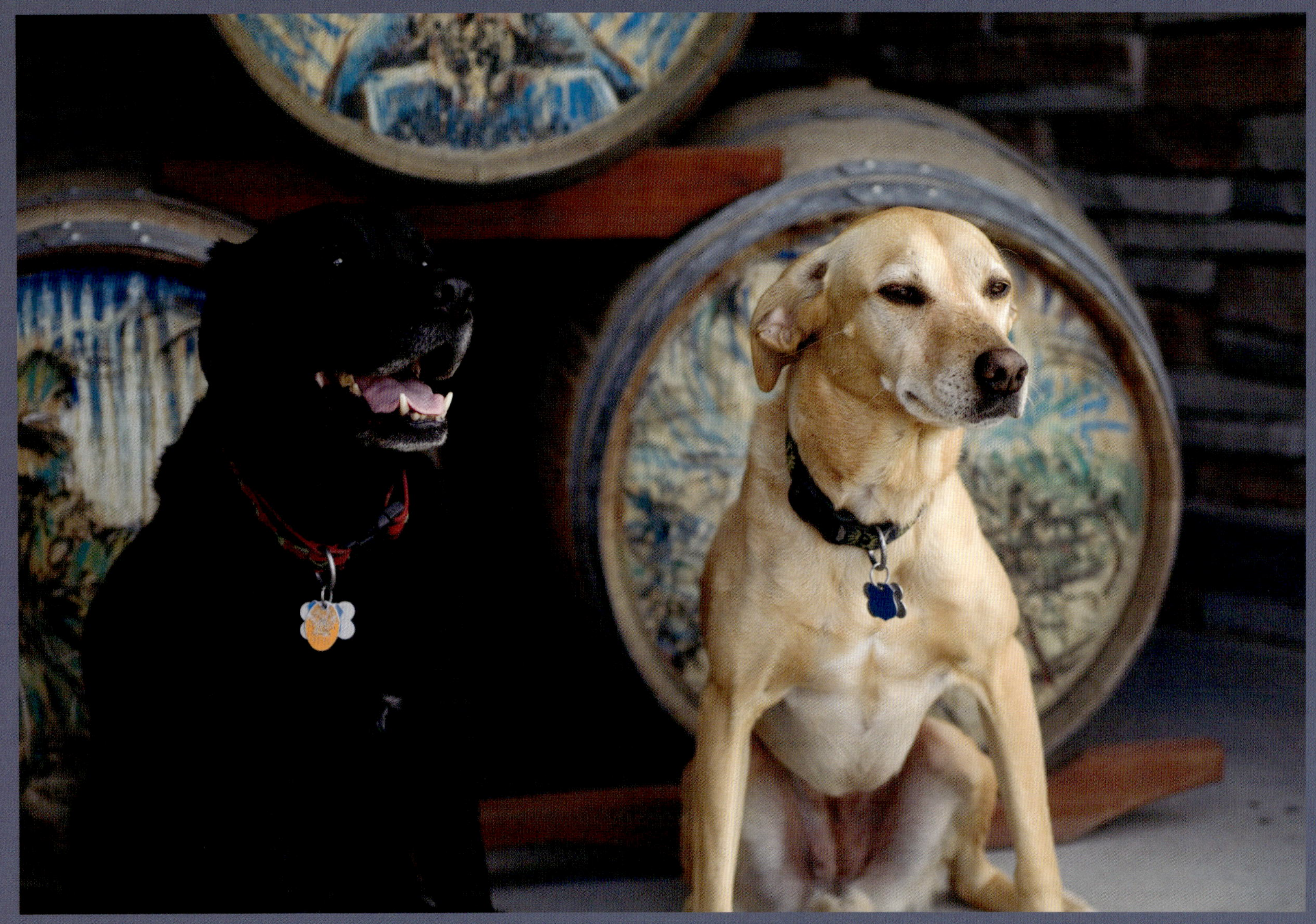

Huxley and Lucy

Isenhower Cellars

Huxley is our 12-year-old Black Lab whom we got as a puppy when we lived in Colorado. He was born for the water and loves to swim after sticks in the Columbia River. Huxley is so gentle that he allows our 2-year-old daughter to hold his leash on walks. Lucy is our Milton-Freewater mutt. She is probably 1/3 Labrador, 1/3 Vizsla and 1/3 crazy. Now 7-years old, Lucy howls for joy whenever guests come to the winery. Strangely Lucy only likes to eat white wine grapes and shuns the red ones.

Brett and Denise Isenhower

Recco and Lalique

Isenhower Cellars

Lalique and Recco are two loved dogs who deal with differed canine complexes.

Lalique, a 4-year-old, came to me via the Newfoundland Rescue Group in Spokane. She has a hard time being away from me and quickly climbs inside any open car door or hatch so she won't be left behind.

Recco, a recently acquired Newfie pup, has a drinking problem. He sticks his feet and most of his face in the water bowl. Recco loves being wet and cool – swimming is part of his nature – and mud-puddles work, too.

Both Lalique and Recco visit the winery several times a week and love the attention they get from our visitors.

Since I have started making wine on my own, both dogs will some day enjoy their "minutes of fame" by being on a label in some form or another.

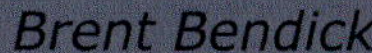

Brent Bendick

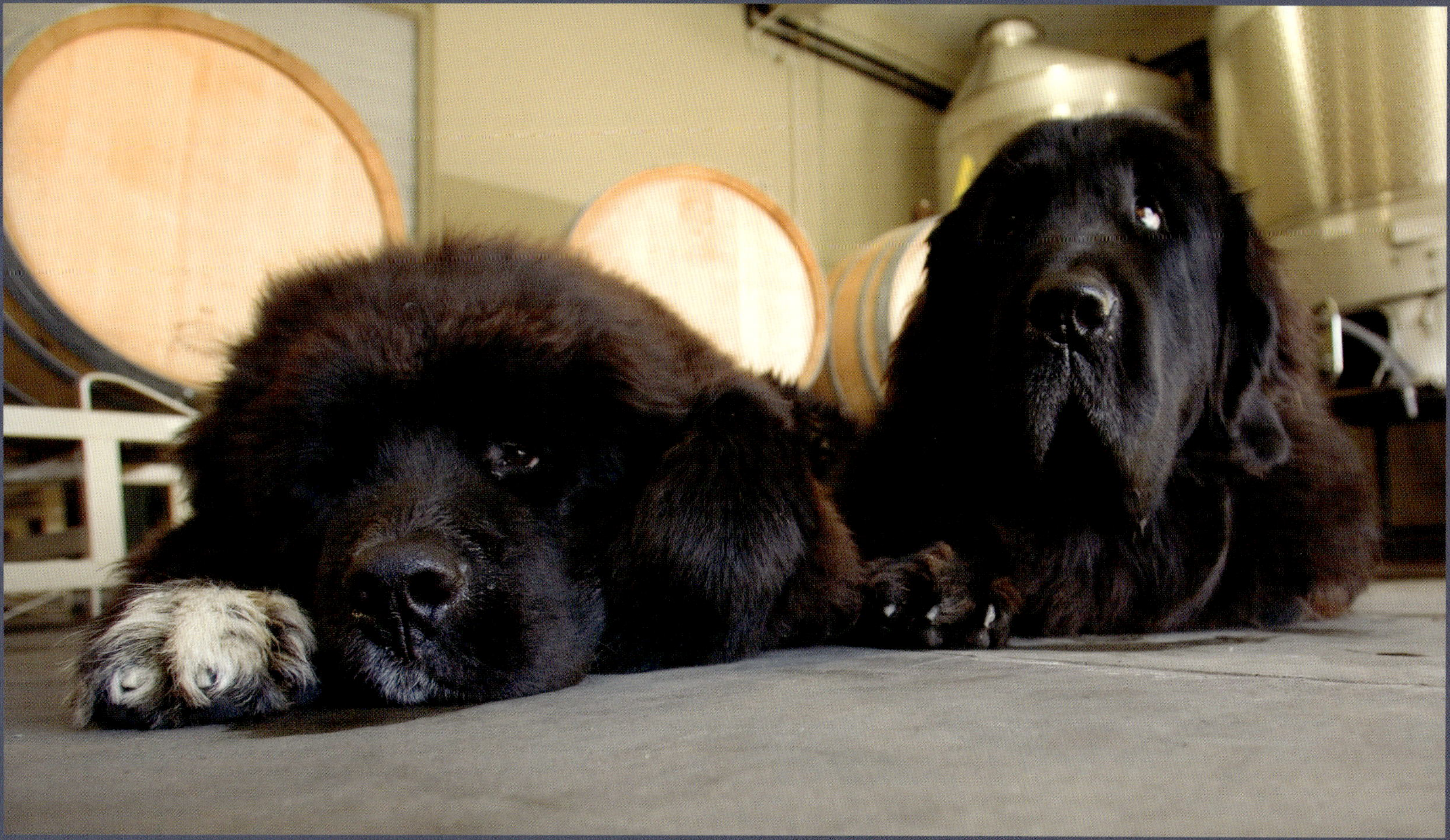

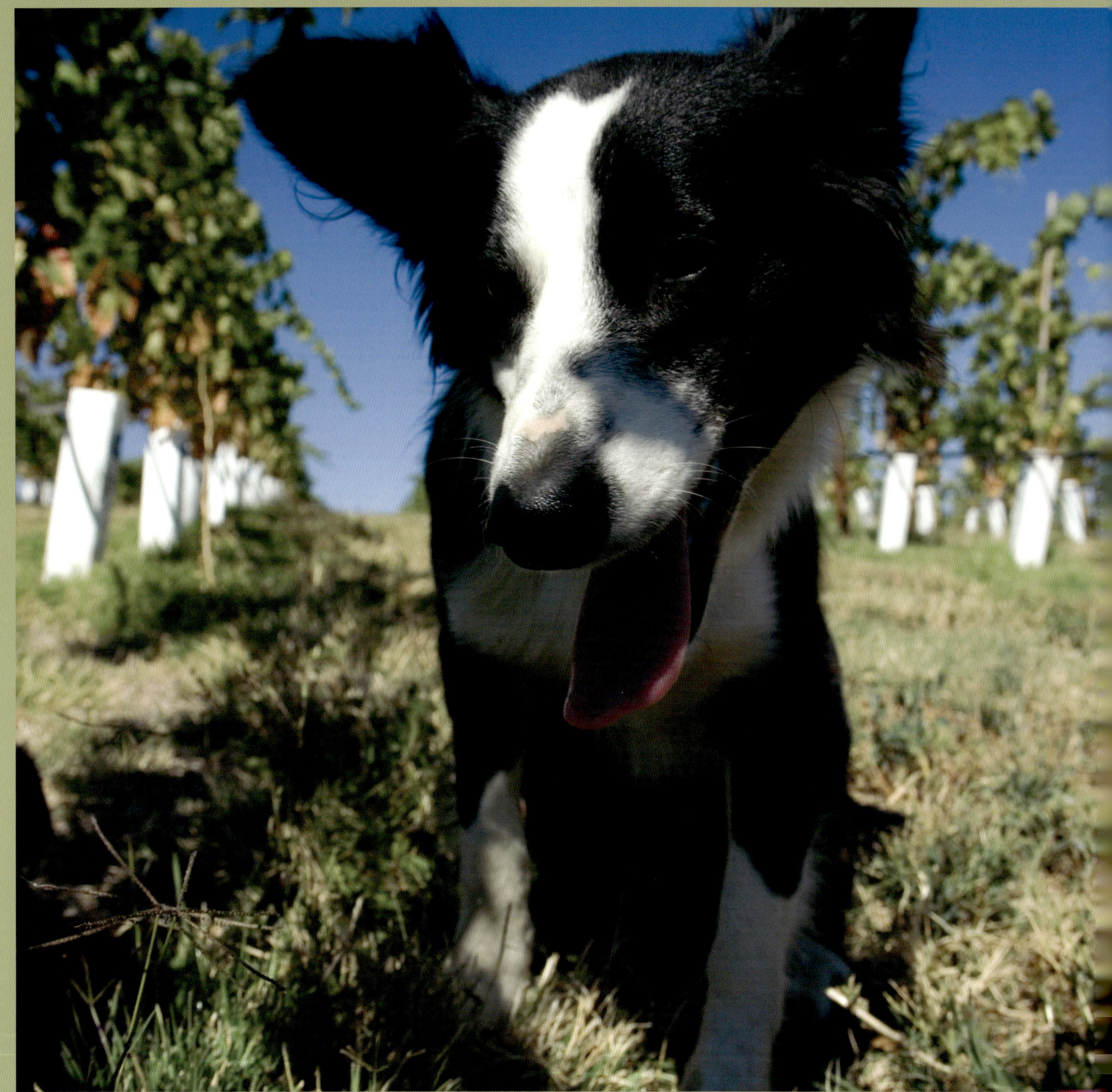

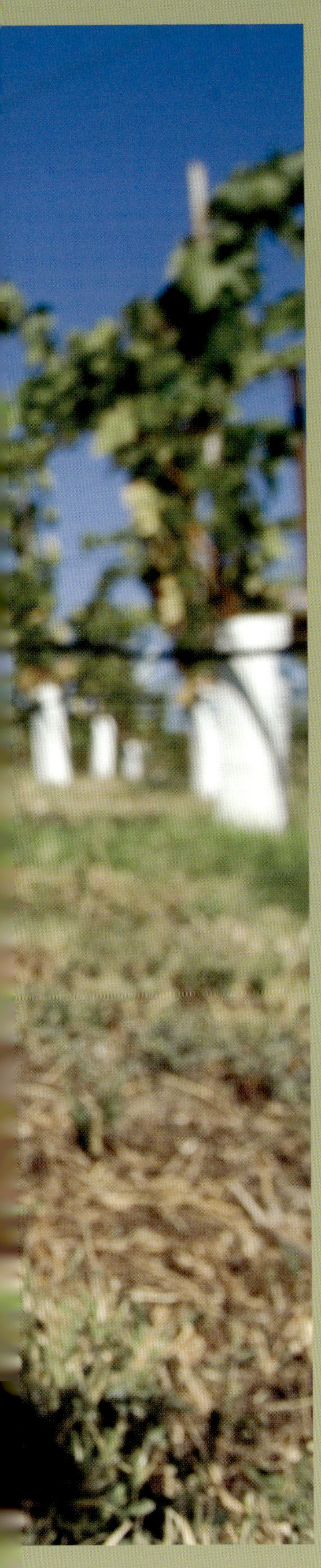

Charlie and Chewy

Gifford Hirlinger

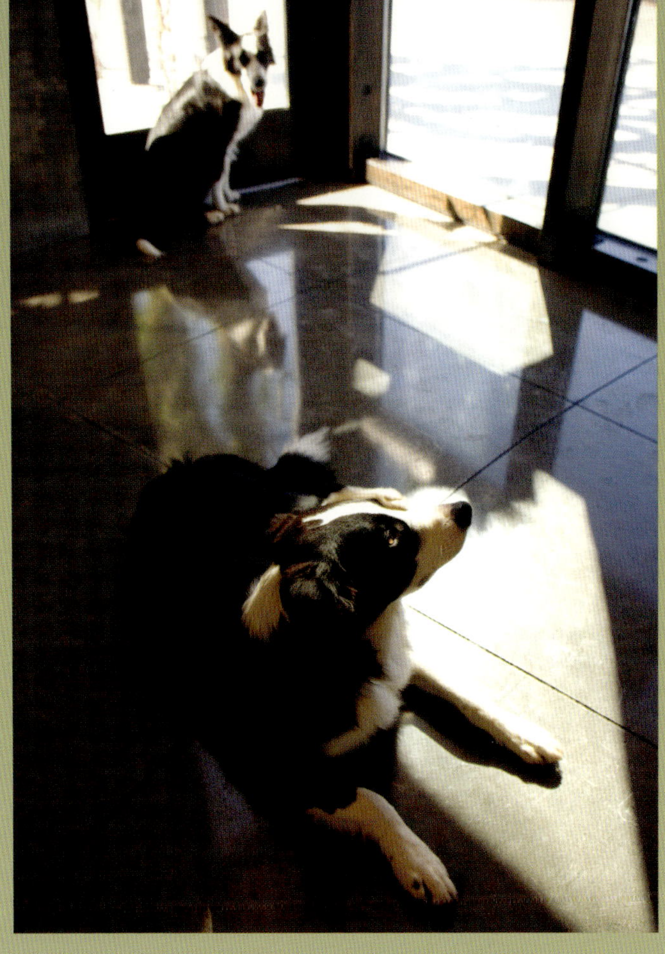

Chewy was first. Apparently worn down by my pleadings for a dog, Pete took me to "see the puppies" at a nearby ranch. We ended up with a bright-eyed bundle of black and while fluff that instantly won our hearts.

That same day, our son Mike – the Cifford Hirlinger winemaker – responded to my excited phone call and came by to meet our new puppy. The next day, we picked out Charlie, Chewy's brother from the same litter.

It's amazing how these two pups became an integral part of life with our family. They accompany Pete and Mike nearly everywhere, monitor the tractor at work, play with our grandchildren and chase off rogue starlings trying to land on their grapes.

Chewy and Charlie are still pups, so their favorite activity is play. They romp around together outside their winery and love to greet visitors.

An no, we haven't named a wine for them as yet – we figure they need to age a bit.

Stephanie and Peter Bergham

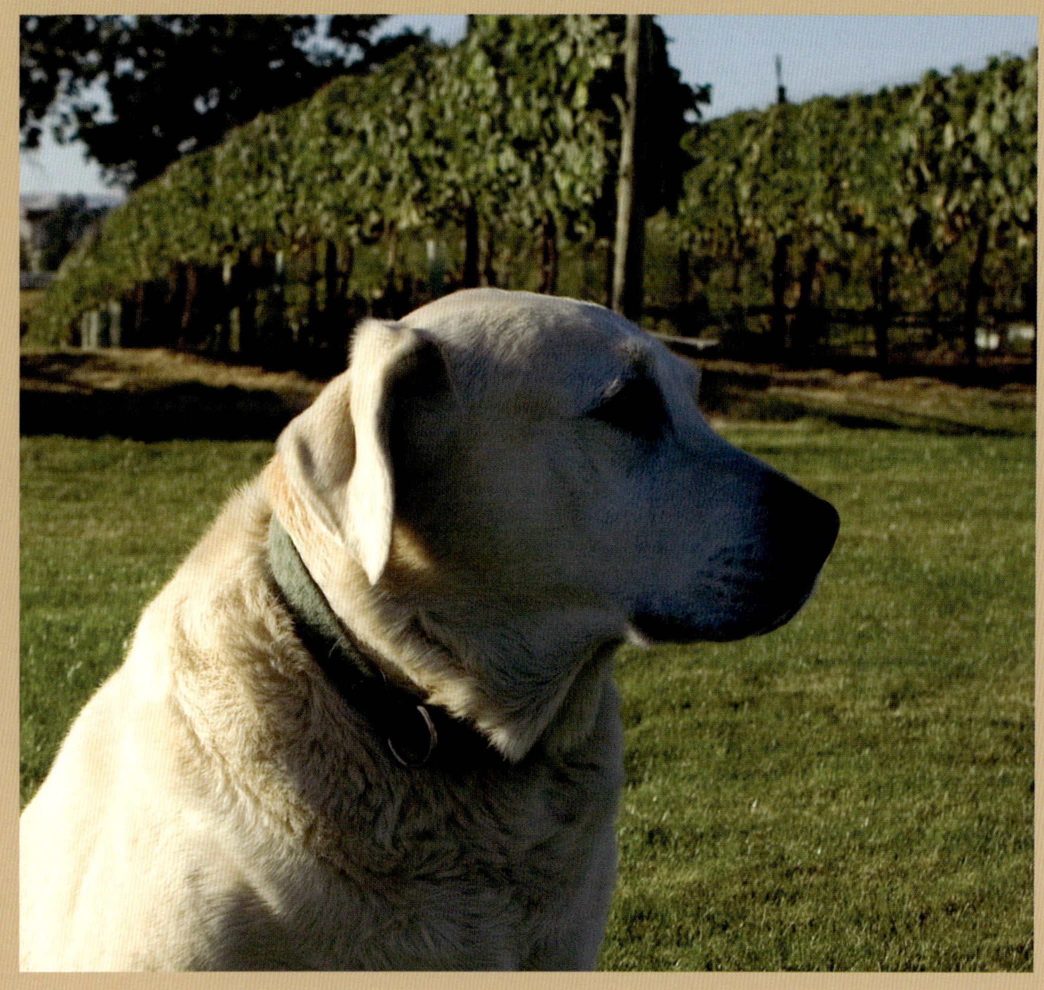

Barrett

Hence Cellars

Barrett was born on the campus of The Guide Dogs for the Blind in California. It was his destiny to be a Guide Dog. In fact, he was "paired" with a family when an illness and the related treatment cost him his placement in the program.

While Barrett returned to his first family, changes there left him home alone all day. They were planning a move. It was time for Barrett to go to "Papa's house."

We've become the best buddies.

Barrett's original family still visits him, but his love now is time with me. He feels a sense of duty as he "guards" my pickup. The vineyard is like a playground, and yet a job, too, as Barrett moves up and down the rows.

Now, Barrett is near 8-years-old and we both at times just like to lay down and take "five."

When you visit Hence Cellars, look for the little gray pick-up, and not far away you'll find me and my old buddy, Barrett.

Willis "Papa" Orchard

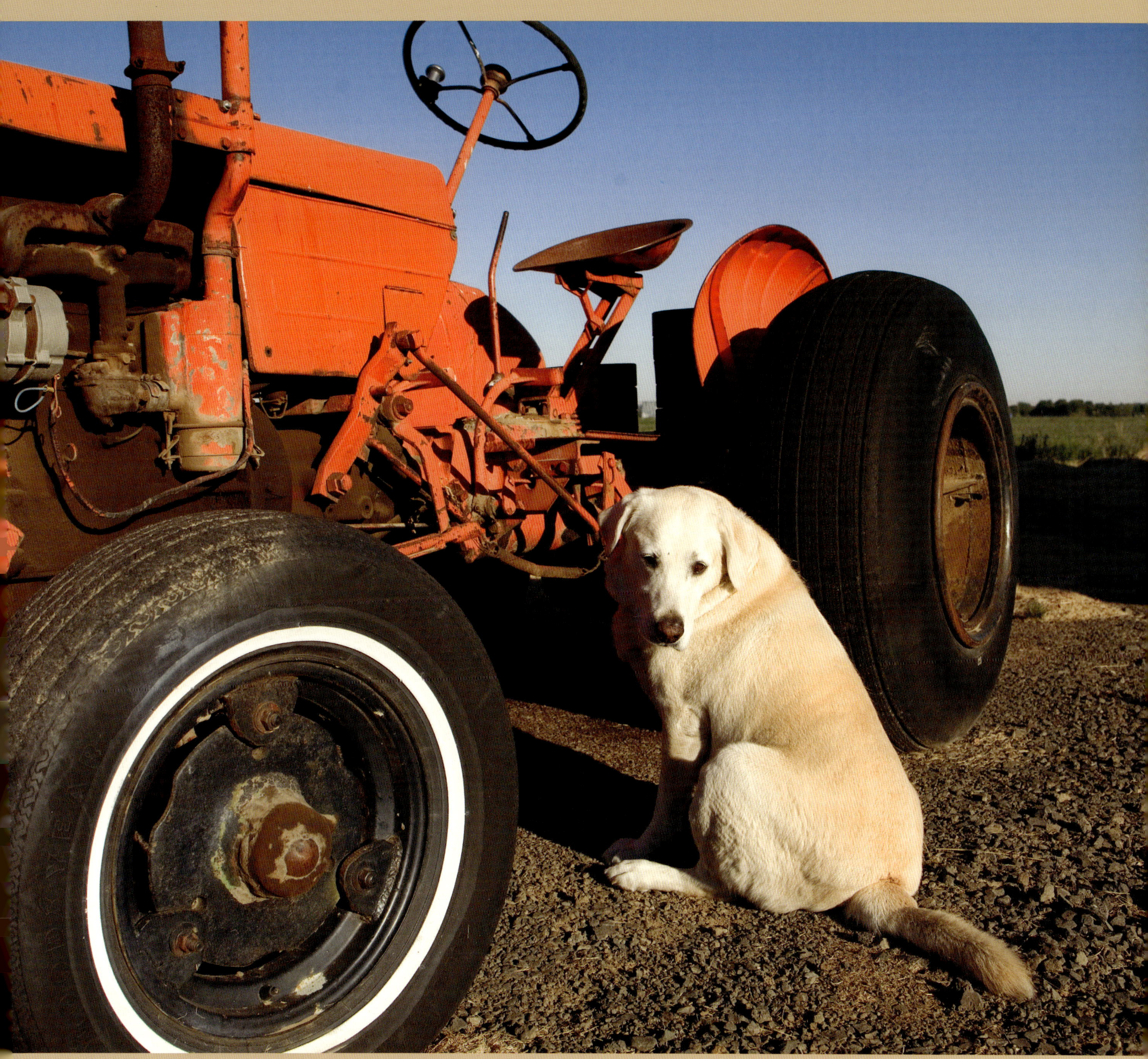

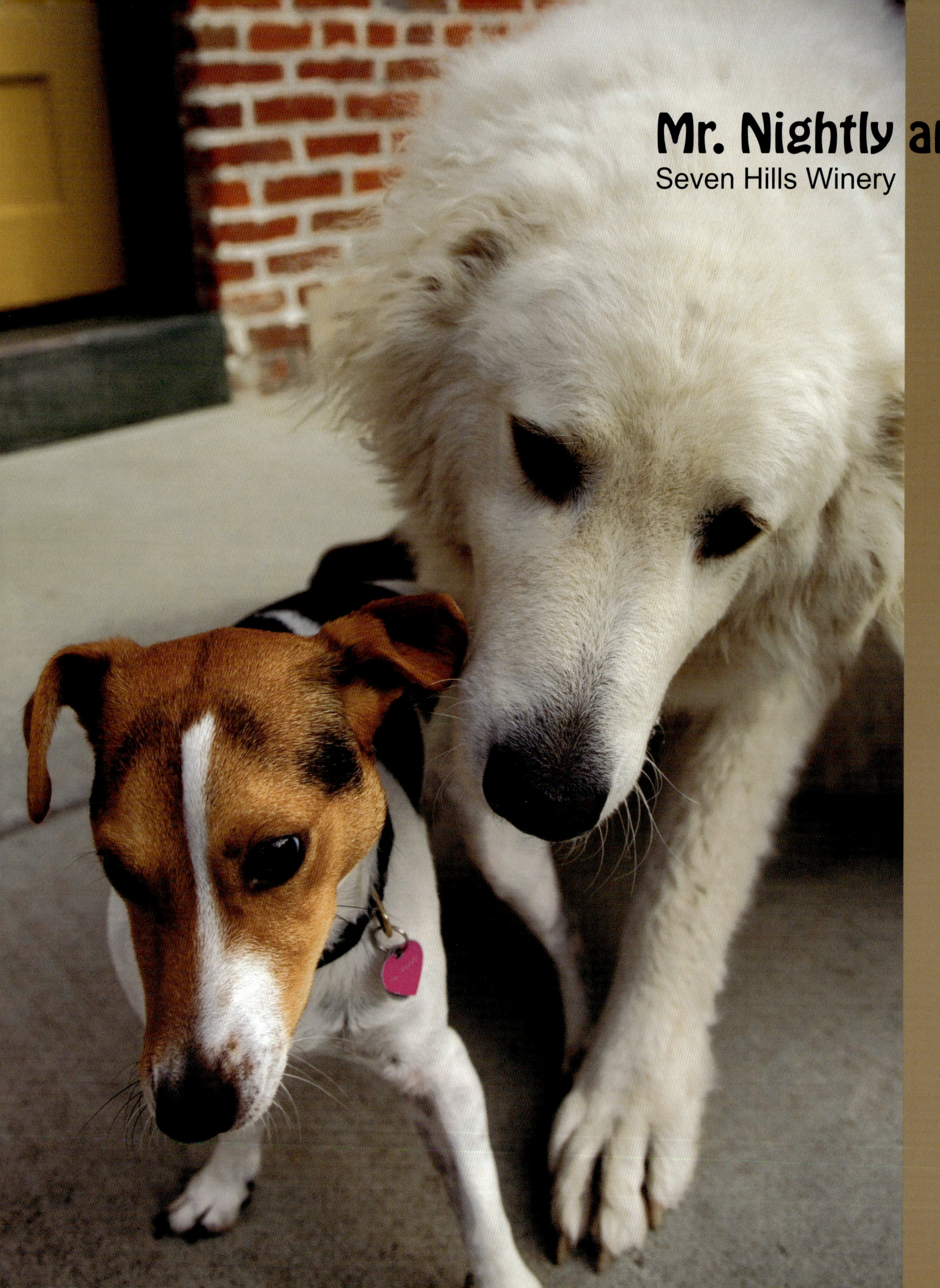

Mr. Nightly and Neve

Seven Hills Winery

Mr. Knightly is a small doggie with a stalwart heart.
He came to Seven Hills by way of the devastating hurricanes of 2005. His mother was found pregant and lost in the wake of the storms and taken by volunteers to a shelter in Georgia, where Mr. Knightly was born. Conditions were so crowded he and his brother were transferred to Washington State, where by virtue of his extreme cuteness and indomitable spirit he captured our hearts and came home to Walla Walla.
As near as anyone can tell, Mr. Knightly is a Parson Russell Terrier with black paw print markings on his back, a toffee colored head and magnificent curled tail.
True to his name, he has the character of the perfect gentleman, greeting man and beast alike with a wag and a nod. While the last thing we expected was to have a winery dog, now we cannot imagine our days without him.

Casey and Vicky McClellan

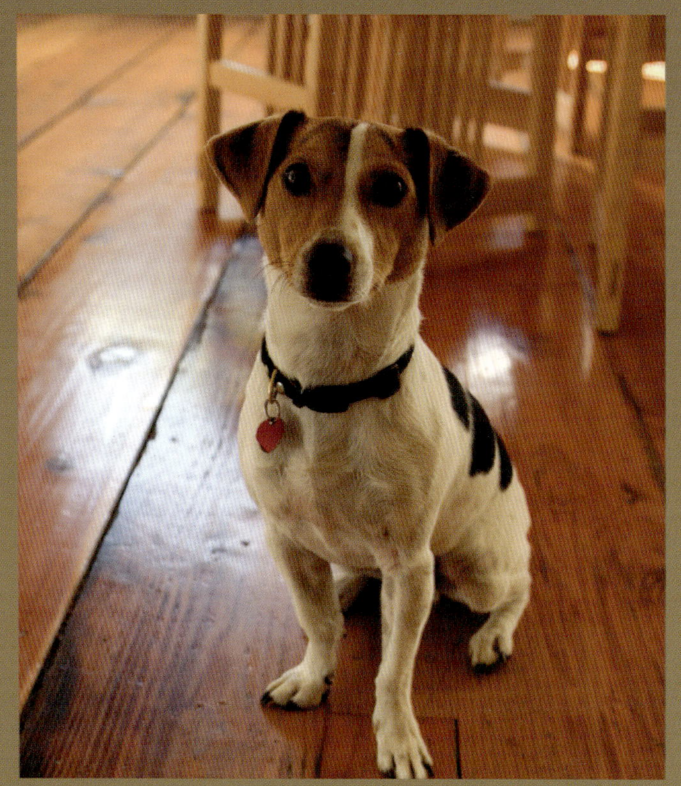

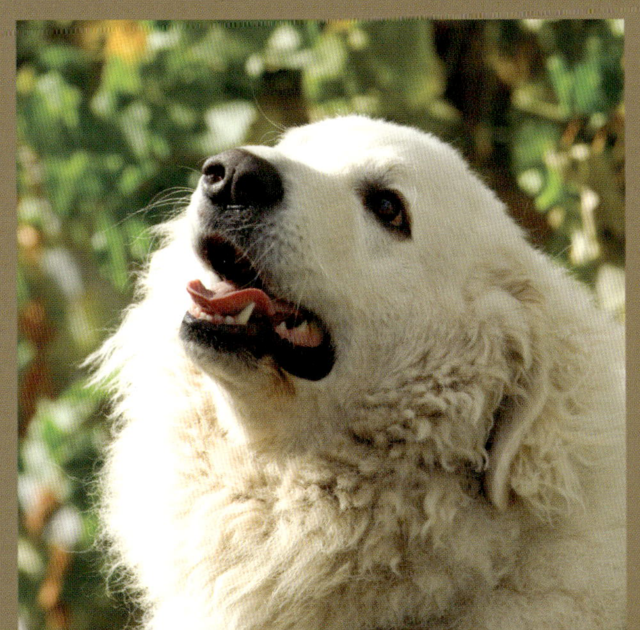

Neve is a gentle giant.
As a puppy, with paws so big he could barely walk without tripping over them, he was careful not to bite or scratch or even to take a treat from our hands too greedily. He respects cats, even bugs, and gets rambunctious only with other dogs and playful children. He is also a kingly dog, sitting on our front porch and giving his most regal look to all passersby.
I have rarely known such an expressive animal. When his food or walk come late, he is capable of a distinctive pout, and when he runs off leash through fields, he smiles as broadly as any ecstatic human. Yet he never whines, barks only when he has a reason, and I am still waiting for the day when he will turn to me and speak in a full sentence.

Haydn and Jen Mouat

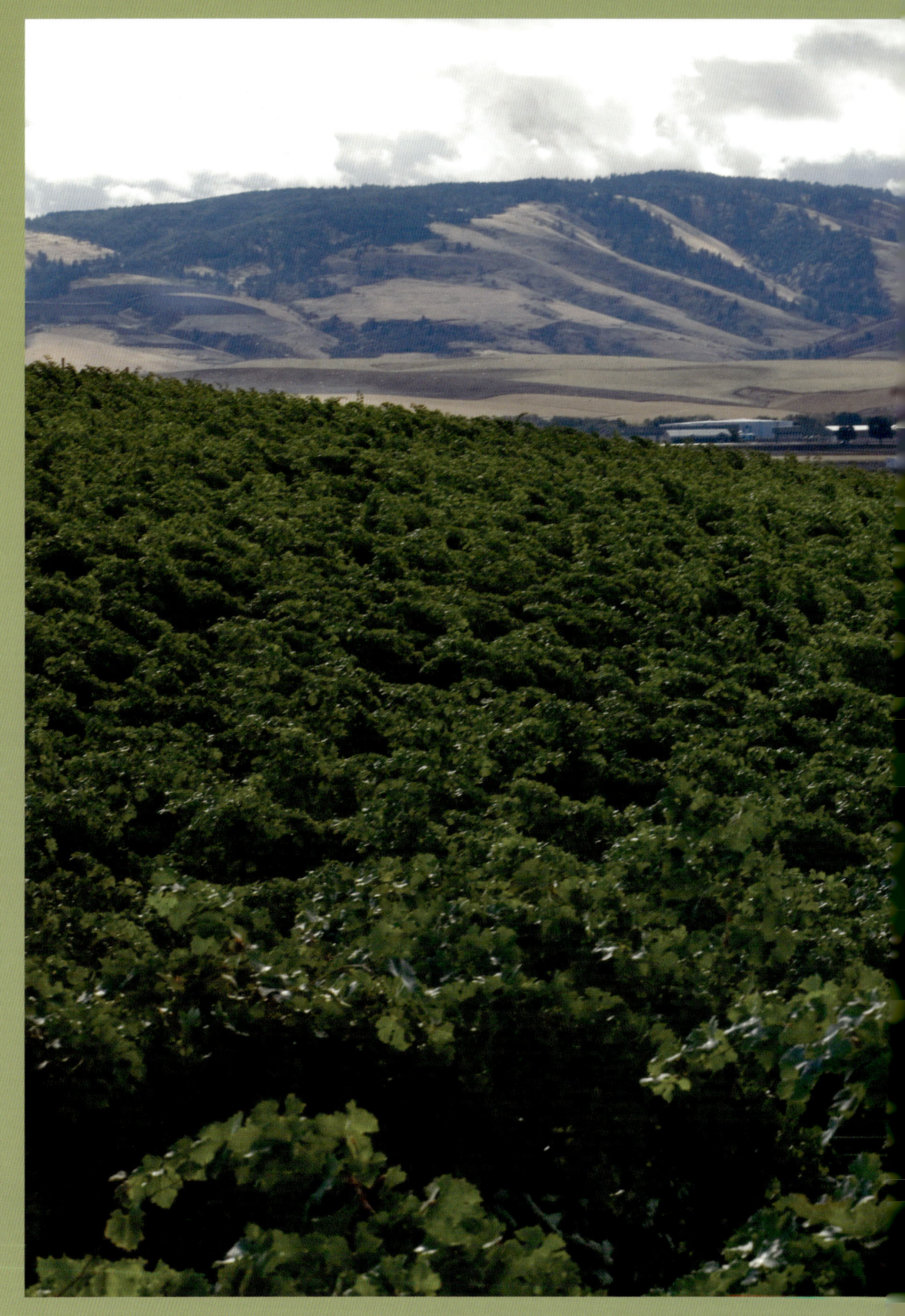

Minnick Vineyard

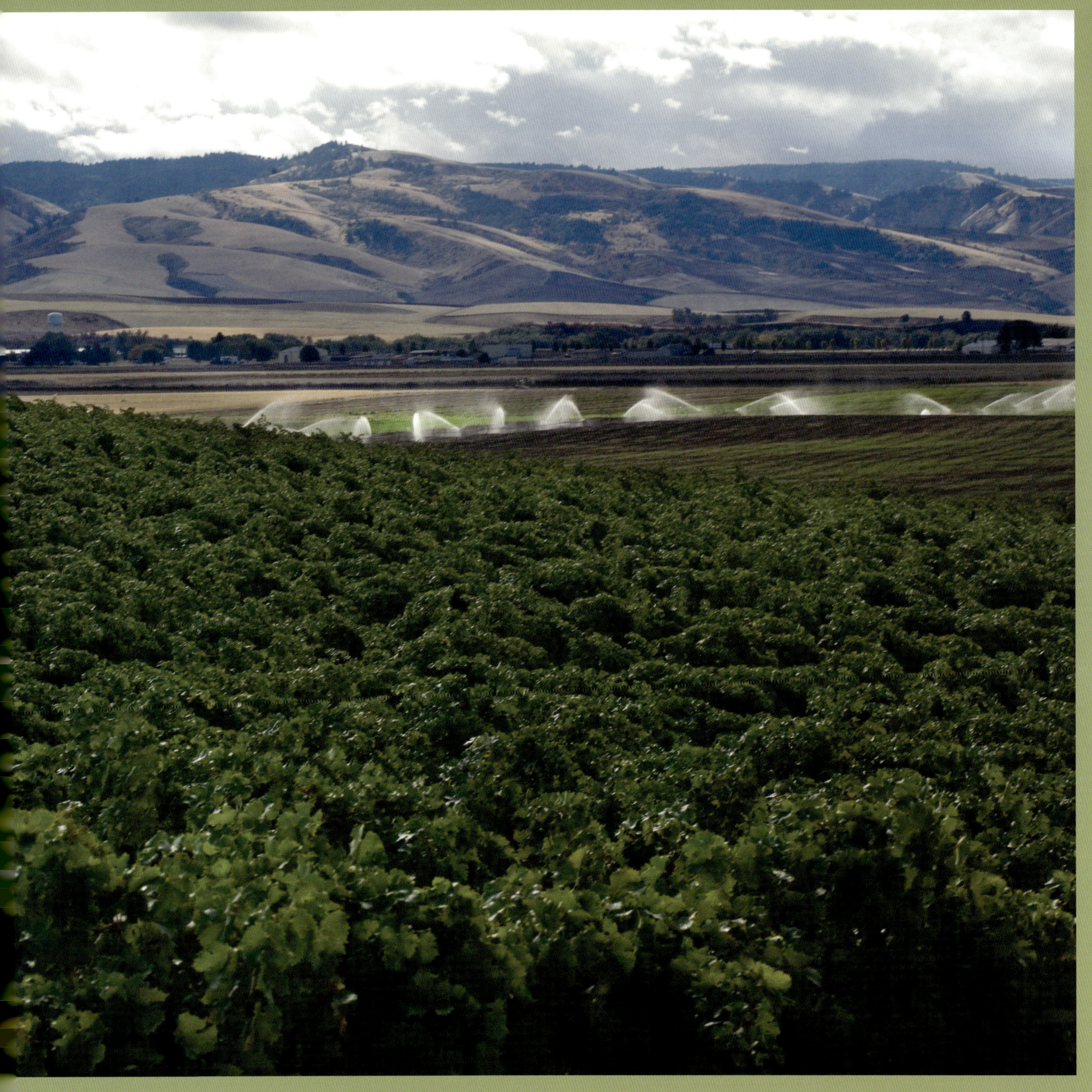

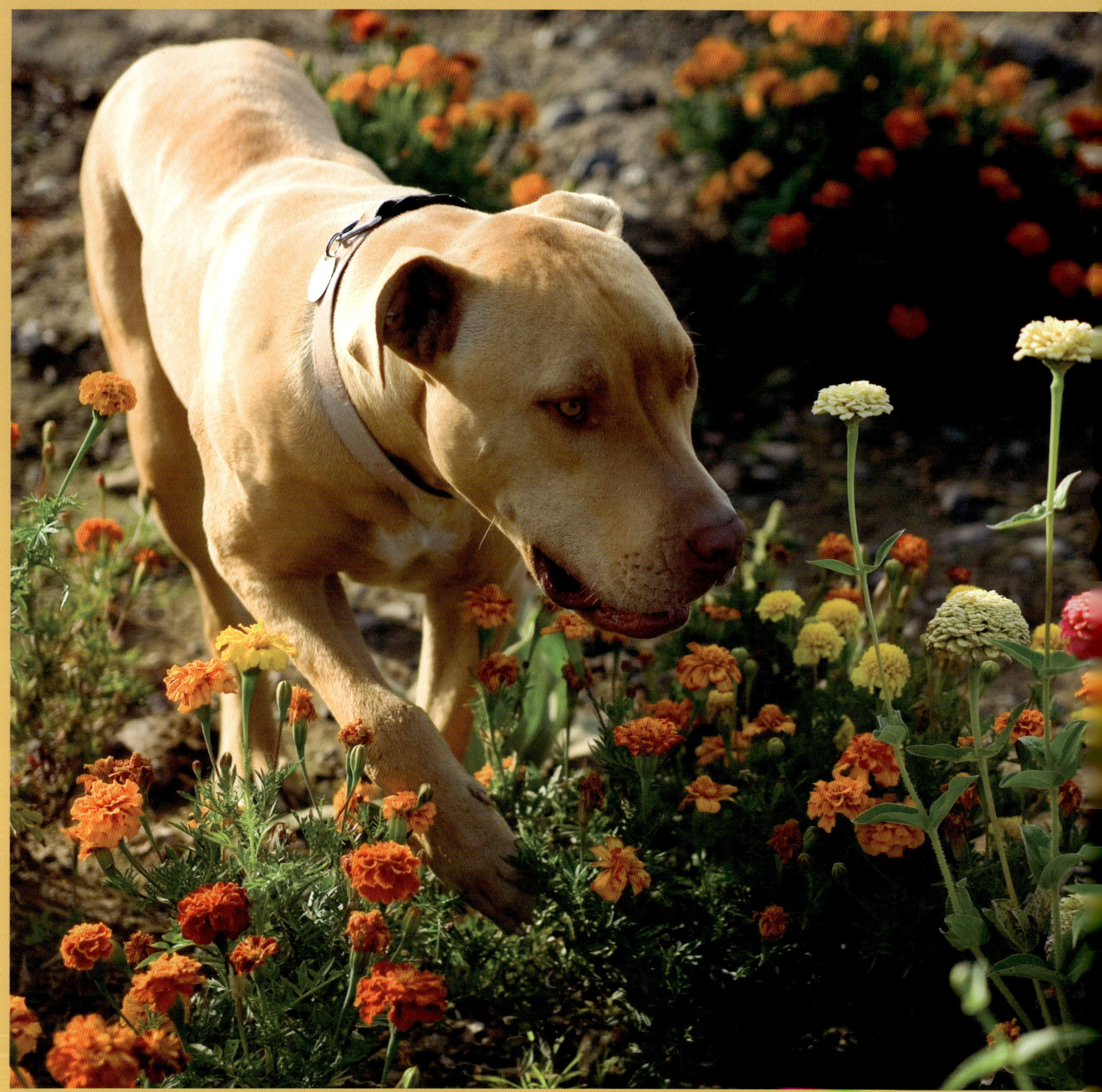

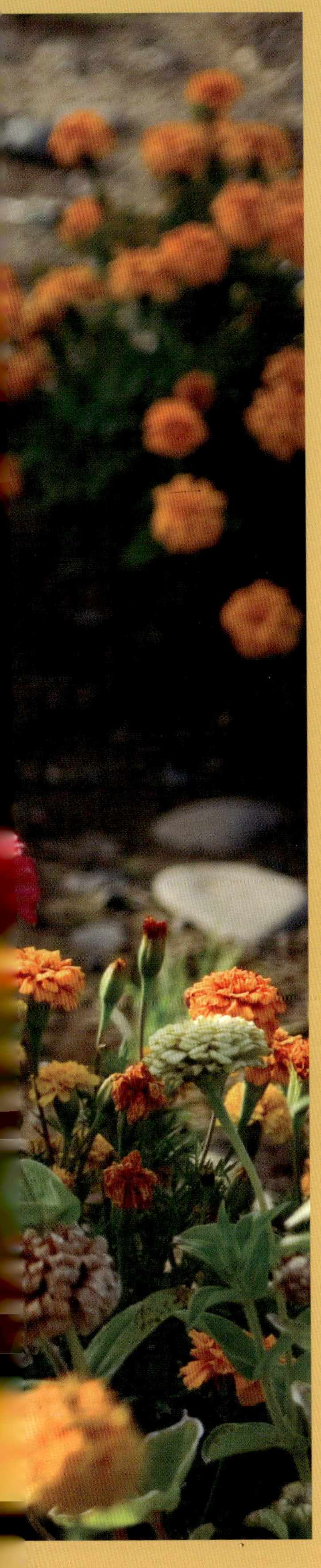

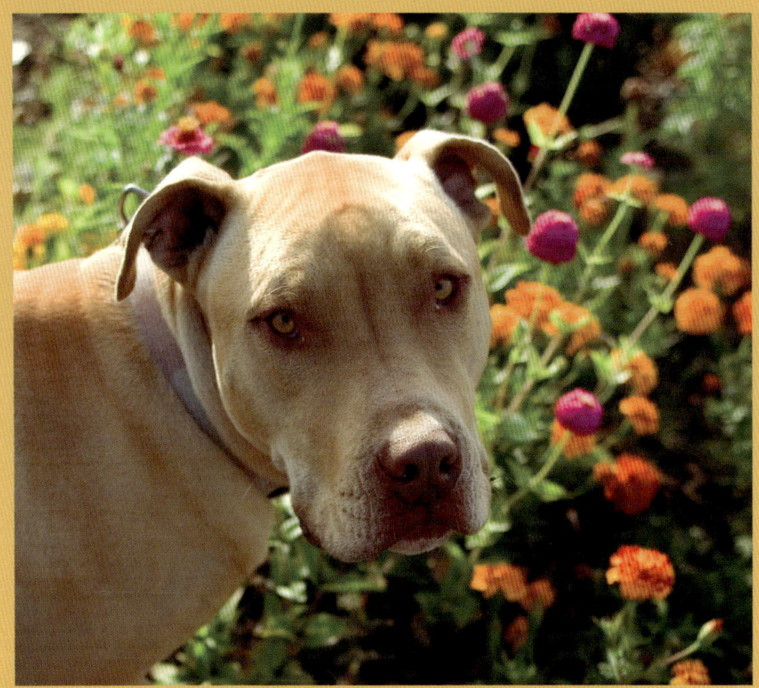

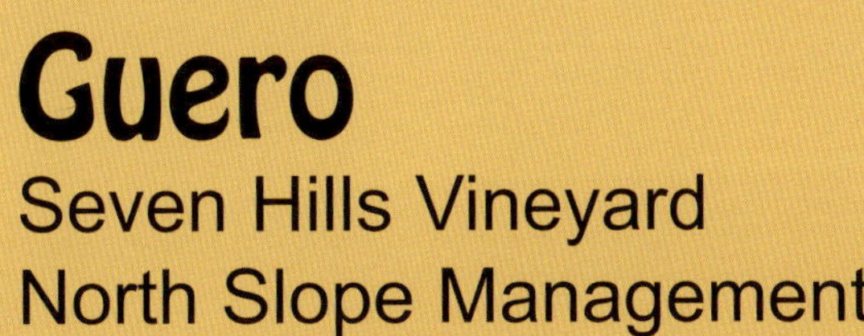

Guero

Seven Hills Vineyard
North Slope Management

Guero Gomez, a 3 1/2-year-old Red Nosed Pit Bull, calls Seven Hills Vineyard home.

When he was 18 months old, his owner, Army Sgt. Roberto Gomez was deployed to Iraq, so Guero came to live with Roberto's parents, Lupe and Rosa and their family.

Although he stands nearly 30 inches tall and poses a unique vision of vigilance and wariness, he is best pals to the Gomez children – Leo, Francisco and Daniel. When they are in school, Guero senses when the bus is about to deliver them home and he's waiting at the road side ready to greet them with big Guero kisses.

While Guero's stature commands strangers to not loiter, it's an appearance that camouflages his sweet temperament. Guero finds comfort and solitude napping in the vineyard's bio-diversity gardens of Zinnia's, Buttercups and Daisies.

Just as Sgt. Roberto Gomez is protecting our security in Iraq, Guero is protecting Seven Hills Vineyard and the Gomez family with a vigilant stare and lots of dog kisses.

Bob Buchanan

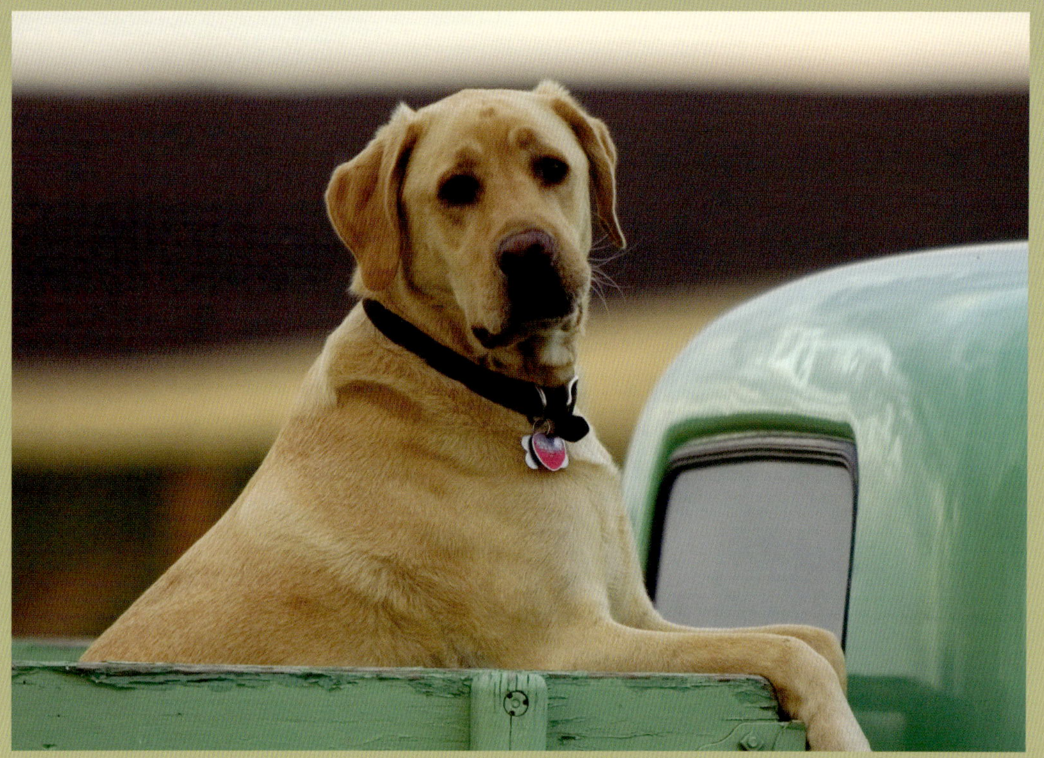

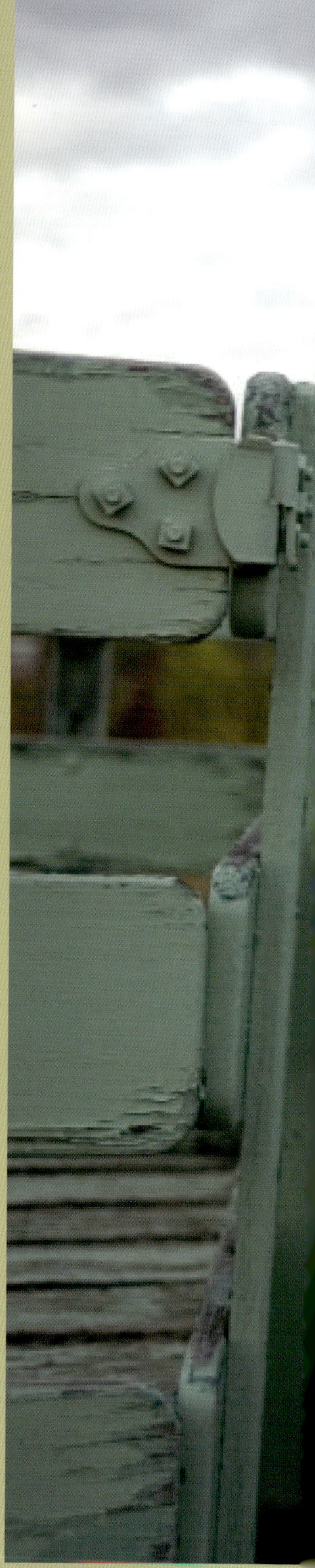

Banjo

aMaurice

Banjo is a great family dog and friend.
Now a 3-year-old Yellow Lab, Banjo was a Christmas surprise for our two daughters when they were 3 and 5.
He is a friendly and well-behaved young lad who doesn't go too crazy unless he sees a tennis ball, a squirrel, a cat, or a person who looks like they need his love (and who might give him a scratch or two).
Because of his personality, Banjo has earned several nick names, including "mellow yellow" and "Eore" (as in Winnie the Pooh's donkey freind).
When we are not too busy with harvest activities, Banjo often accompanies me to the winery, where he patrols the vineyard, chasing away birds and rodents. He loves it rain or shine and I enjoy having his company.

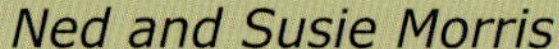

Ned and Susie Morris

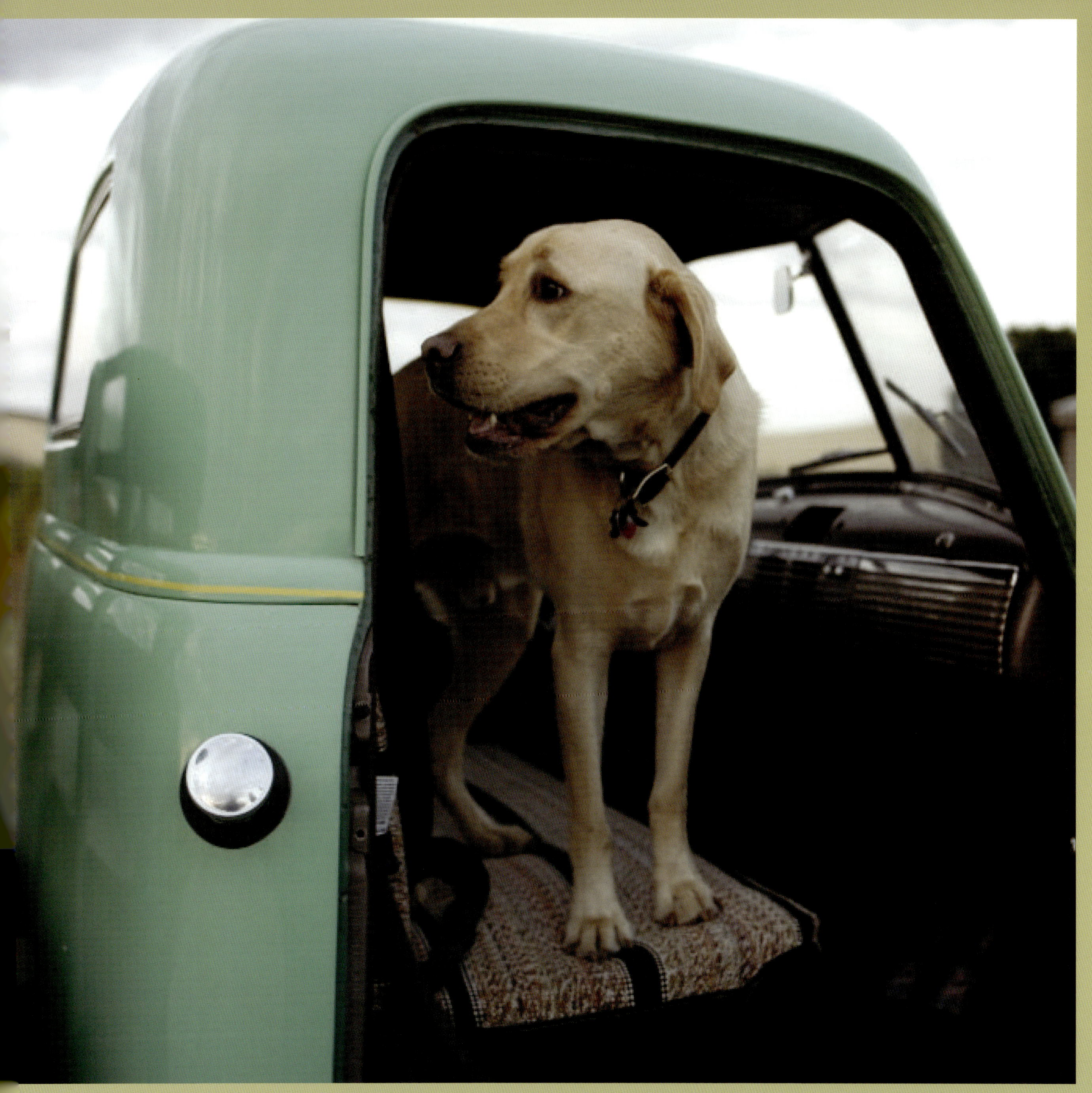

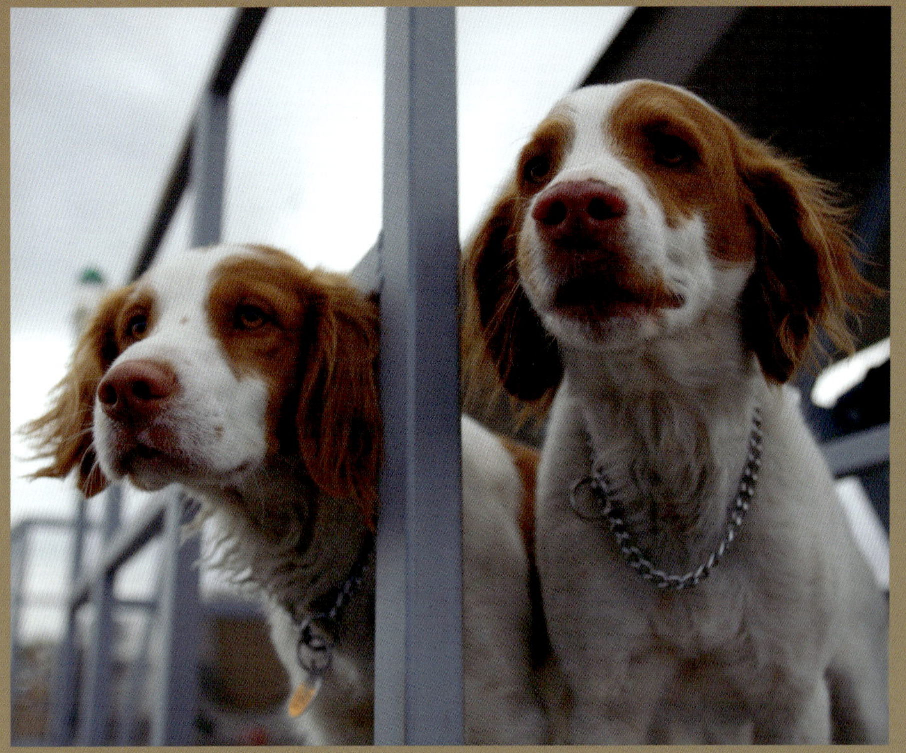

Baylee, Jasper, Chester

Five Star Cellars

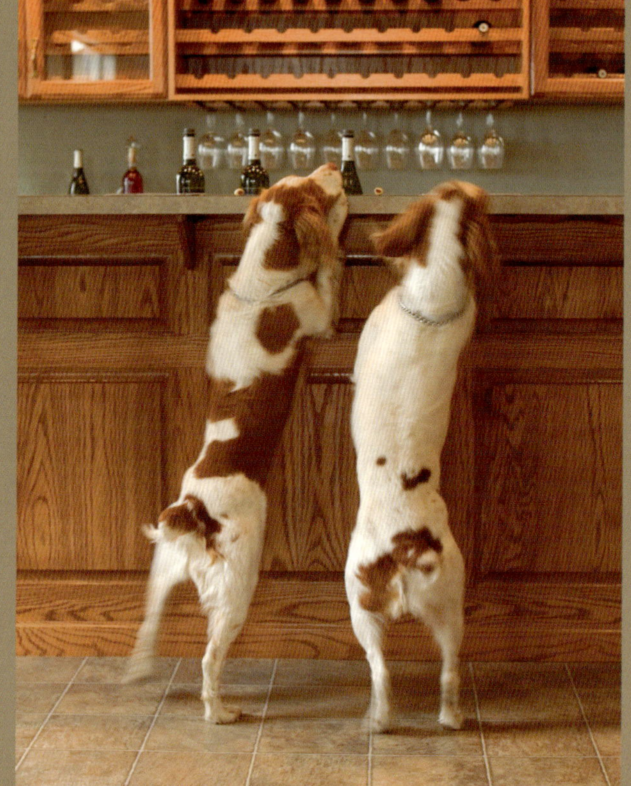

Baylee and Jasper are the "boys" that make sure everything is right at the winery. Both have to inspect everything to make certain nothing is out of place. Part of their vineyard visits include checking the fruit – and for Jasper, that sometimes means taking a nibble from clusters of grapes on the vine. When crush begins, their nightly visits are highlighted by Baylee's moth-chasing and Jasper's Baylee-chasing.

On Sundays, the pair become a trio when Chester joins in. Chester is Baylee's brother and Jasper's Uncle.

During his once-a-week visit, Chester's routine includes a careful check of the winery and the vineyard to make sure everything is in its place.

All three are quick to welcome tasting room visitors and enjoy their attention.

When Fall arrives, the fearsome threesome are all about seeking out the pheasants. They love to go hunting, are excellent at their sport and never fail to help put a few meals on the table.

Matt and Traci Huse

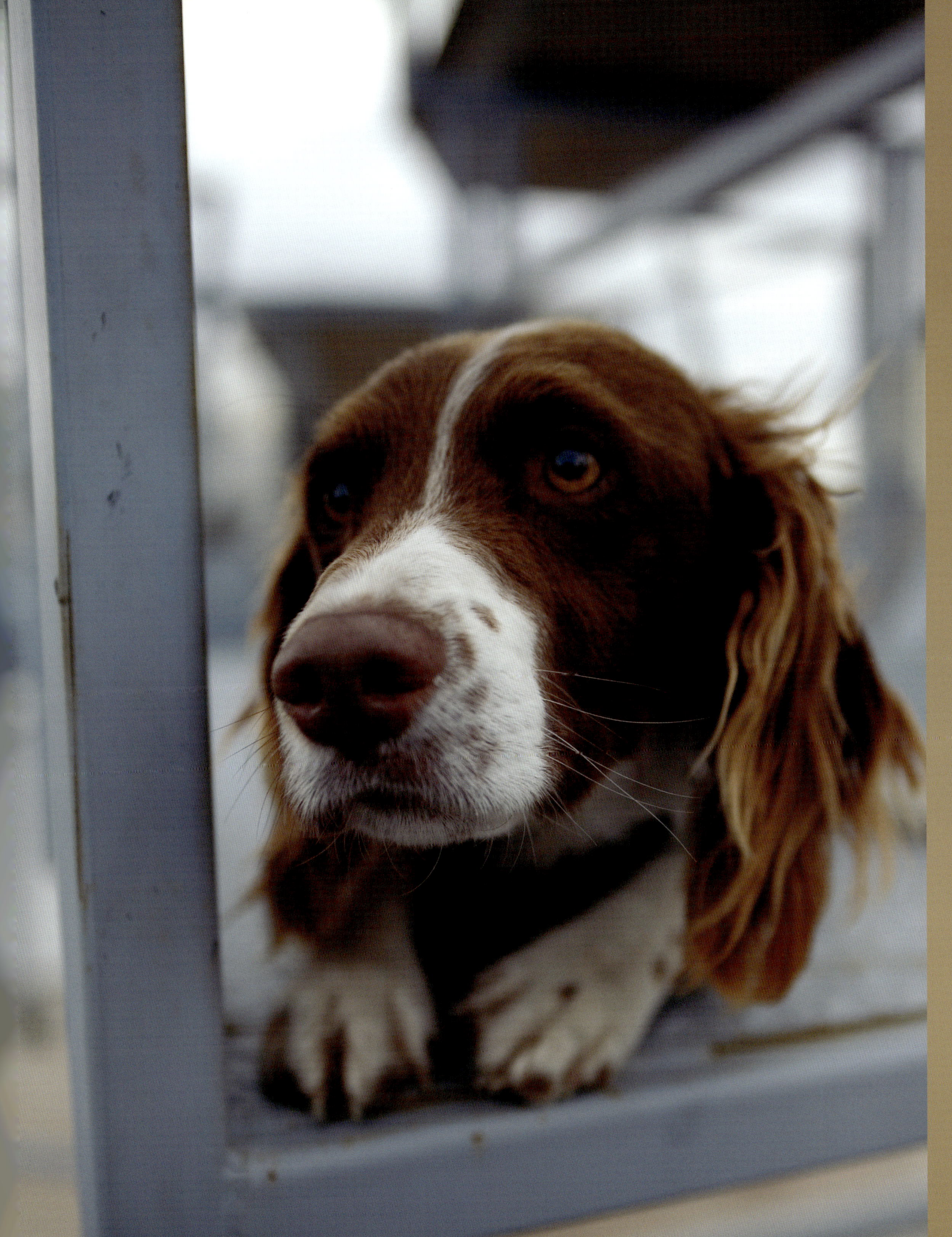

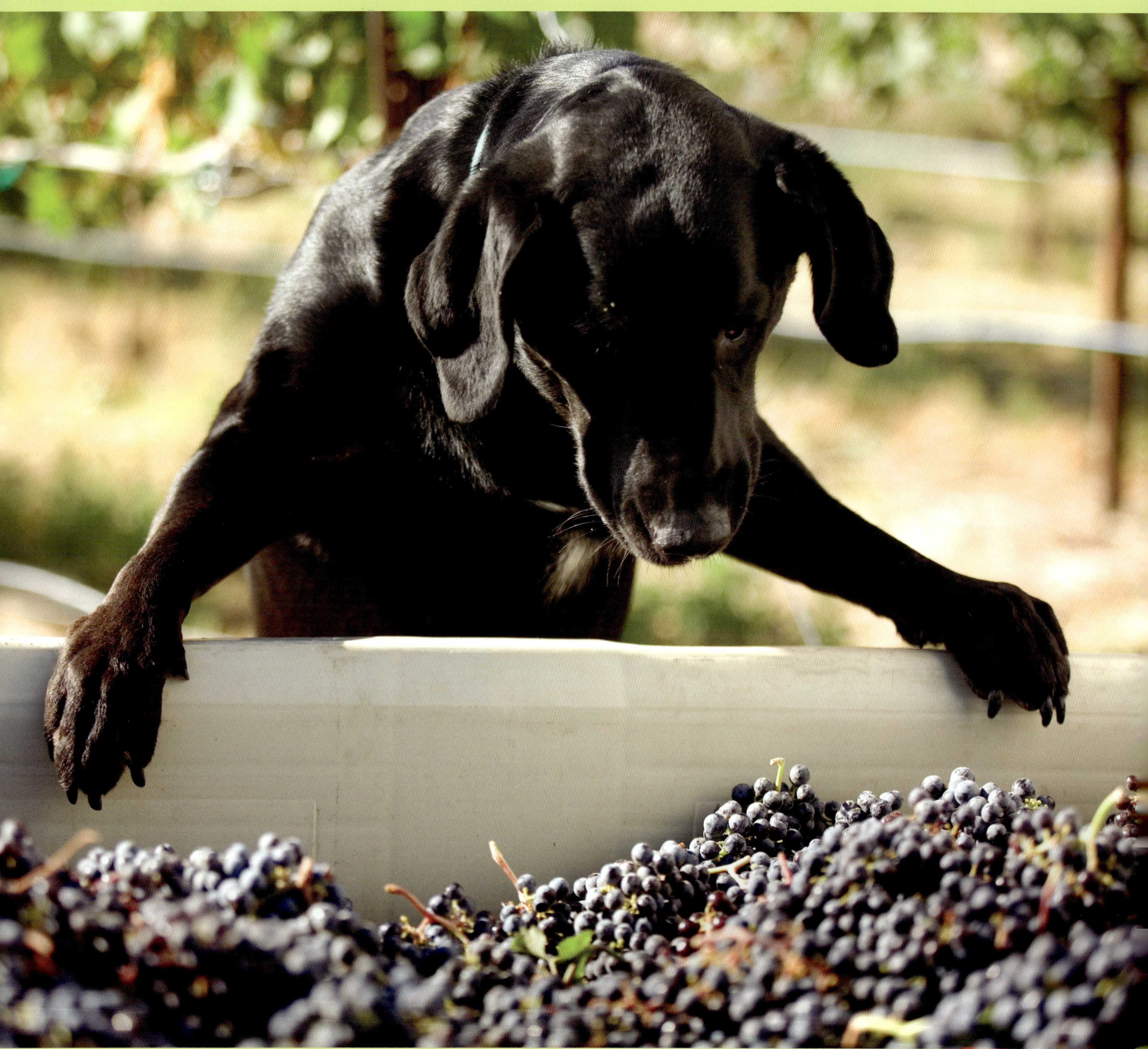

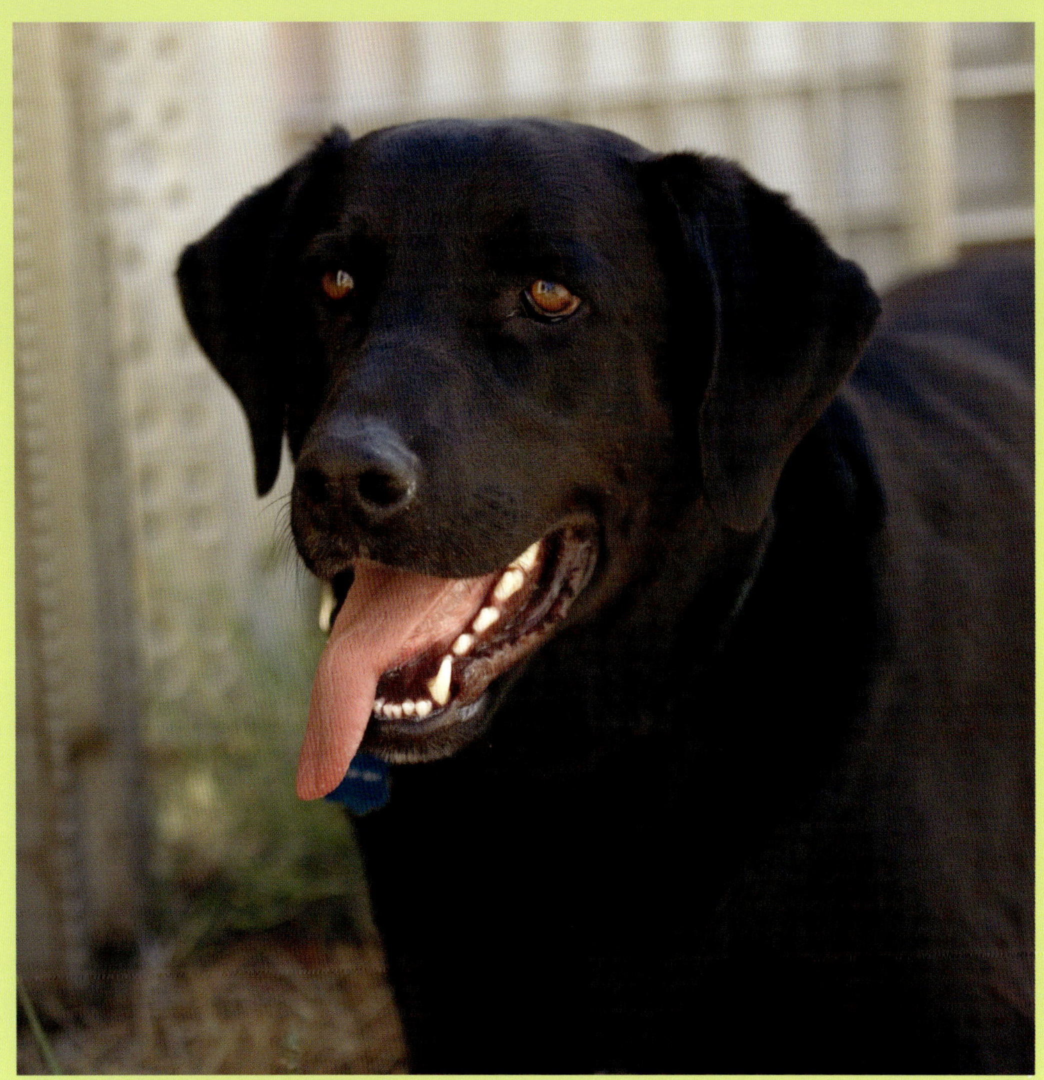

Buck

Dumas Station Wines

A classy winery dog, Buck is not. But our 4-year-old Labrador-Rotweiler mix is loyal, wonderful and silly.

Country life is Buck's passion. Because of that, there are responsibilities at the winery that fit his qualifications. Since Dumas Station is near the Touchet River and in the midst of alfalfa fields, Buck is "required" to conduct a perimeter search for all manner of wildlife, from deer and raccoons to coyote and blue herons. Somebody has to do it, and Buck has a grand time with the job.

While he loves all things "wild," Buck really is a kind-hearted "people person" and doesn't seem to care if they prefer Cabernet Sauvignon or Merlot.

Jay and Debbie DeWitt

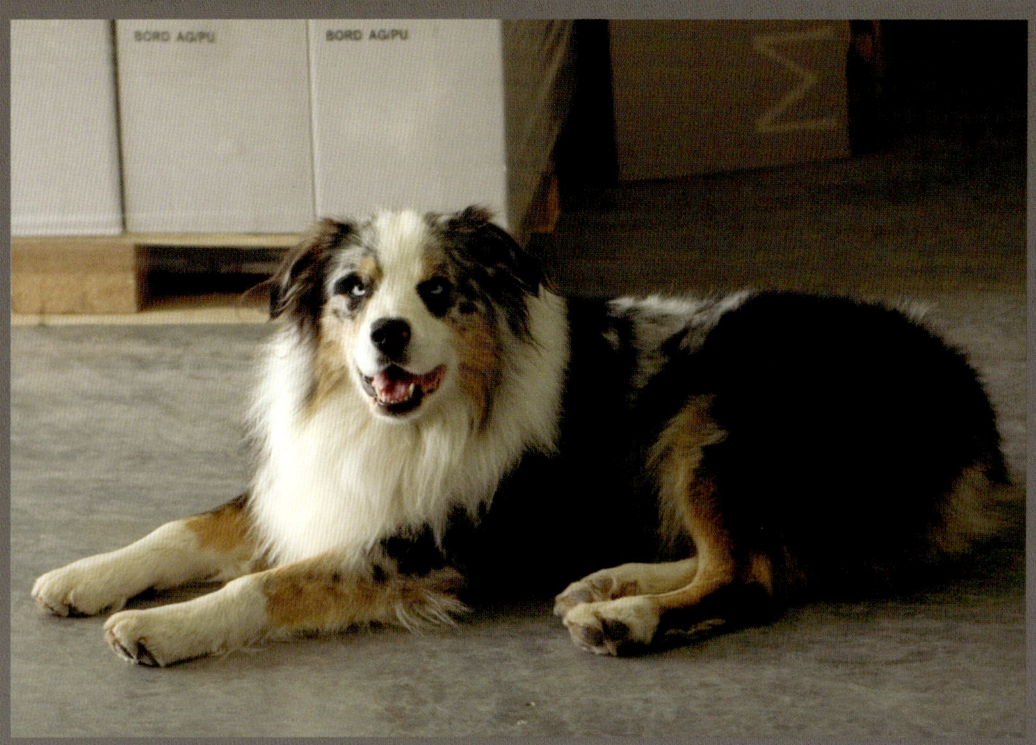

Ranch

Zerba Cellars

I am a 4-year-old pure bred Blue Merle Australian Shepard with blue-brown eyes and I am cute.
I love my family and all of you! I can talk and am bilingual when necessary.
I like to help the workers, the winemaker and I am pretty good.
I do prefer the front seat of the vehicle I am riding in and do not like the back. Am I spoiled? YES!
If not enough attention is given to me I will let you know with a gentle "paw" and treats are always appreciated.
I am at the winery often, but please do not hesitate to ask for my presence if you are visiting.

Cecil and Marilyn Zerba

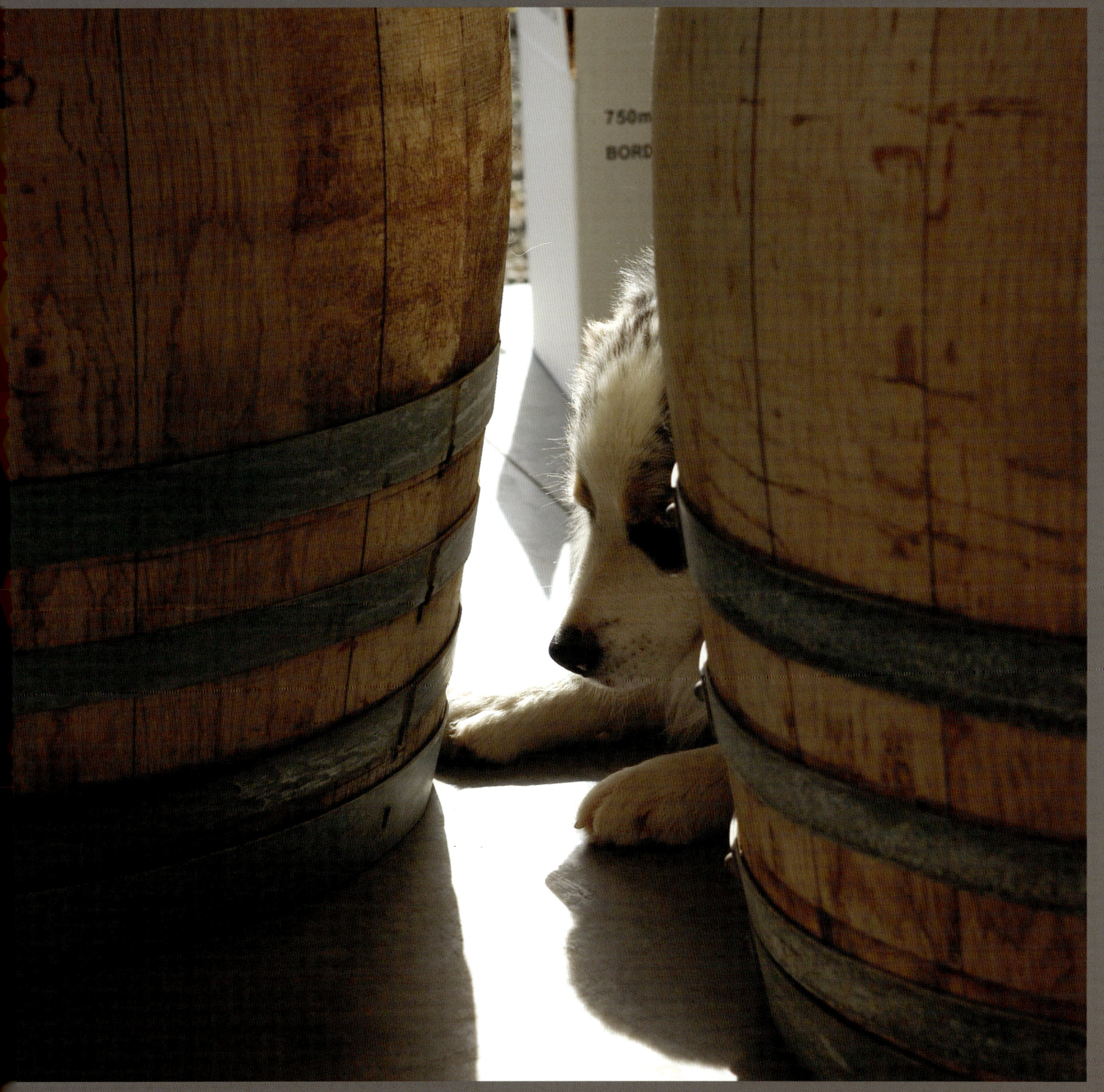
750m
BORD

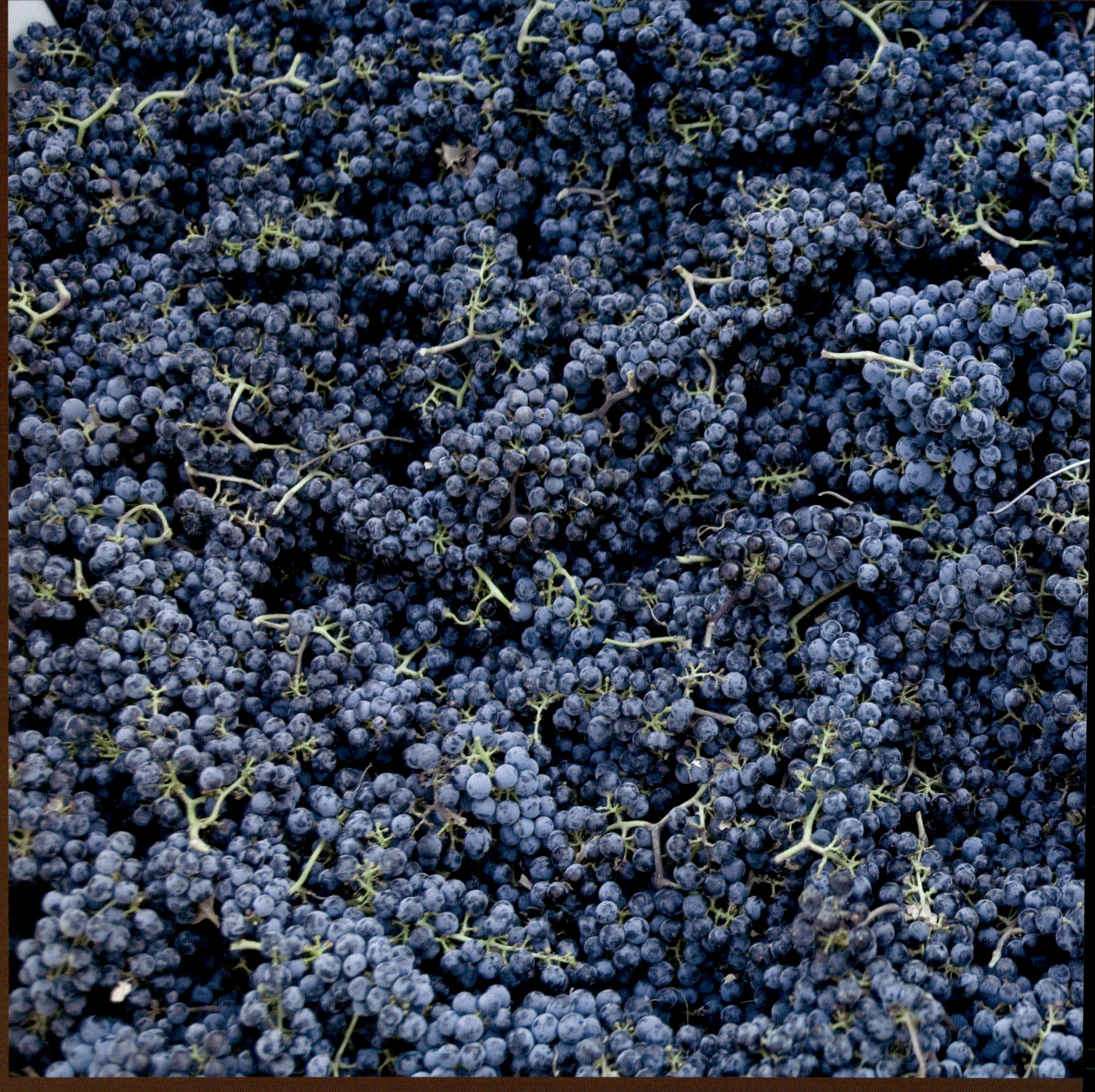

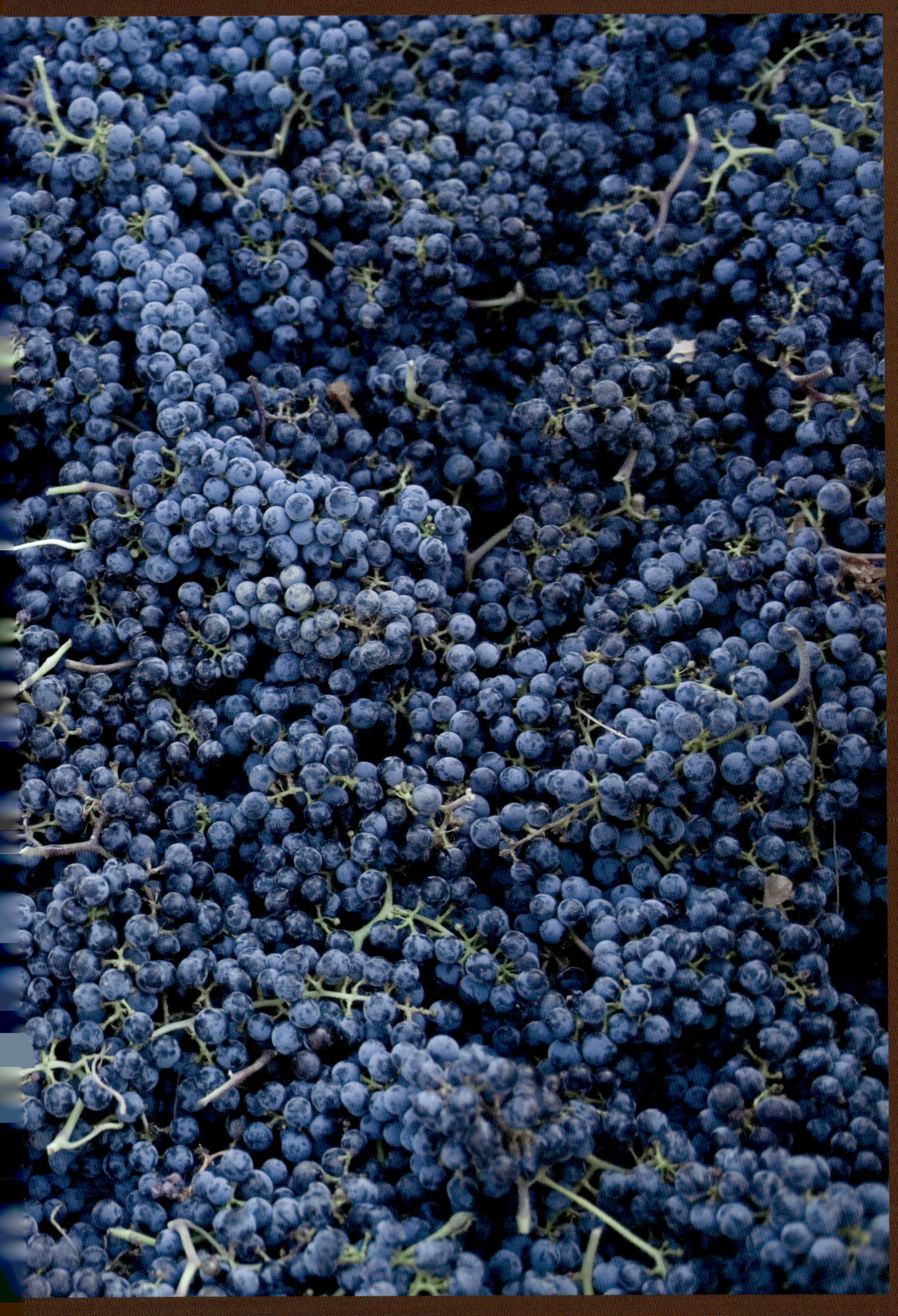

Cabernet Harvest

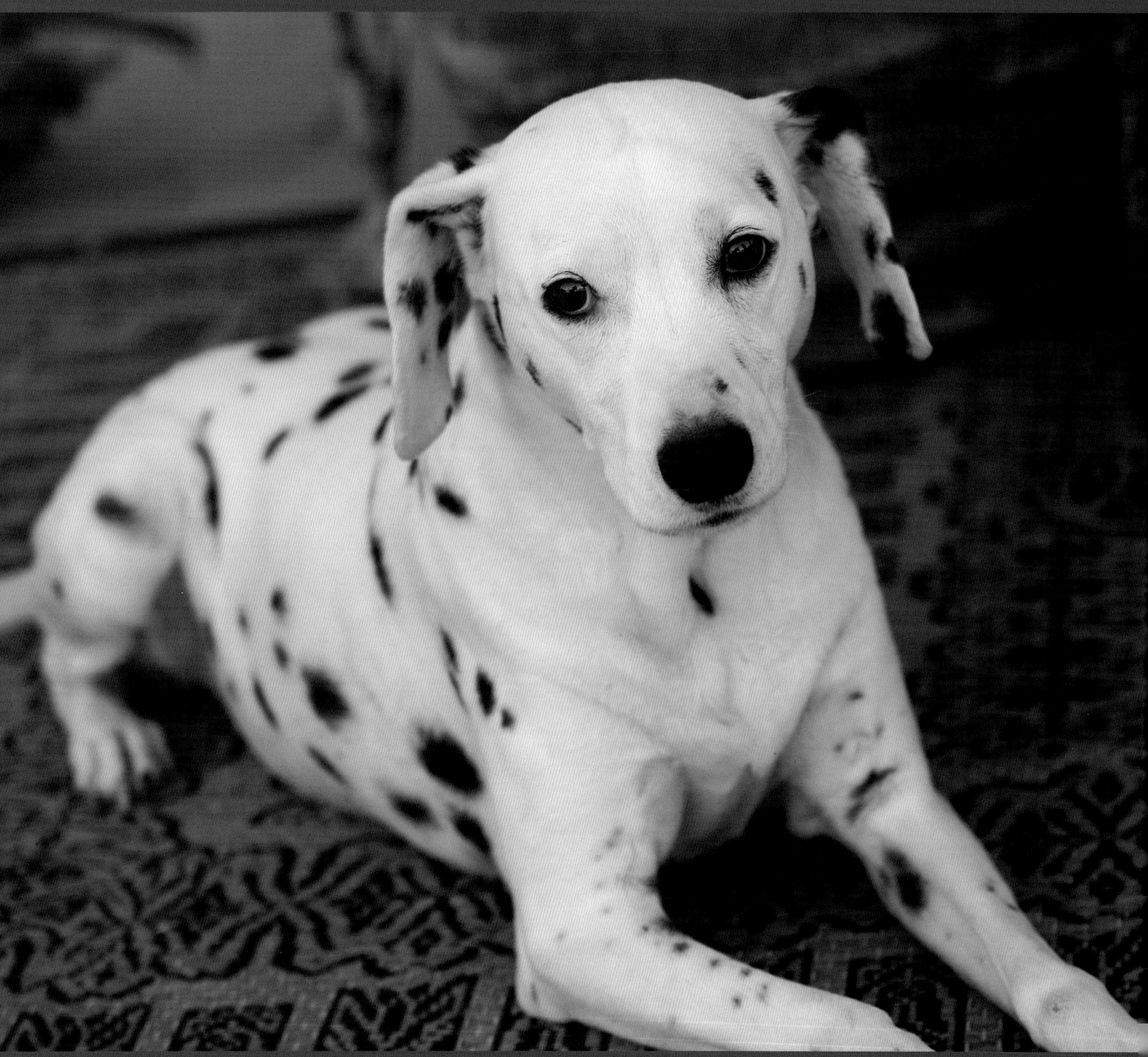

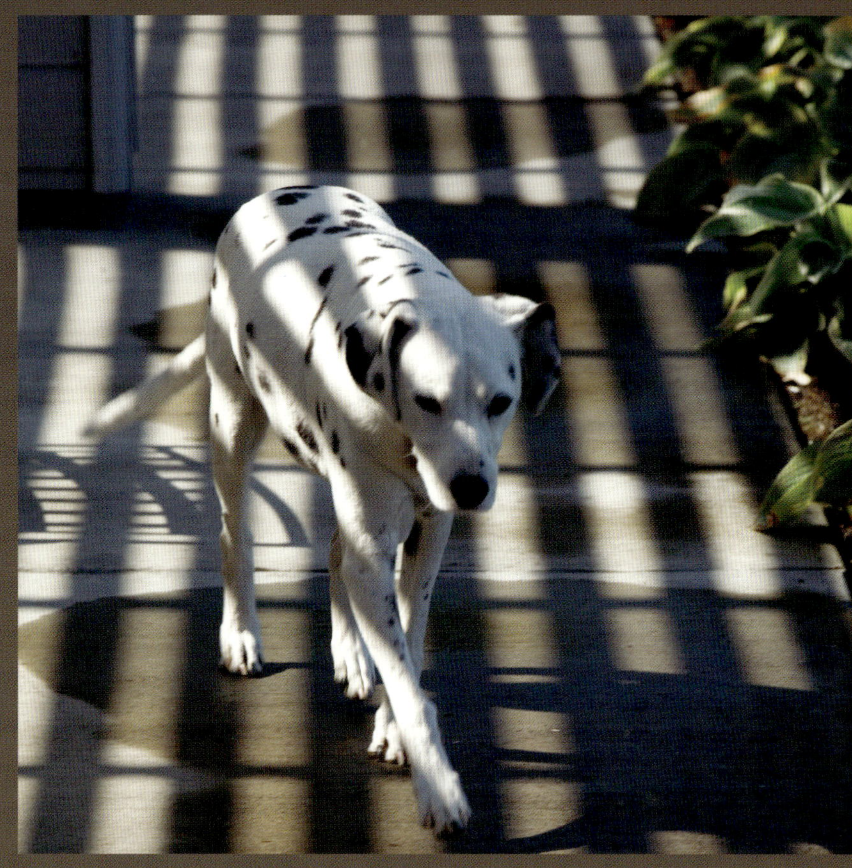

Lily

Skylite Cellars

AKC registered "Dallions Spotted China Lily" – Lily – was born in 1994.
She was chosen for a 4-H project by our daughter Ashley and since has been a part of all the family endeavors.
As a youngster she played, ate and slept only with Ashley.
As a teenager, rather than running through the snow to the family cabin she learned to ride on snowmobiles and still enjoys mountain winters by our side.
As an adult, she accompanies Tom in the truck on wondrous adventures.
As a senior citizen, Lily has earned the pampering of royalty.
She will eat any grape, drink any wine poured, so her palate is not considered when making our wines!
Lily is featured in two "wine" paintings by the famous Michael Stockdale, which is quite an honor.
We know that this will be the last appearance of Lily's long career as a model, after all she is "93." We are so proud and pleased that you have had this opportunity to meet our precious Lily.

Tom and Cheryl Hodgins

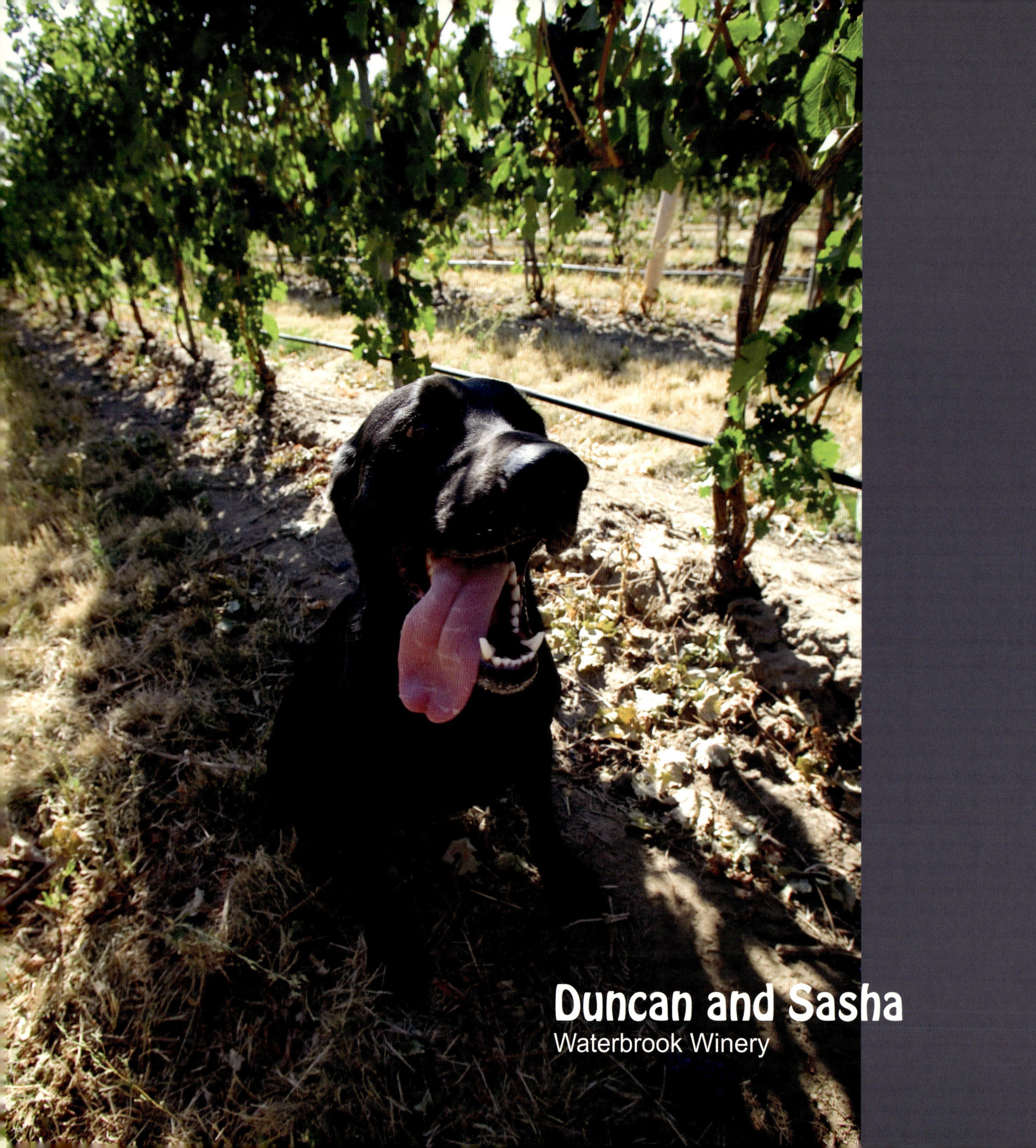

Duncan and Sasha
Waterbrook Winery

Duncan had a rough childhood thanks to my two daughters need for a submissive. partner to wear makeup, nail polish and be a runway clothes model. I saved him more than once from peanut butter on his tongue and two-sided tape on his paws and tail. He managed to cowboy through the early months by taking long walks in the grass kicking up pheasants so I could scare the crap out of them with multiple near-miss shots.

Like most Labs, Duncan likes fetching bungs, chasing birds, playing with kids, spilled wine and beer and going for boat rides.

His dislikes include puppies, staying home, rap music (I assume) and two-sided tape (see above).

Duncan has been "working" at Waterbrook for three years and still greets guests with enthusiasm and sometimes kisses. Visitors always complement Duncan on his fetching ability as well as his need to be between their legs (his comfort zone). Duncan is sure to be a fixture at Waterbrook for many vintages to come.

John Freeman

Our "Princess" was born in Northern British Columbia, Canada, on a compound uniquely dedicated to allowing Huskies to breed naturally without human intervention. Although still a puppy, Sasha has mastered the skills of catching field mice and quail, in addition to devouring expensive leather footwear. At the winery she is best known for getting in front of the forklift, eliminating over the cellar drain and many "time-outs" in the car.

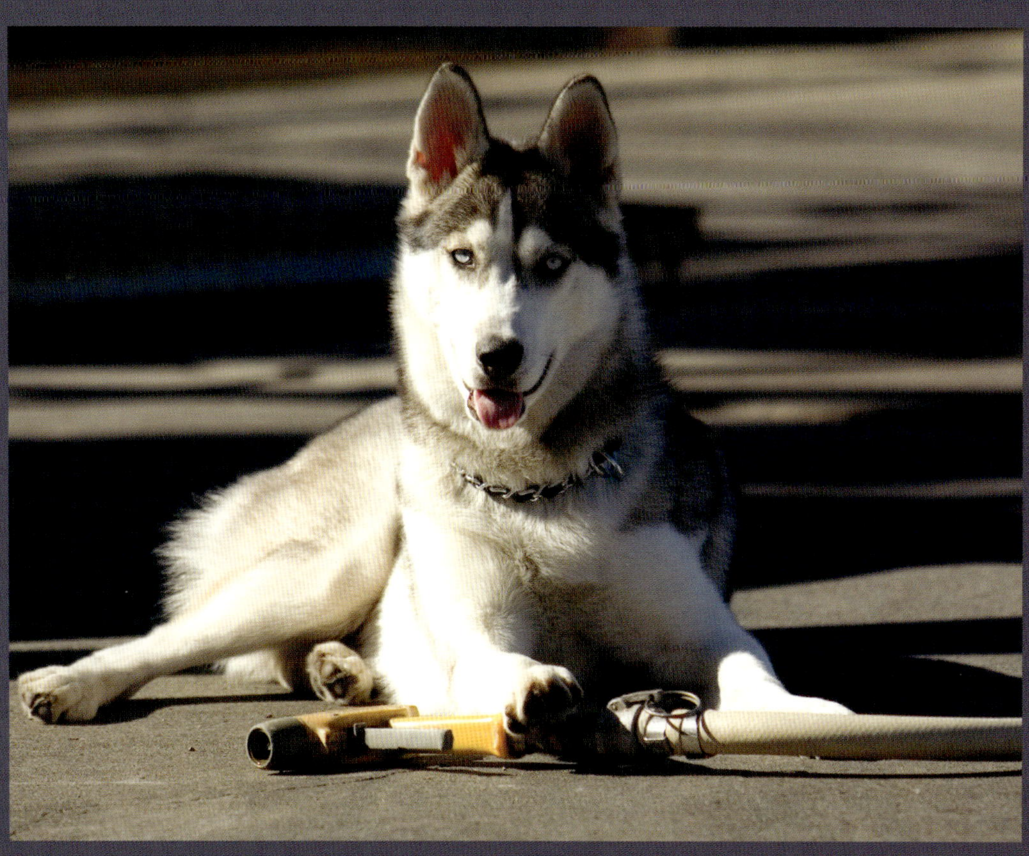

Sasha has developed a discerning palate and to my dismay very much enjoys feeding on vinifera fruit; Syrah being her favorite!

Peter Devison

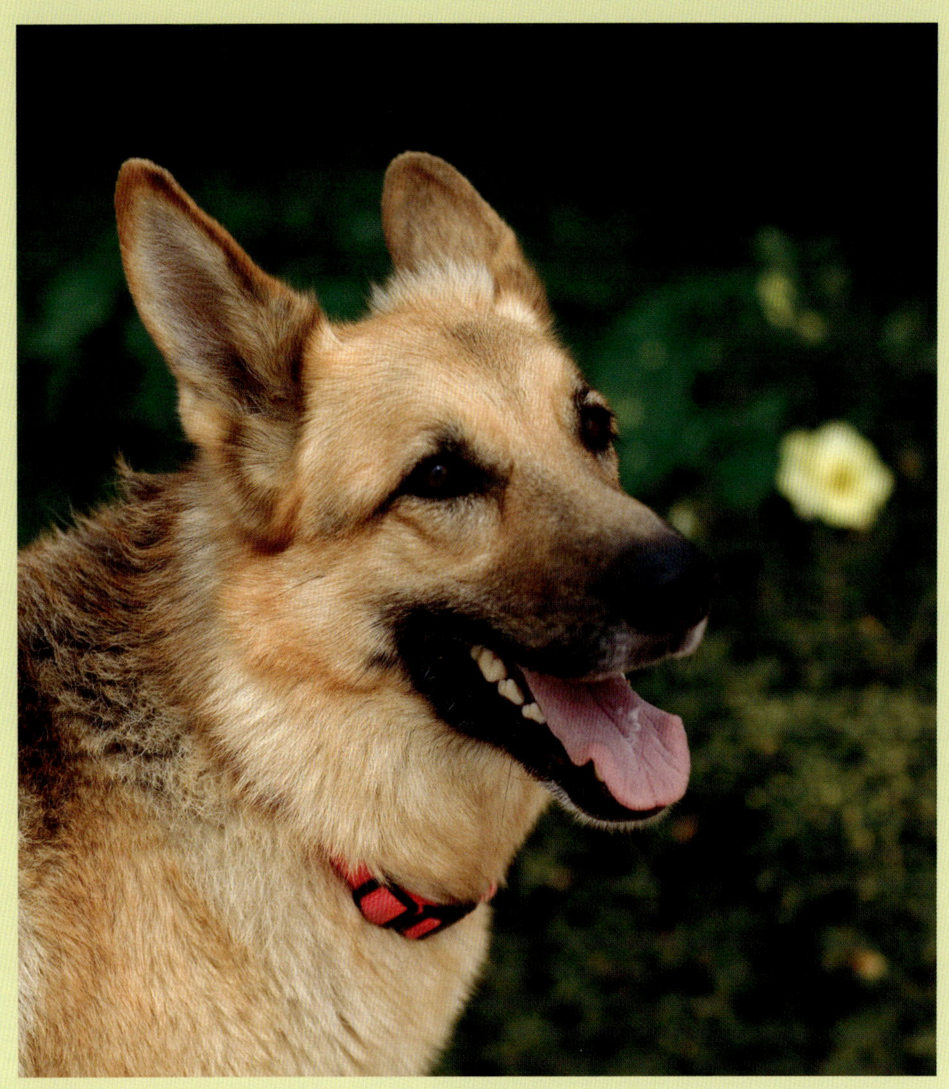

Sage and Rhys

Spring Valley Vineyard

Geyera's Desert Sage aka "Sage" is our 5-year-old black & tan German Shepherd. Her job is to work on the ranch taking care of us, herding the horse, helping with sprinklers and monitoring the crew. Sage is Dean's constant companion on his "ranch rounds" and is quick to work the crowd when visitors come.

Williams Derby Rhys aka "Rhys", a 7-month-old Blenheim Cavalier King Charles Spaniel, came to Spring Valley to give Shari company while Dean and Sage are out in the fields. Sage wasn't so happy about that at first, but now thinks he's pretty OK. Named for Shari's Welsh Great Grandfather Rhys – Katherine Corkrum's (Uriah's wife) father – Rhys loves to sit in your lap, go for a ride in the car, play with his toys, walk around the ranch checking every rock, dirt clod and bird, and receiving "oooh's" from the folks who come for wine tasting.

Dean and Shari Derby

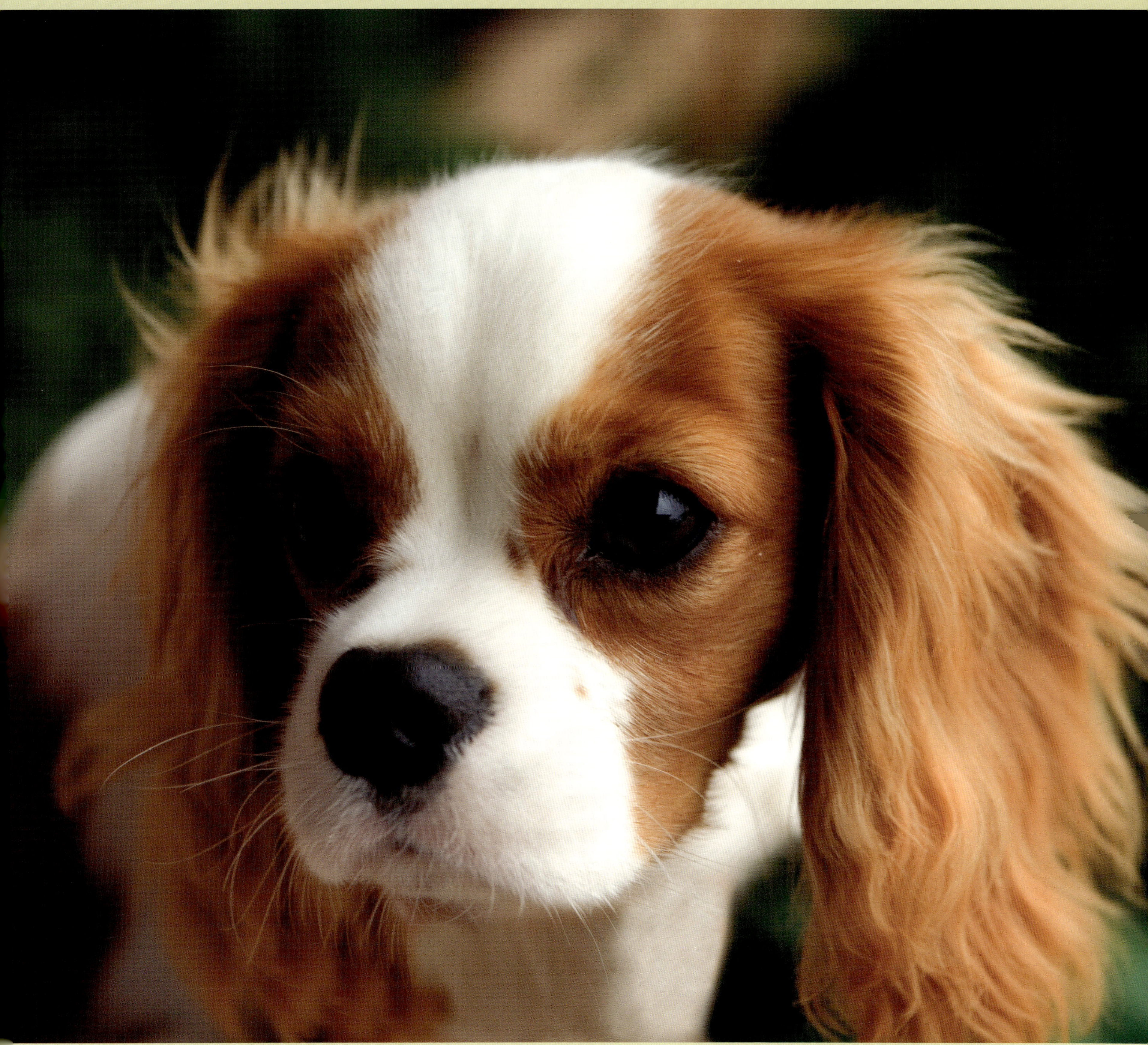

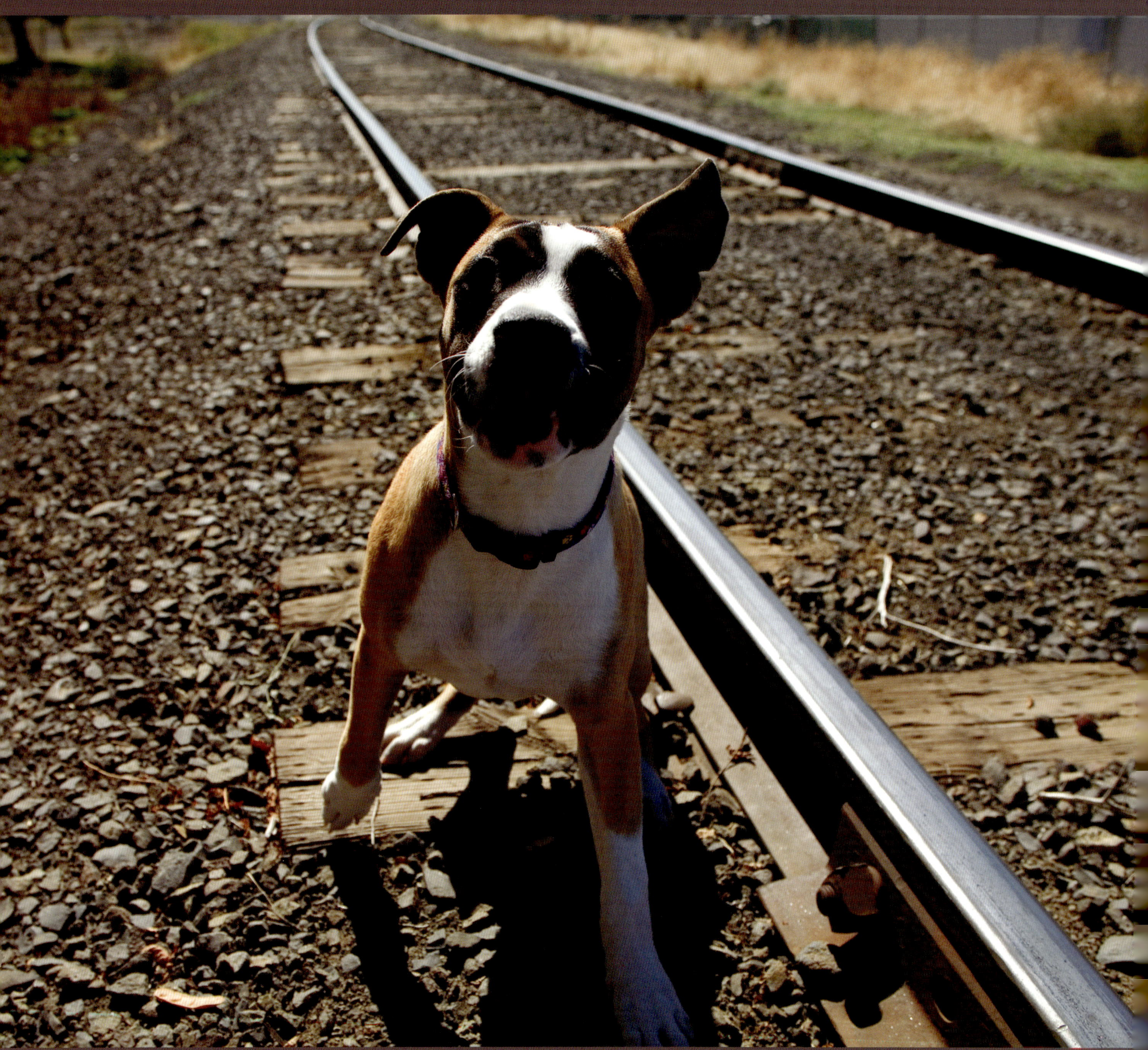

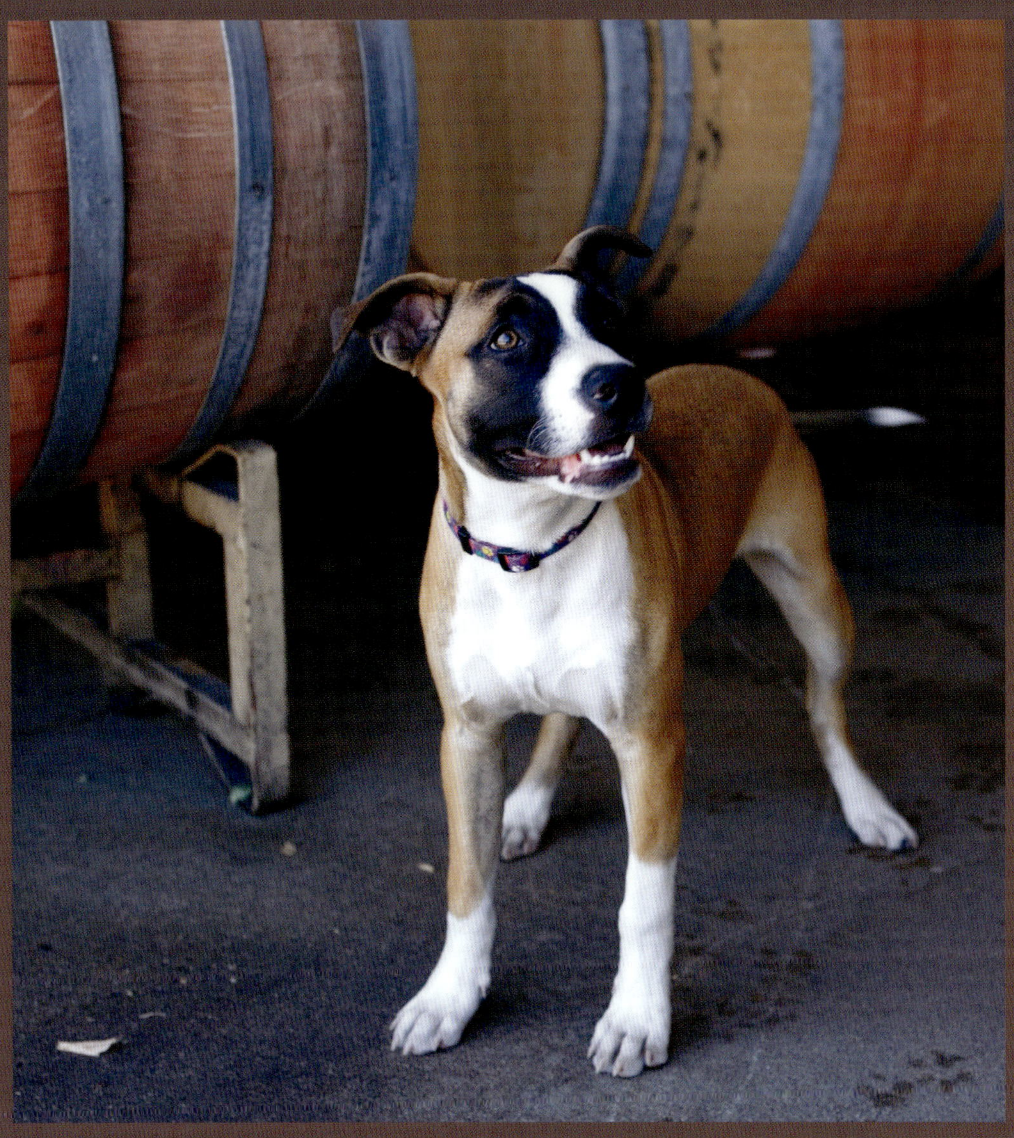

Rosie

Canoe Ridge Vineyard

One morning she was just there...a Boxer/Pit Bull pup on the street in front of the winery. She was without a home, maybe without a hope. For safety's sake, we brought her inside, away from the passing traffic.

Of course she wasn't Rosie then, but the Canoe Ridge crew fell in love with her, decided to adopt her and agreed to give her an appropriate winery name.

An early suggestion was "Corkie." Then our wine maker, Chrisophe, decided she would be "Rose"" – after the wine – and we'd call her Rosie.

Because of her wonderful personality and sweet disposition, Rosie has captured our hearts and she is, for certain, one of us.

Rosie is at the winery during the day, then goes home with one of us at night.

Becky Stanley

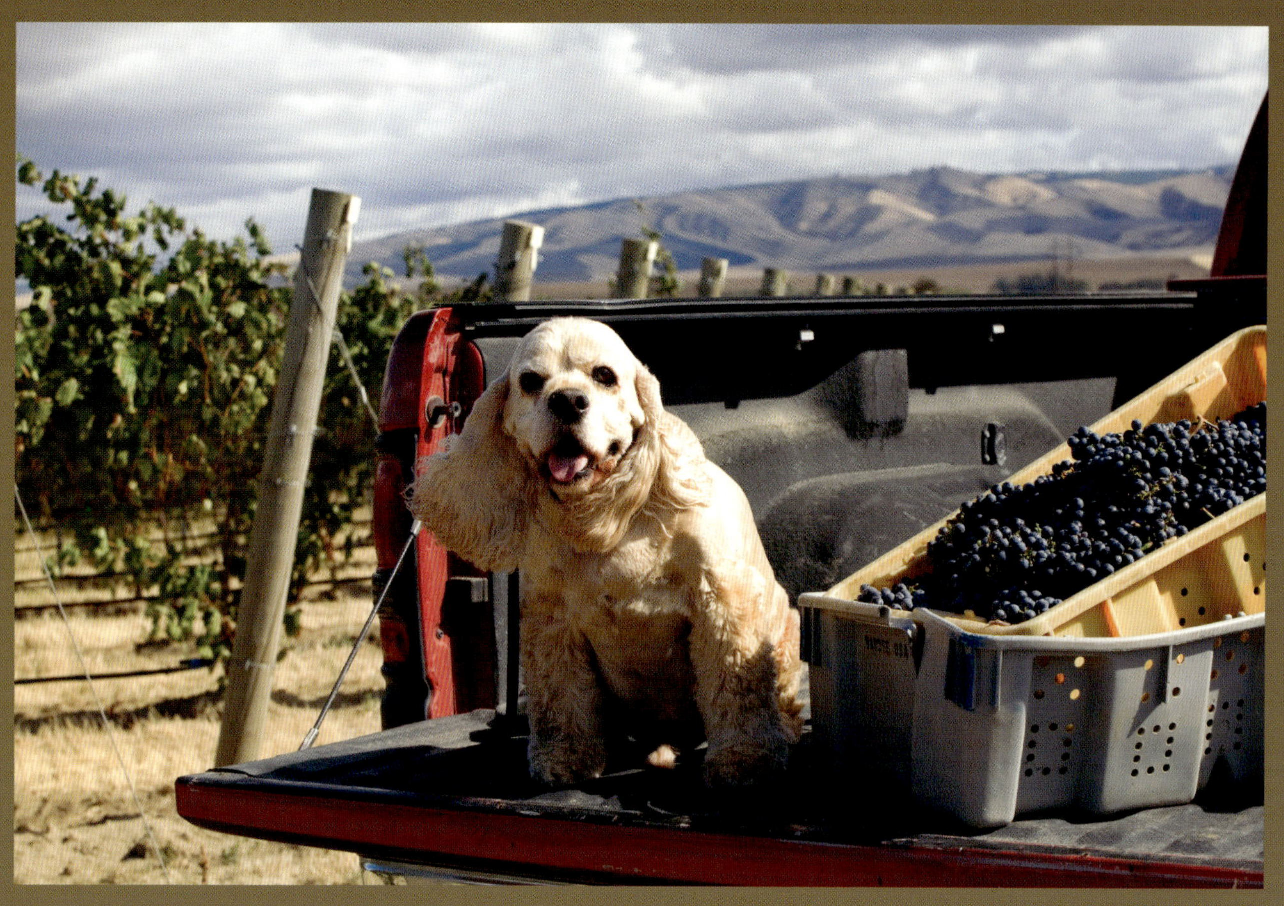

Sadie

JLC Winery / Spofford Station

I found Sadie in a vacated home. She was apparently unwanted and in very sad shape, so I took her home. The veterinarian confirmed she was 5-6 years old and in need of care. Sadie turned out to be very happy and good-natured.

She is a town and country girl. At the vineyard, her nose is always down as she hunts the rows for a meandering pheasant or rabbit. She waits by the truck doors for the workers and sometimes makes it into the cab for a ride, otherwise, she is happy to join the crew at "lunche" for anything that might fall from the table.

When guest visit the winery she always gives them and introductory sniff and tail wag.

Generally, wine visitors fall in love with her.

J. Lynne Chamberlain

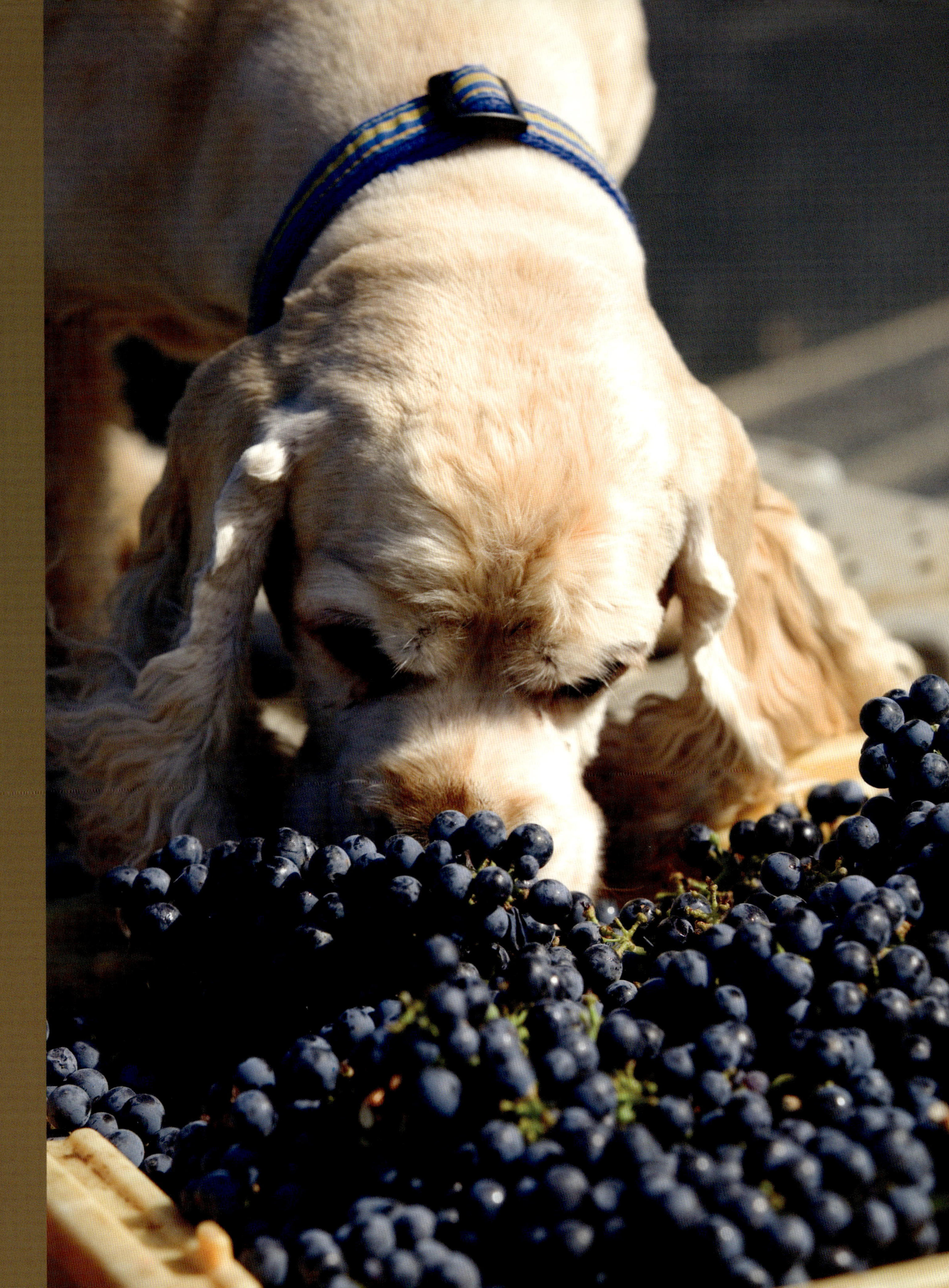

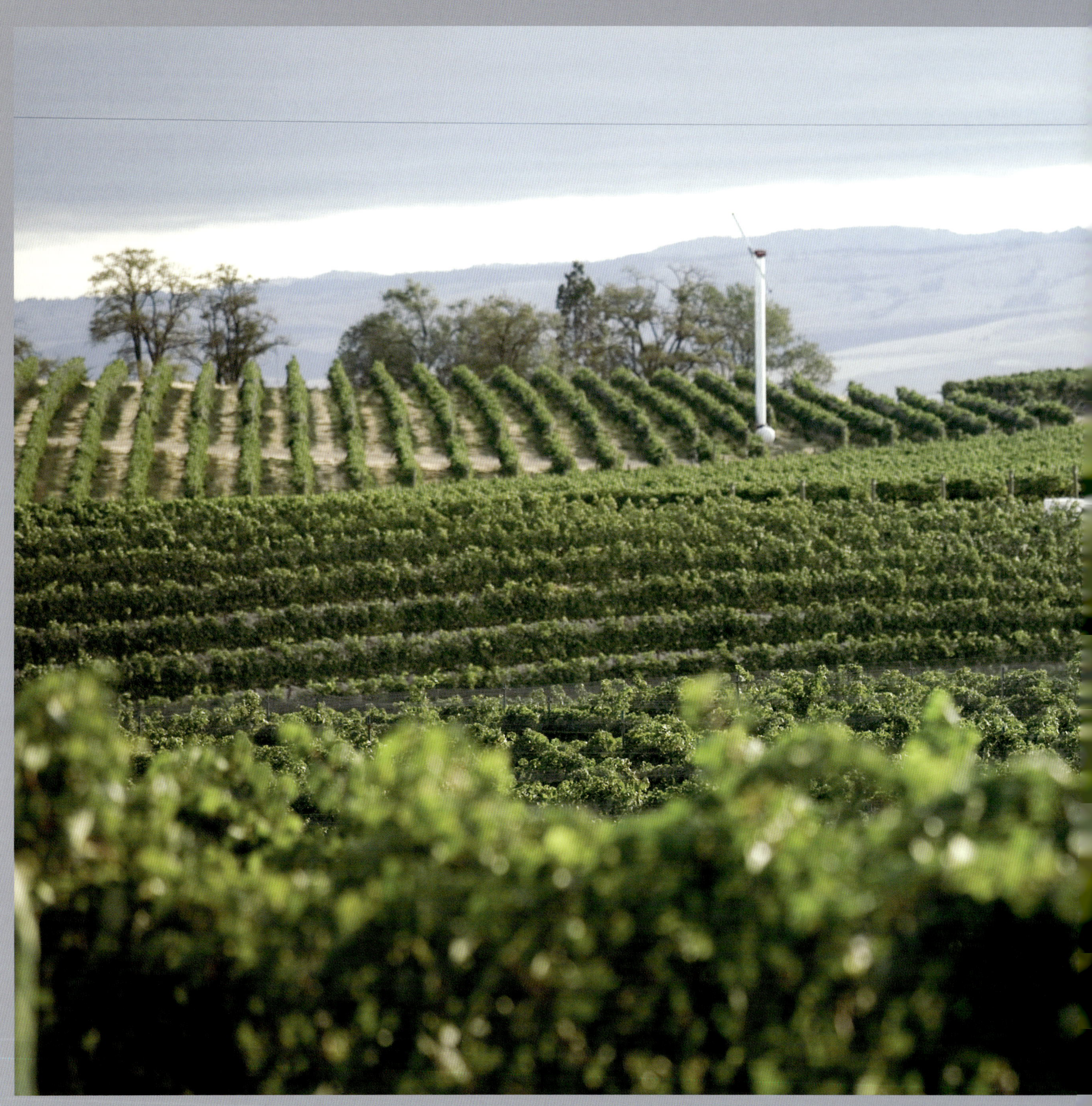

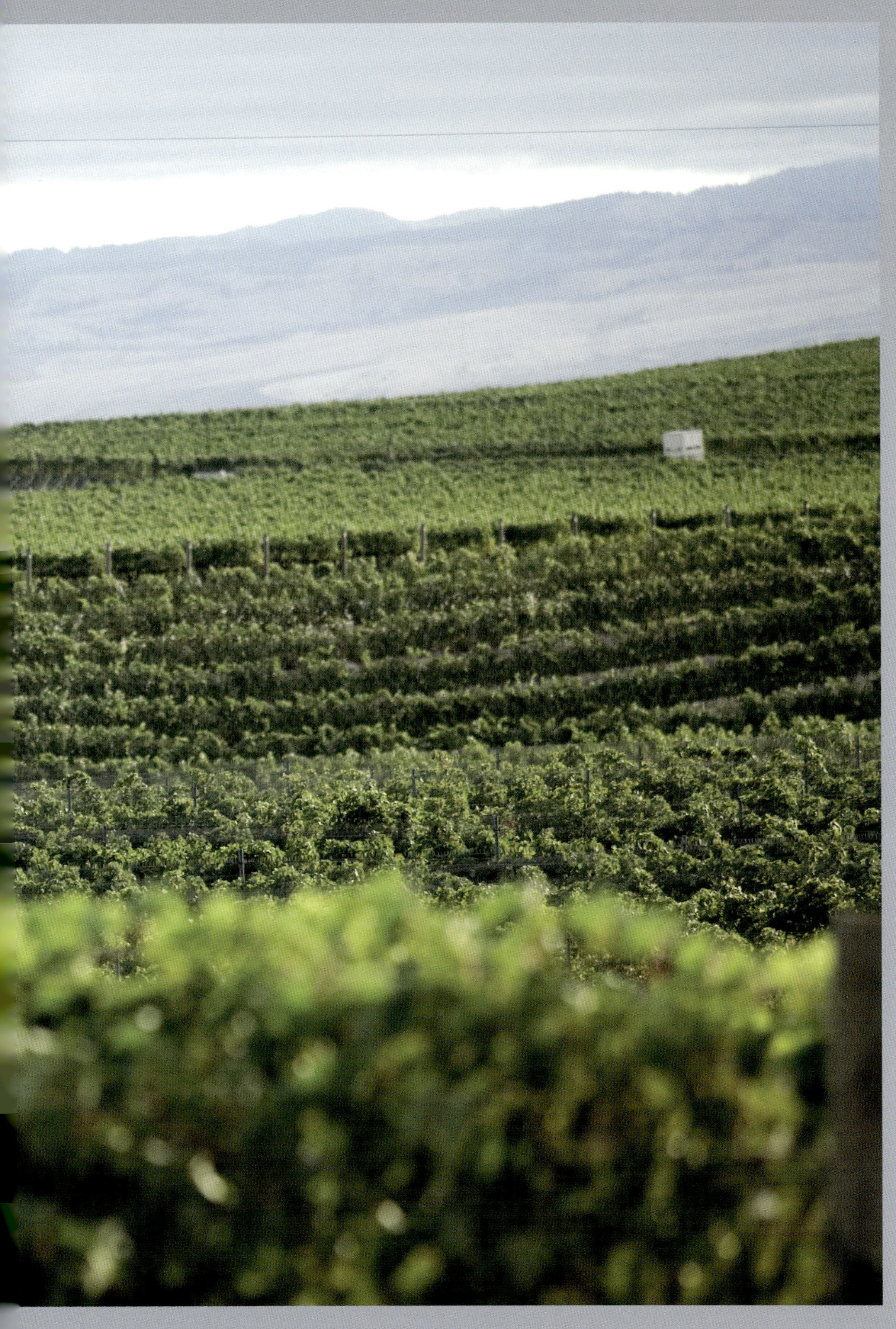

Seven Hills Vineyard

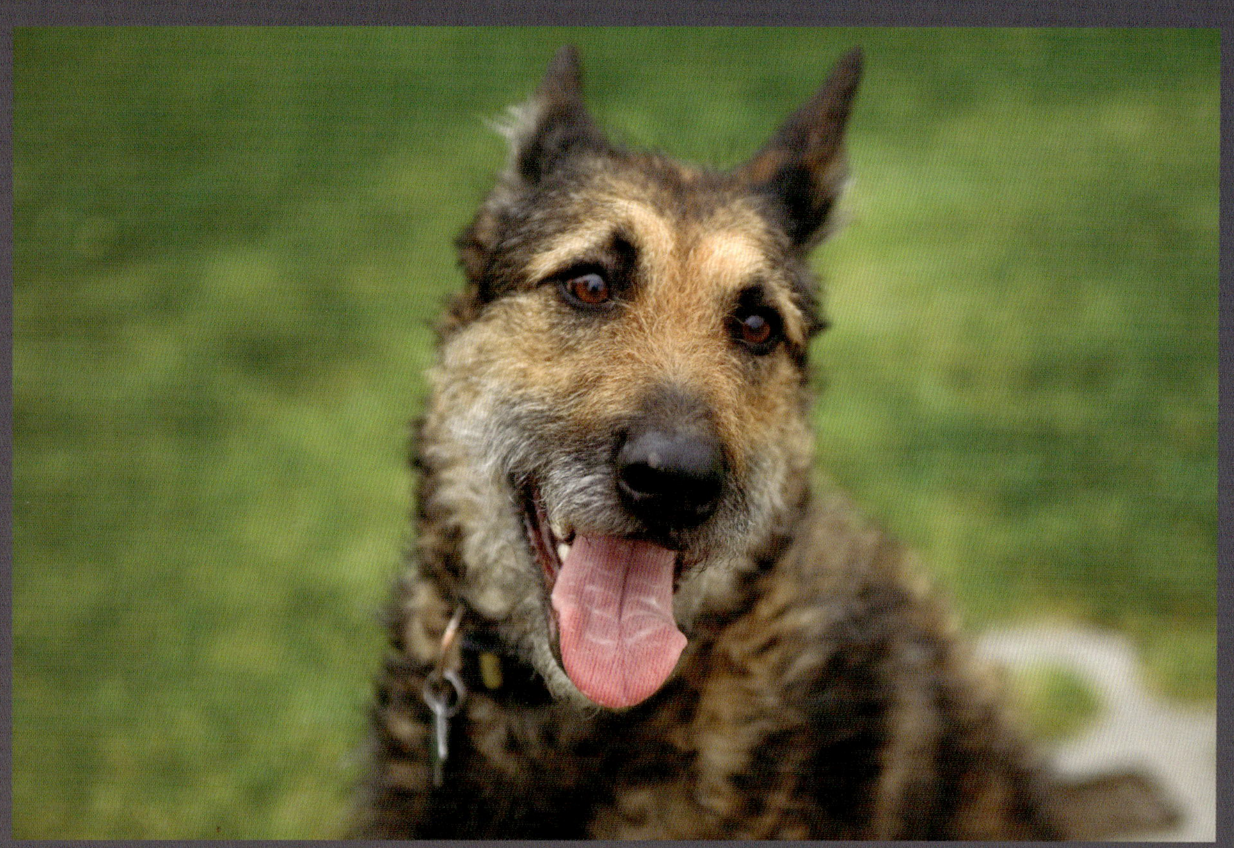

Lucy and Bella

Abeja

Despite their varied interests and mixed pedigrees, Bella and Lucy are best friends. Bella, a Lab/Boxer, enjoys fork-lift rides, supervising crush and greeting Abeja guests. Lucy, a Belgian Herder, is more shy, prefers the quiet of her kennel to the hustle and bustle of the winery. Bella believes Abeja's four cats are good company. Lucy believes those same cats are good for the chase, so they stay clear of her whenever possible.

Both of our dogs are good athletes – Bella is a jumper who excels at the standing high-jump, while Lucy is a born runner and can be seen tearing around the property at break-neck speeds.

Near dusk, the Abeja dogs gather in the wine barn to share their adventures and a "nose-nuzzle" or two while we toast the day with a glass of Cabernet.

John and Molly Galt

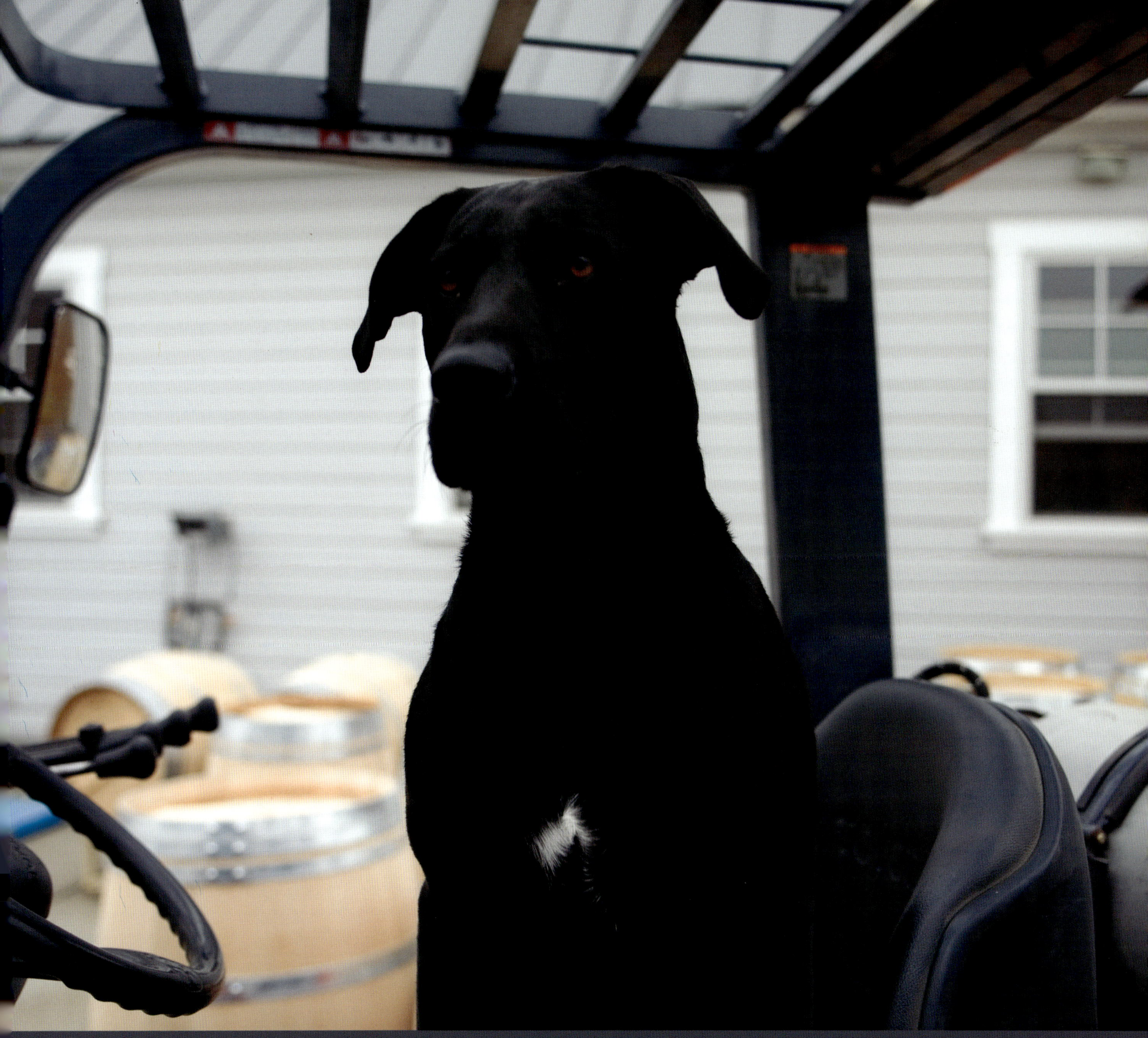

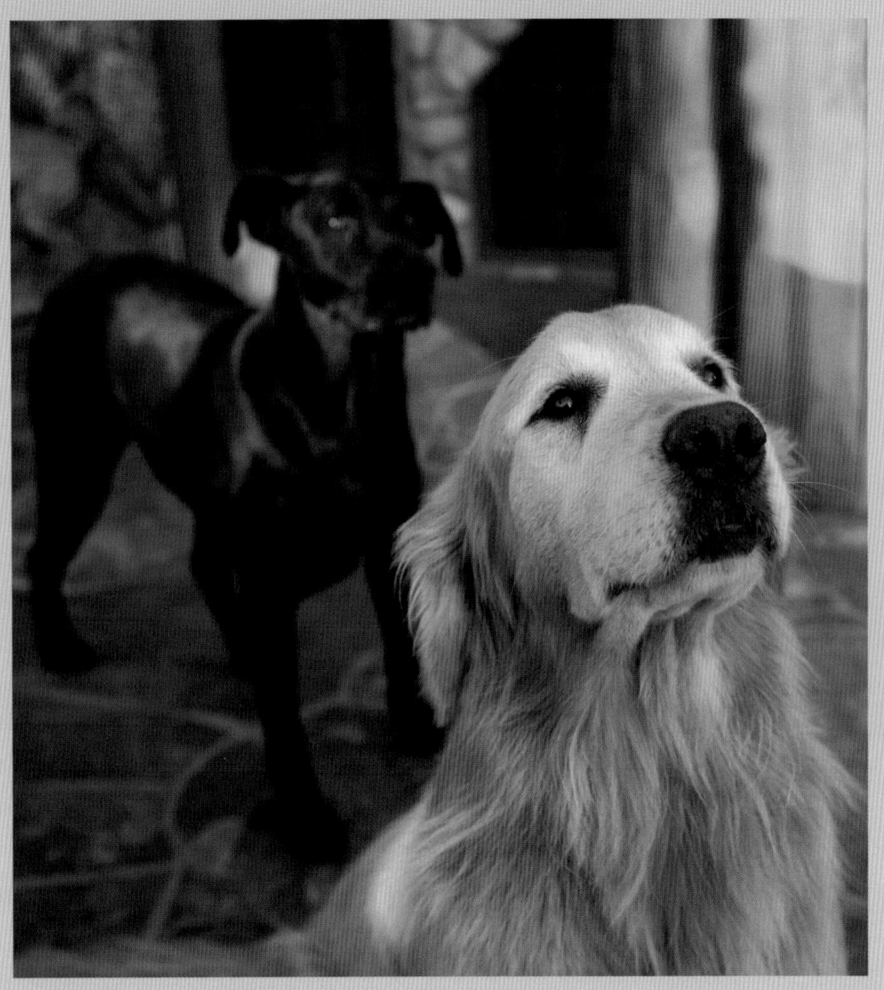

Dudley and Chevy

Basel Cellars Estate Winery

Chevy, aka Sir Top Hat Chevy is a 9-year-old Golden Retriever.
Dudley, a Black Lab mix , is 4-years-old.
The daring duo start their day with breakfast, then move on to their Estate Vineyards, Pheasant Run.
A company truck comes by to check on the crew and the pair hitches a ride to Basel Cellars, where they greet guests and receive their daily messages.
If by chance they miss their ride to the winery, there just happens to be another winery next door. They'll make sure they are on the door mat, so indeed they will not miss out on their daily messages.
In the early evening, Chevy and Dudley join their owner and or neighbor for a walk through Pheasant Run and surrounding vineyards.
This is the life of a Vineyard Dog.

Greg and Becky Basel

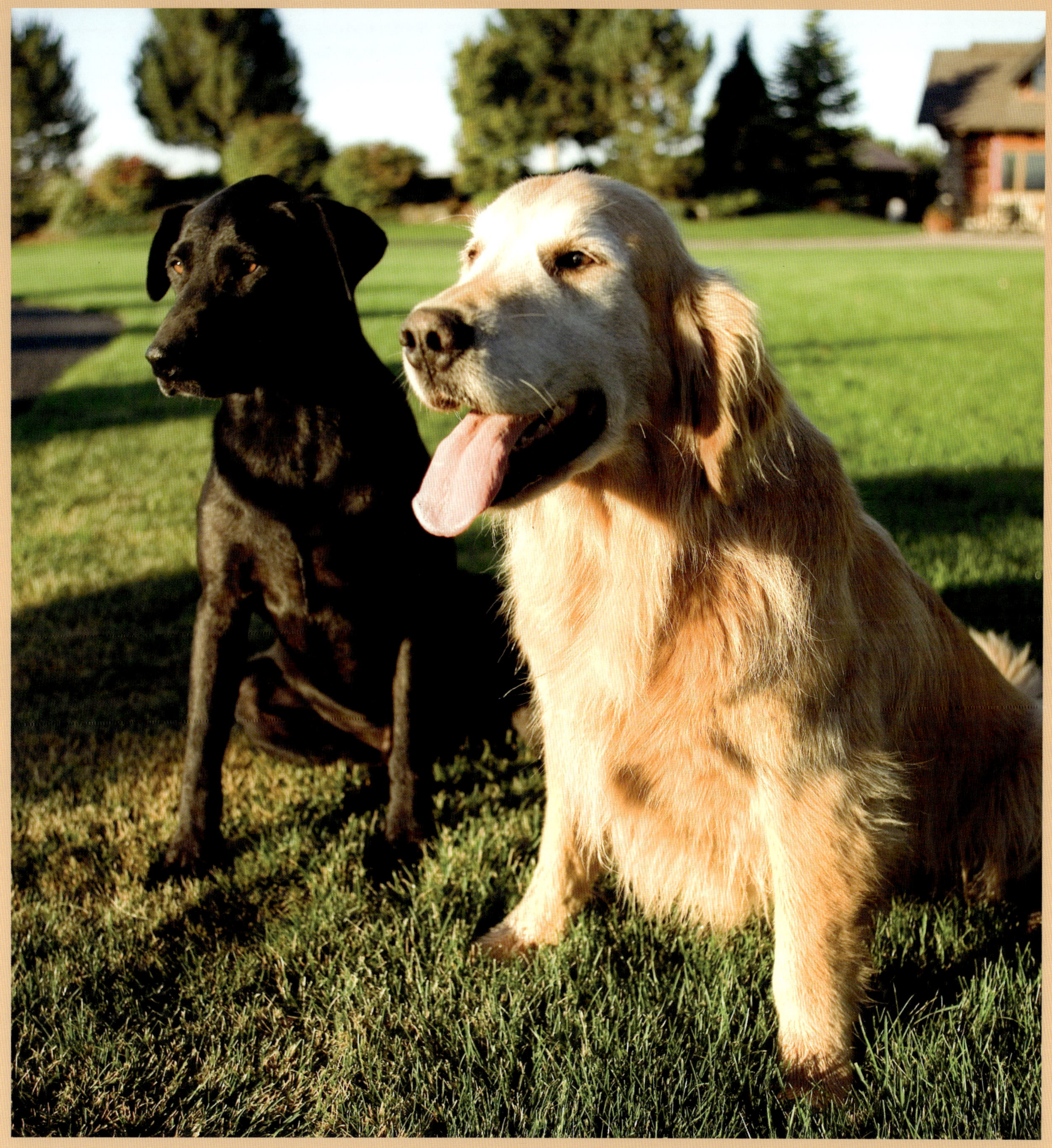

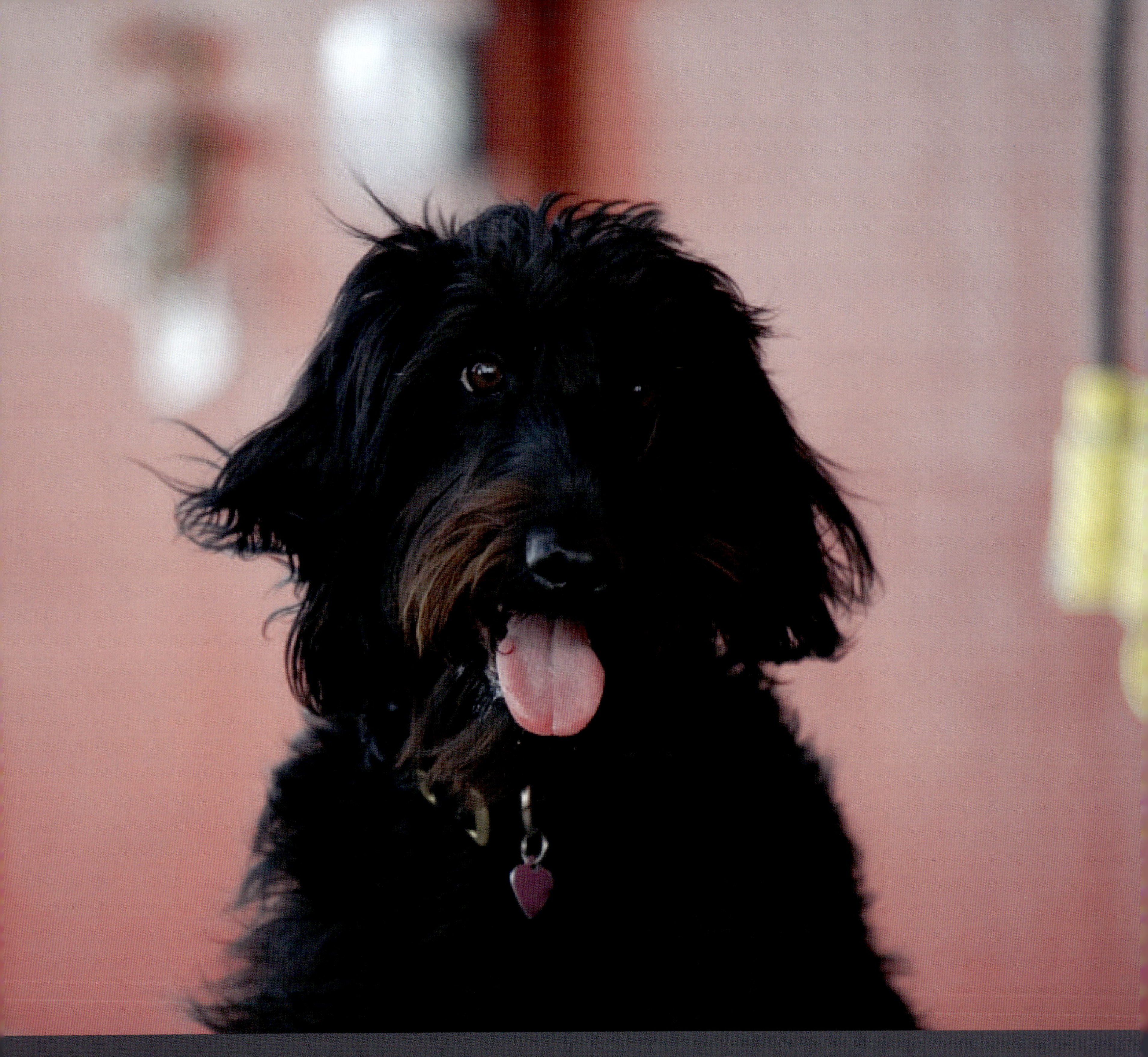

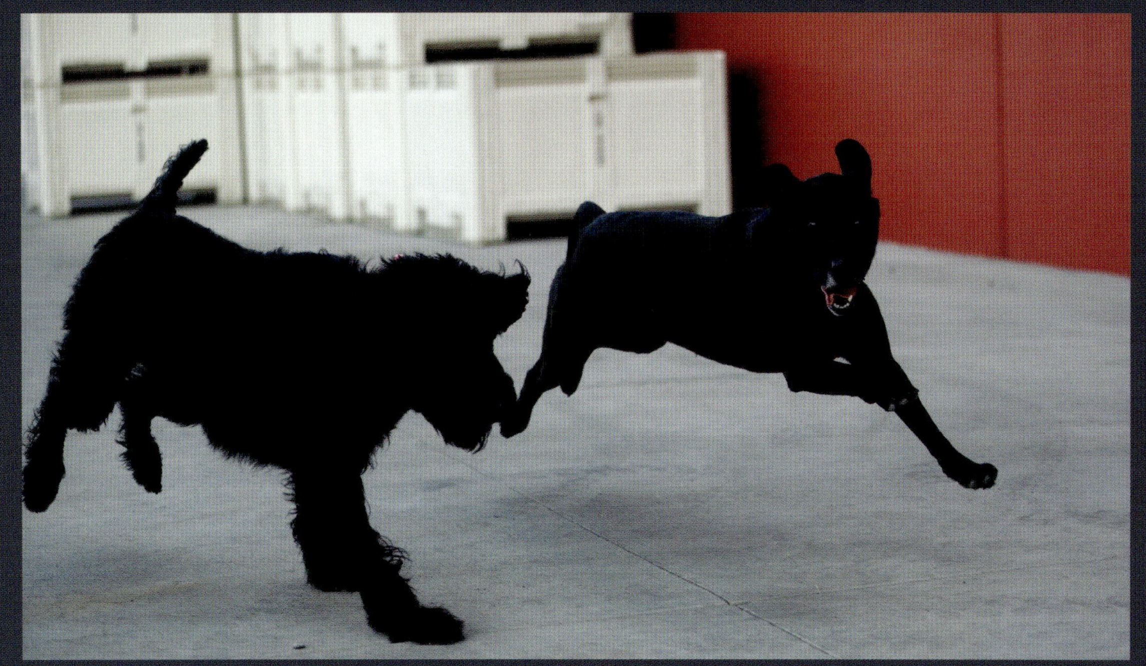

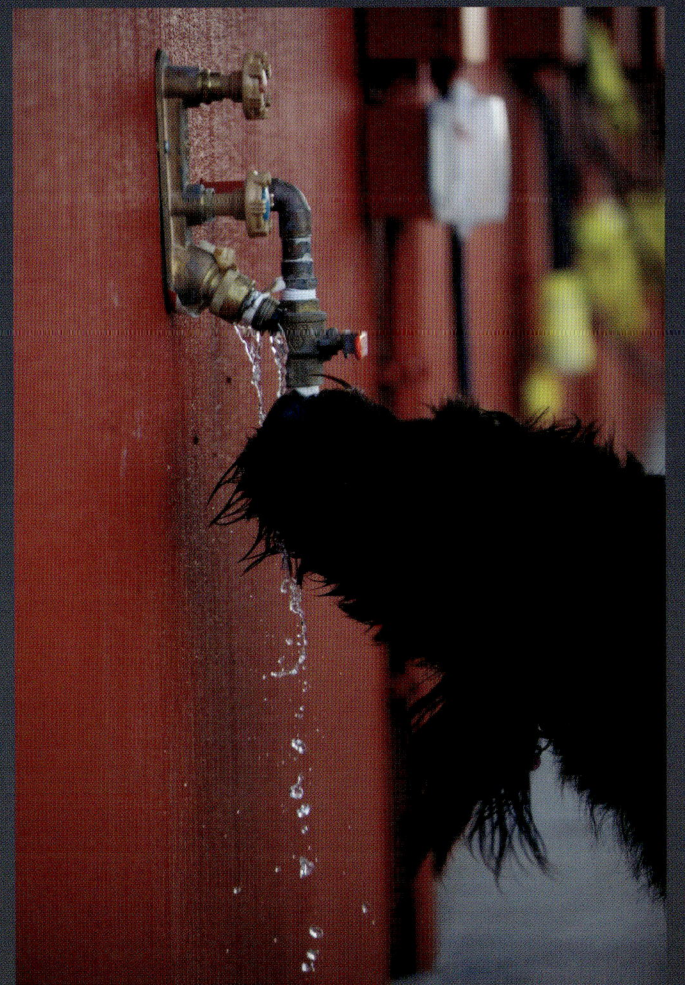

Lucy and Salsa

Long Shadows Vintners

Lucy is a 1-year-old female Labradoodle. As a labradoodle she tends to have the faithful qualities of a Labrador Retriever and the gentle nature of a Standard Poodle.

My wife Jennifer and I got Lucy when she was six months old from a woman who was trying to find a home for her. She had been with four different families.

We couldn't have found a better companion. She loves people as well as other dogs. Lucy especially loves it when Gilles' and Marie-eve's dog Salsa from Forgeron comes to play.

David and Jennifer Marshall

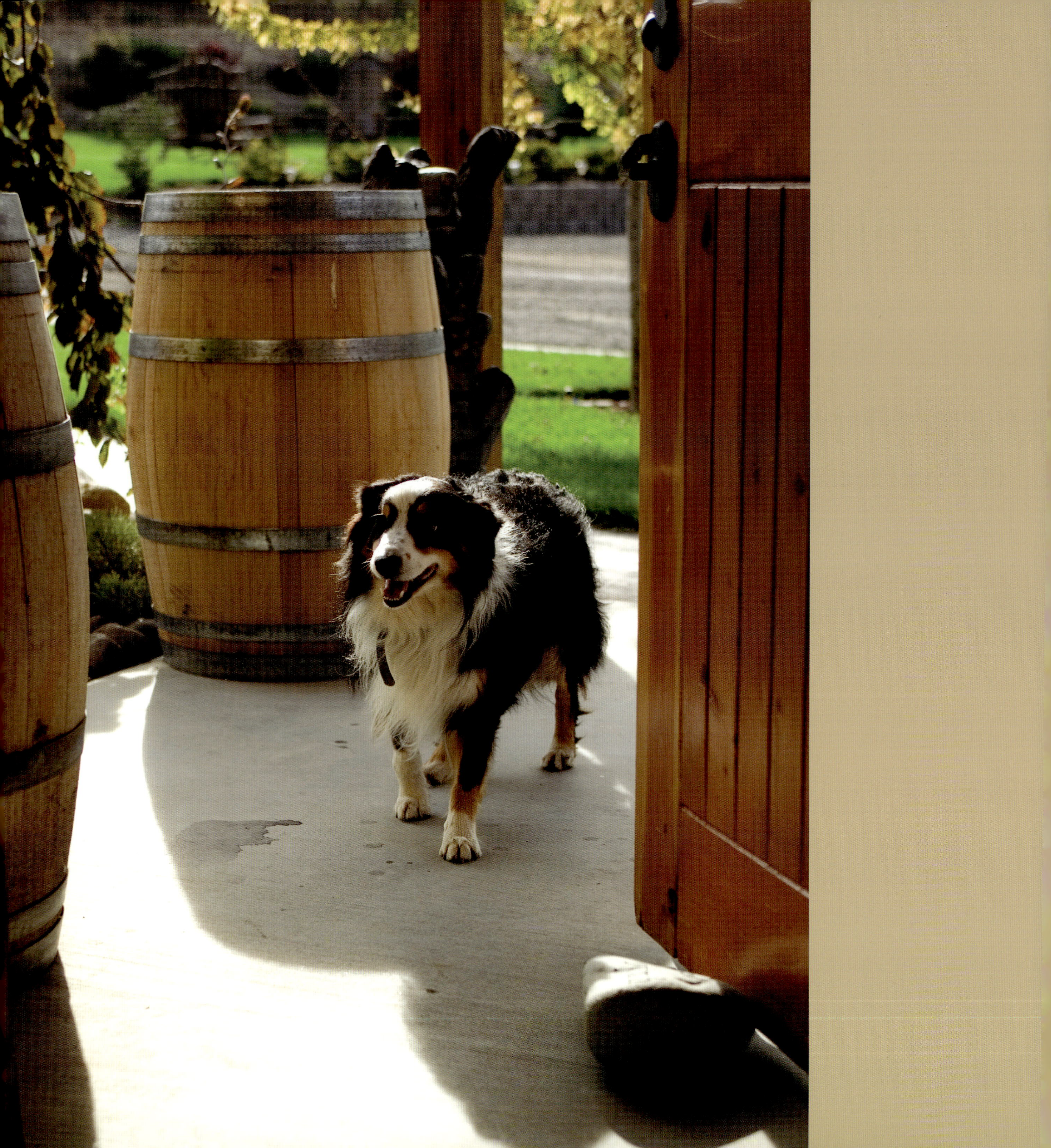

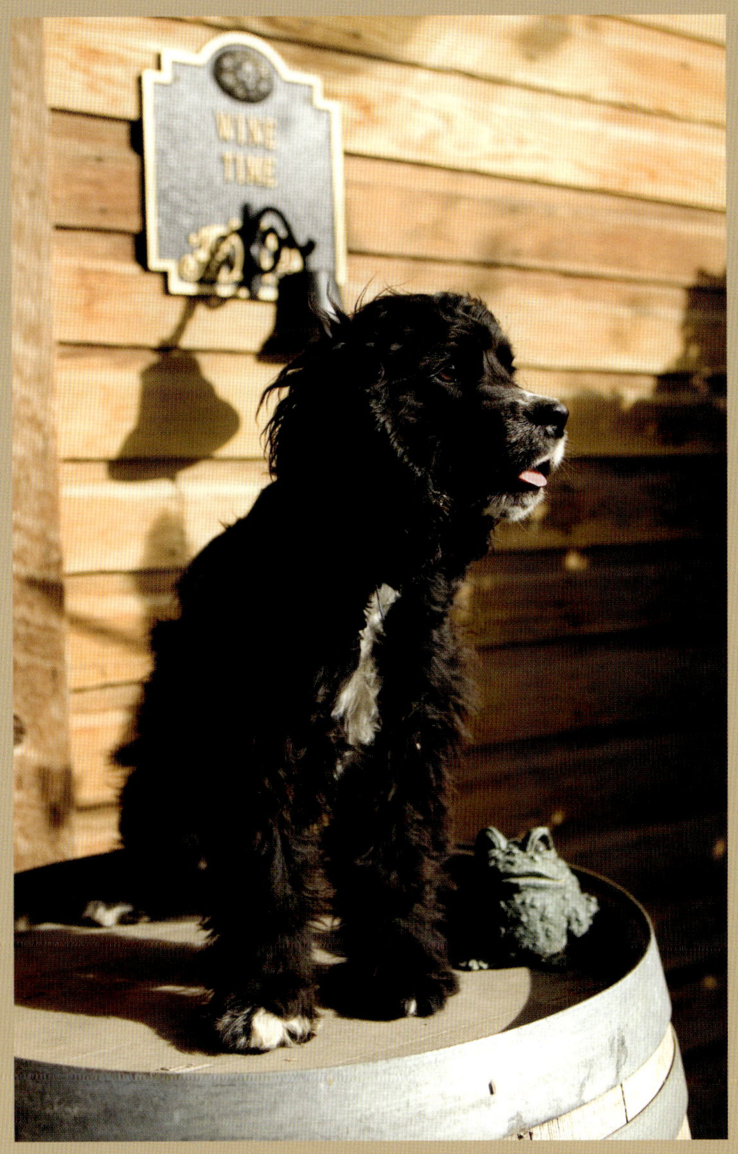

Amy and Vader

Beresan Winery and Waliser Vineyard

Joe – aka One-Eyed Joe – is an Australian Shepherd that "found" us about 10 years ago. He brought his Border Collie girlfriend, Amy (camera shy), with him. She is deaf, so you can call her whatever you want. They will seldom come to anybody (a dog biscuit helps), but let Debbie, owner of Beresan Winery, come outside and Joe is right there looking up at her with his one eye. What a loyal dog.

Tom and Debbie Waliser

"Vader" is your normal puppy with vast amounts of energy. He has three activities that take up most of his time – eating, chewing and barking.
His favorite foods include thinned wine grapes, pig ears and dog biscuits.
Chewing (we love this phase) on anything and everything laying around, including plastic (toys), rocks and a wide variety of wood products.
His final love is barking. It can be intimidating, even when you're just ten inches tall. But the vineyard crews are not going to leave the vineyard even if he is...
"Darth Vader"
His two best friends are Noah and Caven who he loves most of all.

Tim Pratton

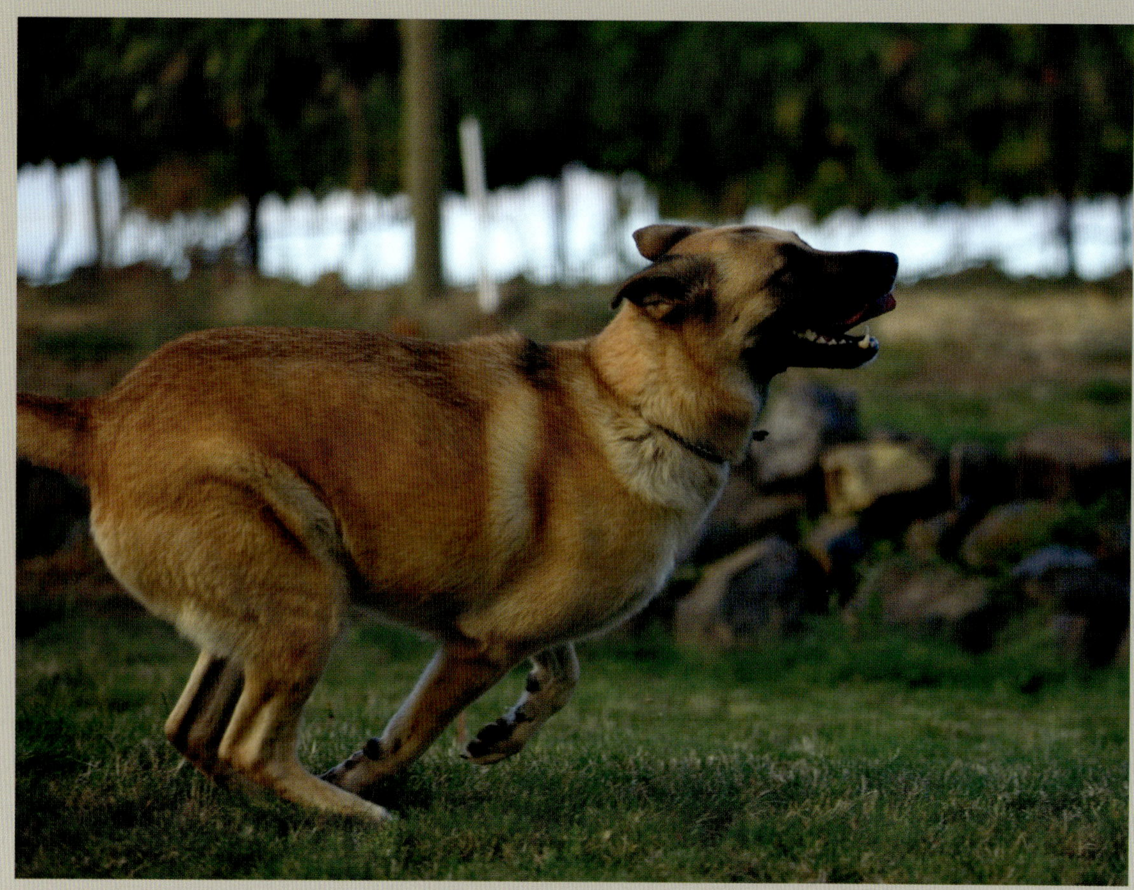

Bella

Stephenson Cellars

Bella is a 6-year-old German Shepherd whose mother was a purebred German Shepherd and her father, too, if a couple of fence-climbing coyotes hadn't beat him to the punch.

She has a strong work ethic, but without large animals to protect, Bella herds her cats, farm equipment and cars filled with potential customers. The joy she exhibits performing these tasks makes it pointless to scold her.

I have also observed that when guests survive her barking, sniffing greeting, they welcome wine to drink.

Bella's contribution to my happiness cannot be overstated. I work strange hours, in unpredictable weather, occasionally in grumpy moods. Unlike normal humans, Bella is thrilled to get in the truck, go to work and keep me company.

I often hear people describe being accepted, forgiven and never abandoned by the deity they worship. I'm not an organized religion guy, but I understand what they are talking about.

I have Bella.

Dave Stephenson

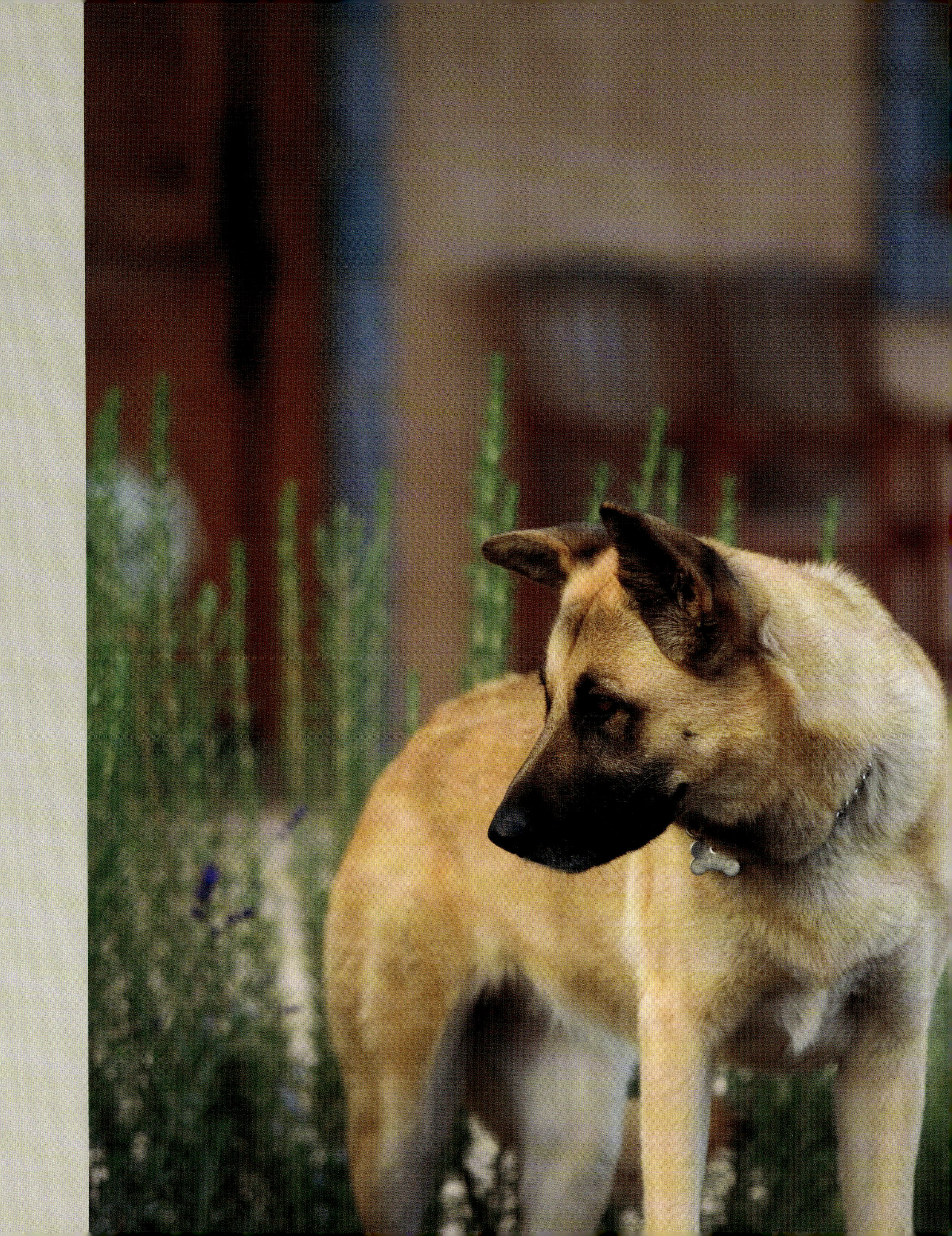

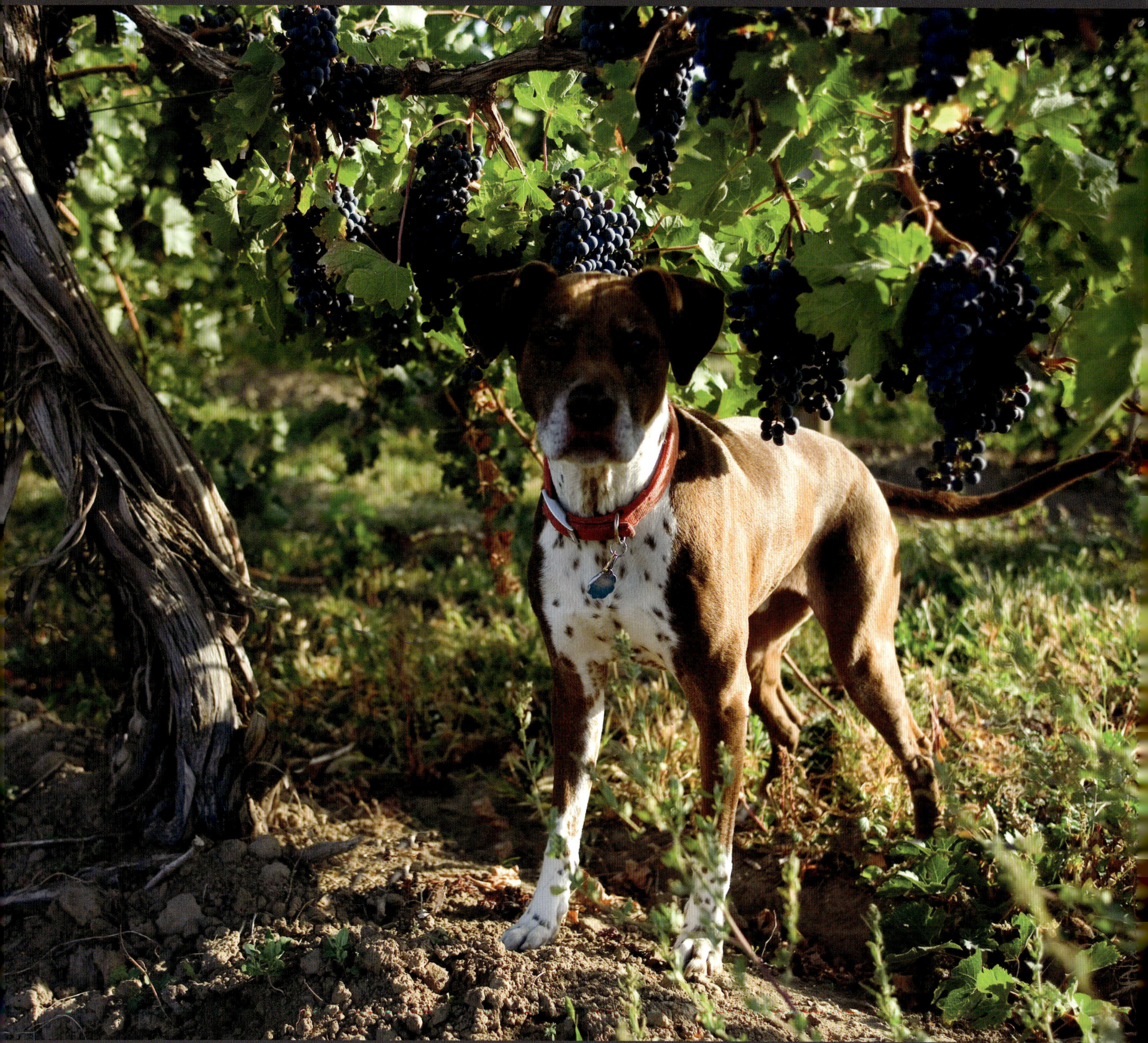

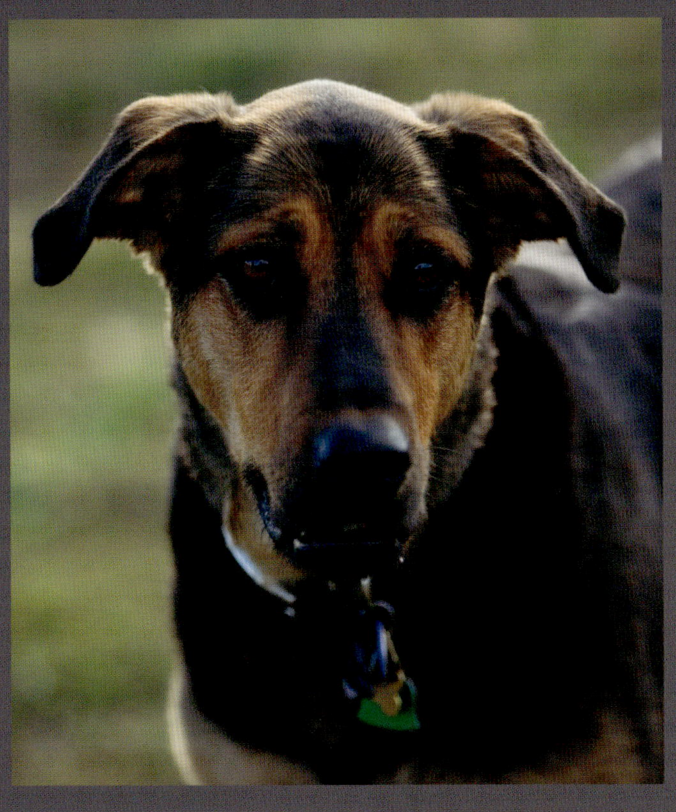

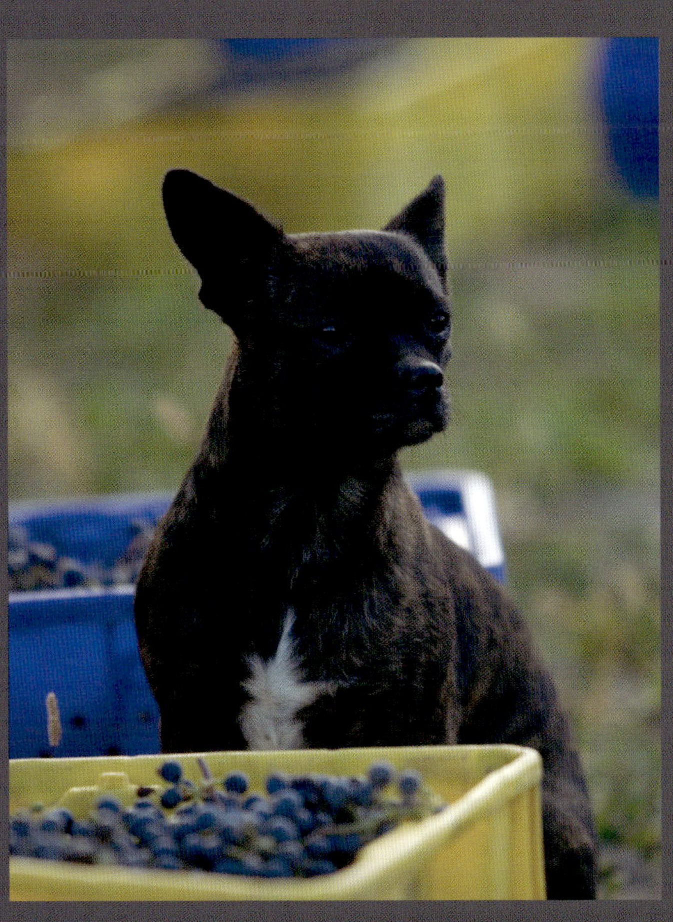

Bozco, Kayla, Meca

Windrow Vineyard

Bozco is our German Shorthair-Boxer mix. Rescued from an abusive home, he is an energetic and irrepressibly happy dog. He loves keeping deer off the property, which was a surprise to us since he had never seen one before coming here.

Kayla, a German Shepherd-Rottweiler mix, was adopted from the pound at eight weeks old. Within days of moving to the vineyard, she became protector of six kittens abandoned by their mother. That was a job.
Kayla likes chasing golf balls – three at a time, please – and swimming in the canal which runs along the property. But her favorite activity is being "one with the vineyard" – rolling in anything on the ground - grapes, deceased skunk, whatever.

Meca belongs to Esteban Albarrañ, our vineyard manager. A Chihuahua, her job is to run circles around all the workers and vineyard critters. Meca keeps smiles going all around, an important role in any vineyard.
All our dogs assume every visitor is here just to see them. The open space and coming and going of guests, workers and delivery people contributes to a very healthy lifestyle for these pals.

Jan and Doug Roskelley

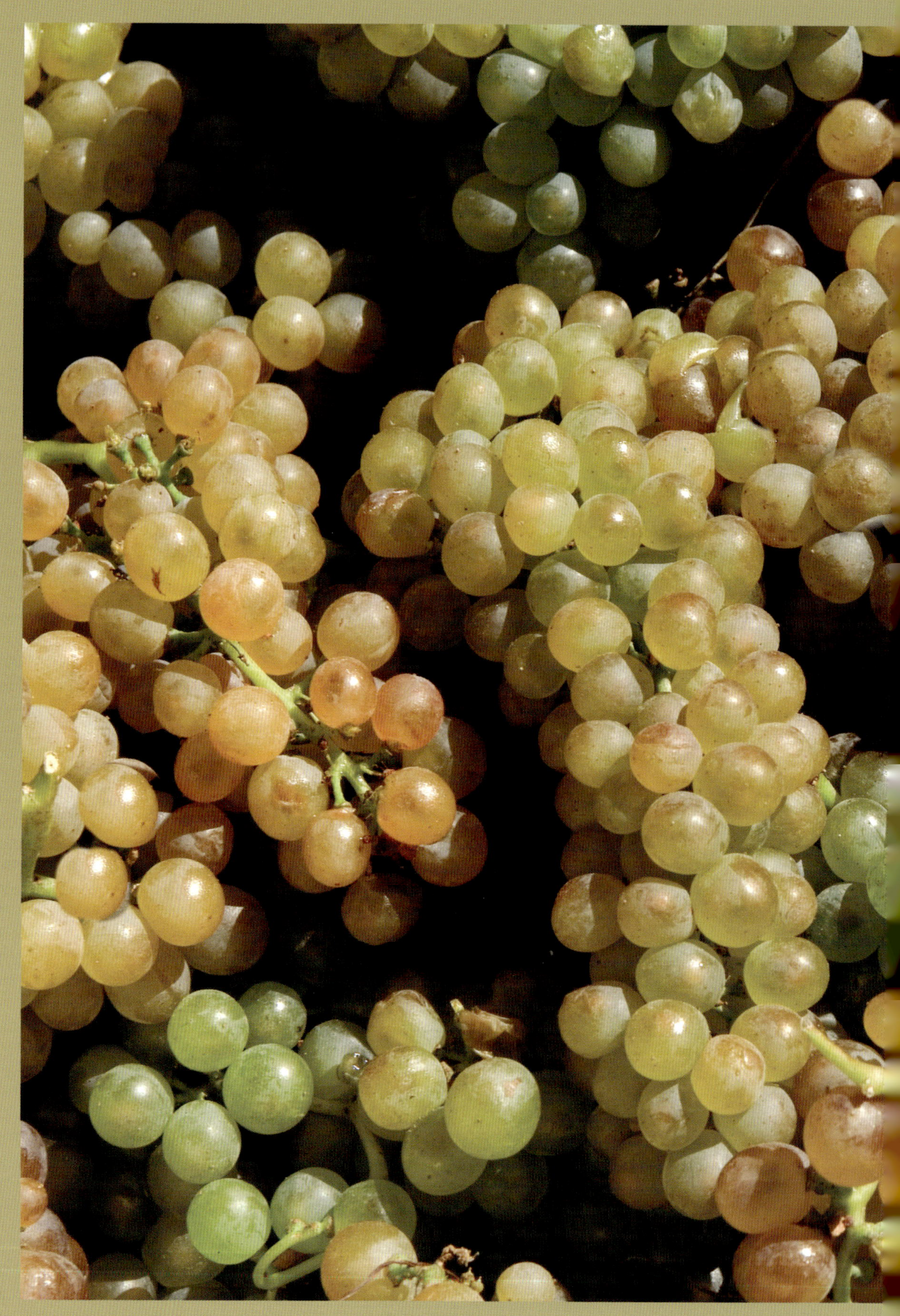

Chardonnay Harvest

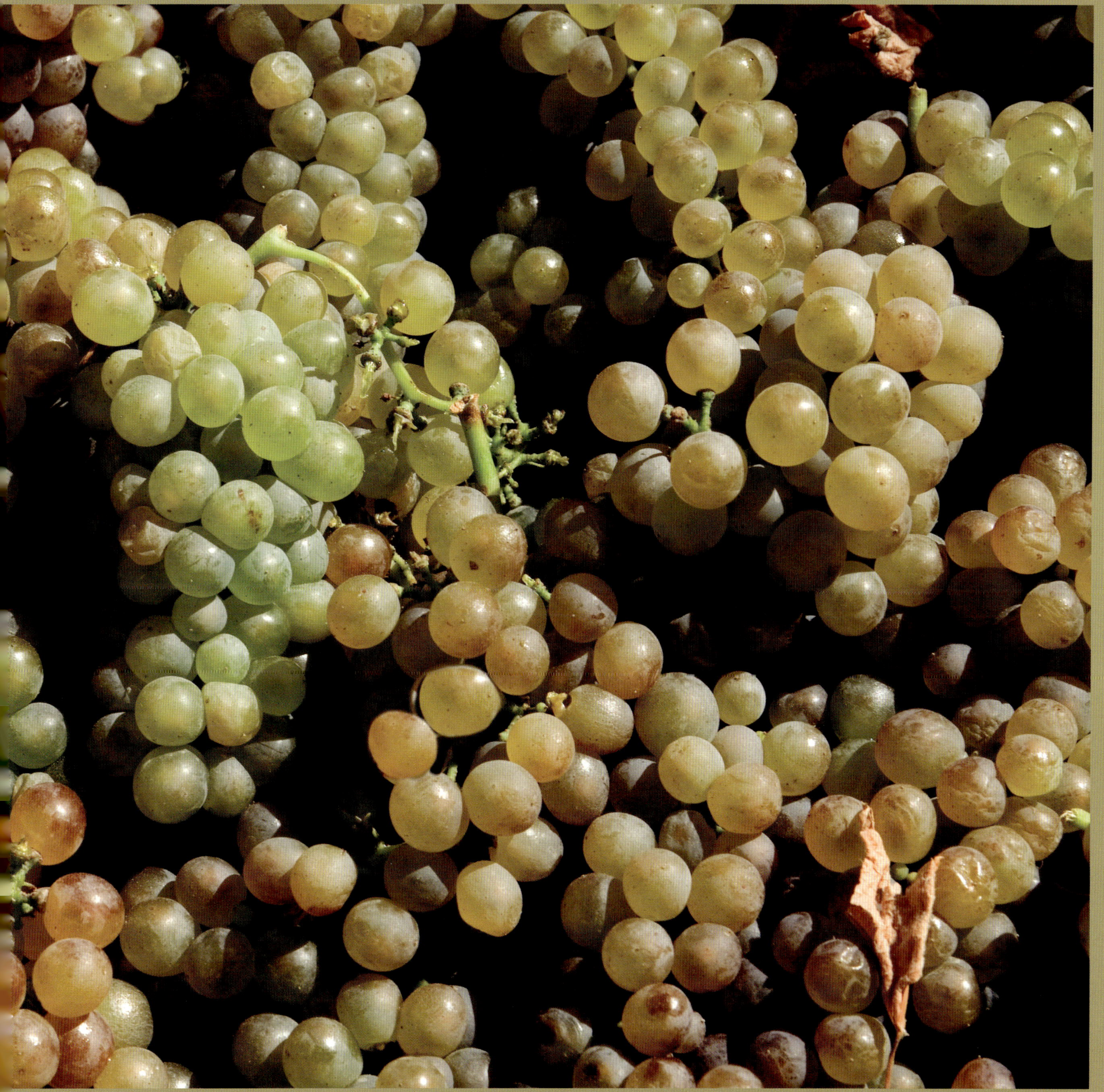

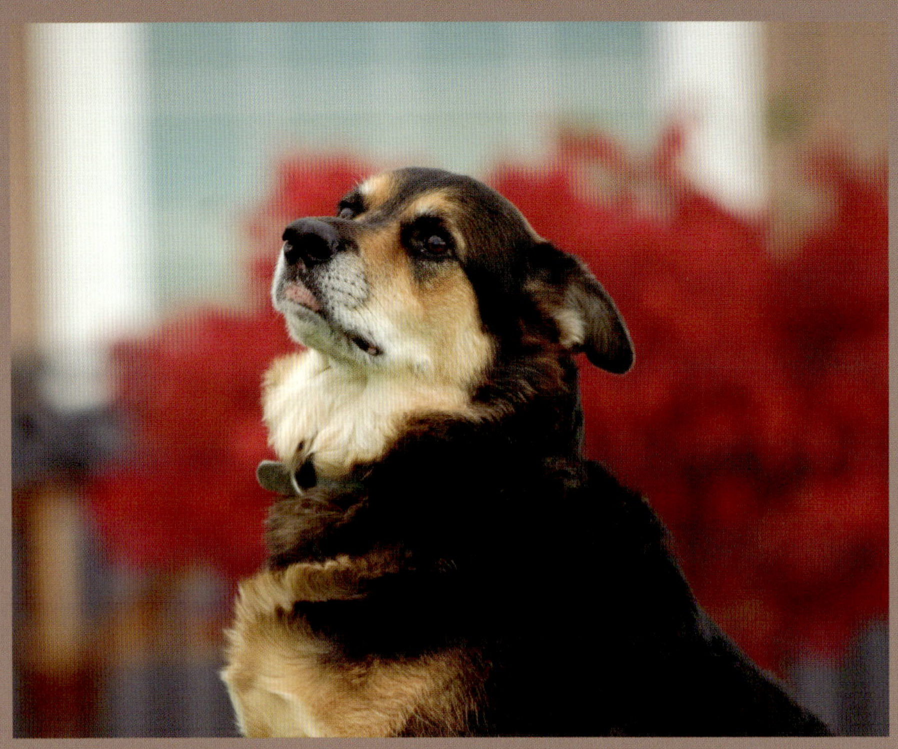

Brewer

Trio Vintners

Brewer – a German Shepherd and Rotweiler mix – started life as a "cute little puppy" sharing a studio apartment with my son, Ian. After a year or so, Brewer had outgrown his space and, for the first time, accompanied Ian to our home.

Ian pleaded with us to give Brewer a yard to run in. Brewer has been my faithful companion ever since.

While he is cautious with strangers and has a big bark, once Brewer decides you are "all right," he is very friendly.

Brewer loves walks along Walla Walla's tree-shaded streets, tricks me into playing keep-away with his favorite ball and is always ready for a treat – a dog biscuit, hot dog or sandwich.

Because of its unique odors, the winery isn't among Brewer's favorite places. But he loves the open fields around the winery buildings and gets to hang out with me when the tasting room is closed and I have outside work to do.

Tim Boushey

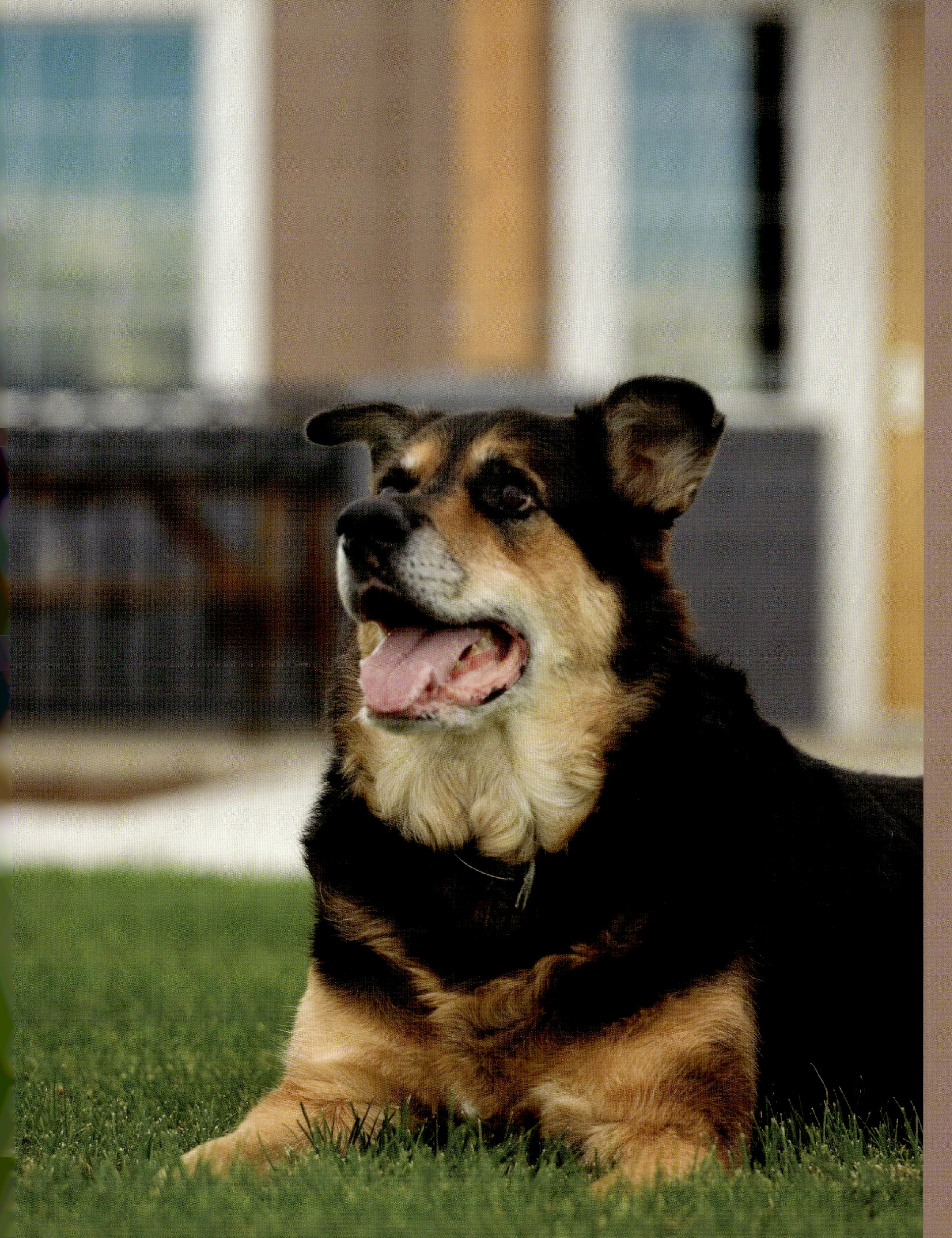

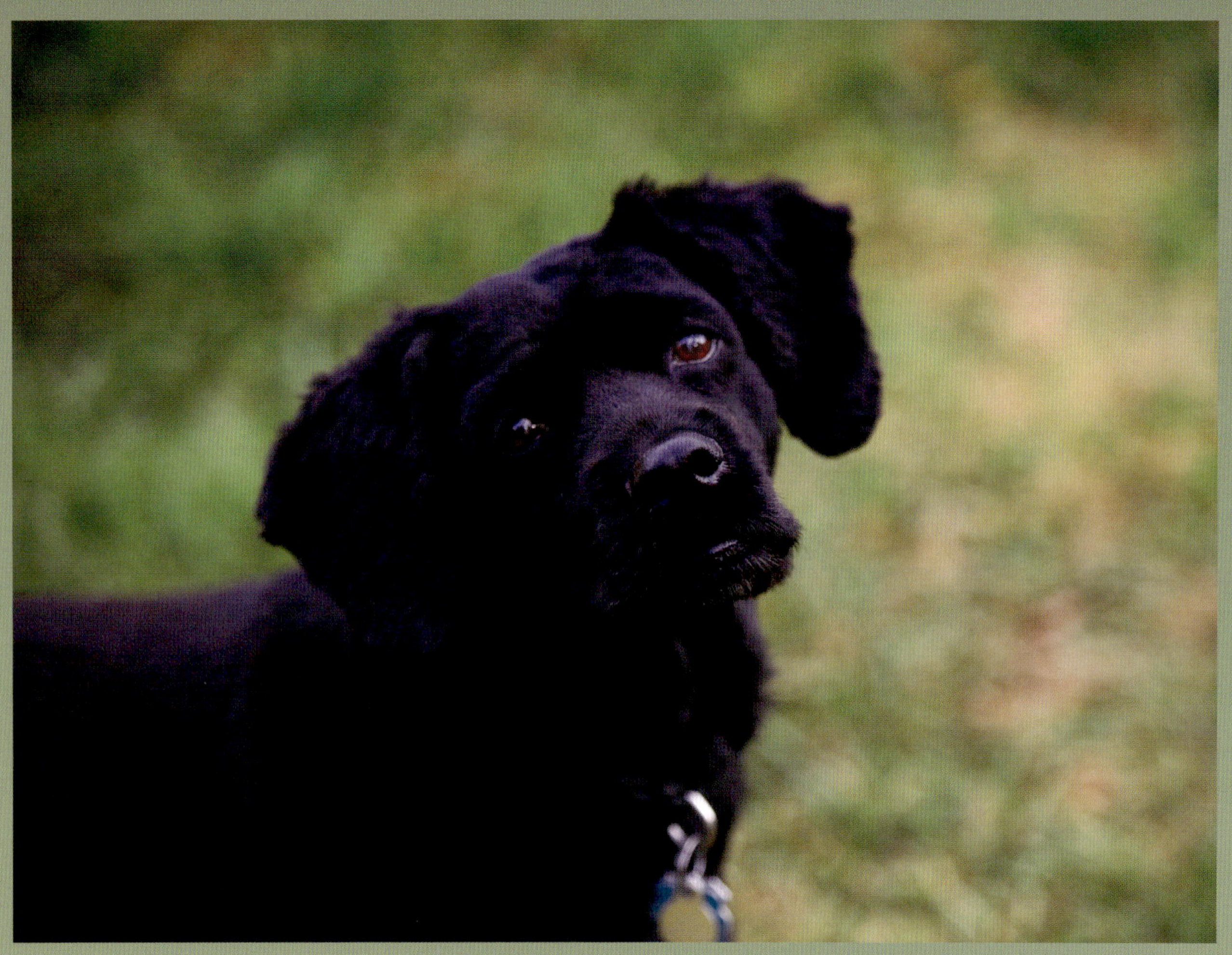

Mattie

Yellowhawk Cellars

Mattie was rescued – personally selected – from the Blue Mountain Humane Society because she was the only dog that was not barking.
Now, Mattie is my doorbell at the winery, letting me know with her harmless bark when someone comes. Appropriately for a winery dog, Mattie loves to eat grapes and watch crush from the rooftop. She also exercises by chasing squirrels and running with the horses.

Tim Sampson and Barbara Hetrick

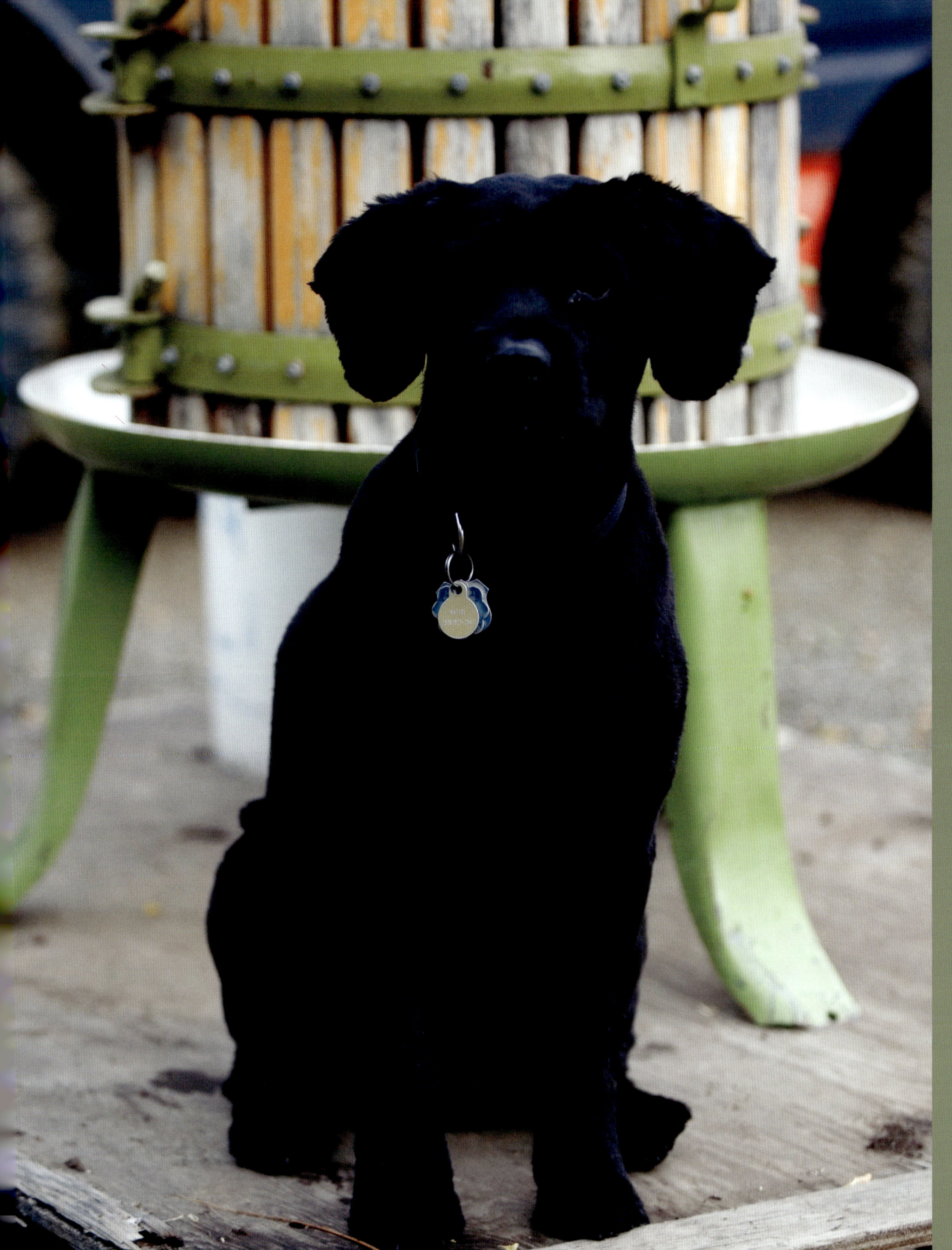

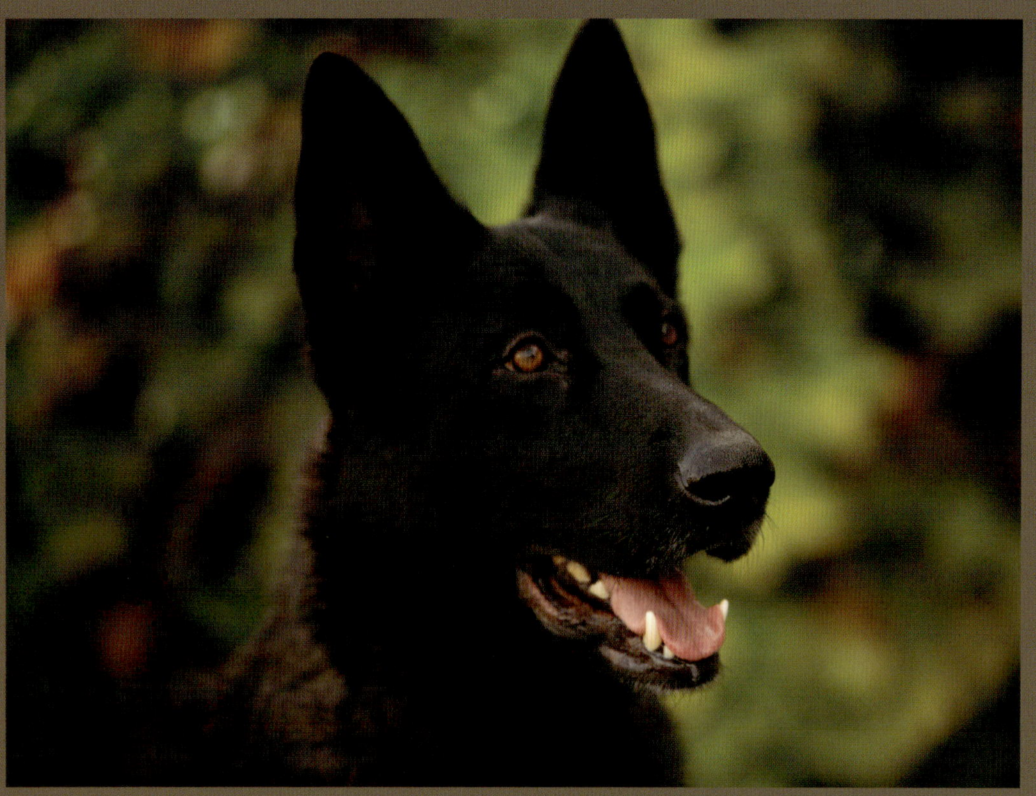

Hagrid

Amavi Cellars

Hagrid's home at Amavi Cellars is a far cry from his original destiny. The pure-bred black German Shepherd was first selected from his litter to become trained as a drug-detecting police dog. We convinced the breeder to let him come with us.

Now the 6-year-old Hagrid - named after the character in the Harry Potter book series - is our constant companion. He travels with us on regional wine-selling travels, lounges about the winery and basks in the attention given him by our many visitors.

When he's not "at work" at the winery, Hagrid moonlights as a teaching assistant in trainer Susan Overfield's dog-obedience seminars.

Ray and Diana Goff

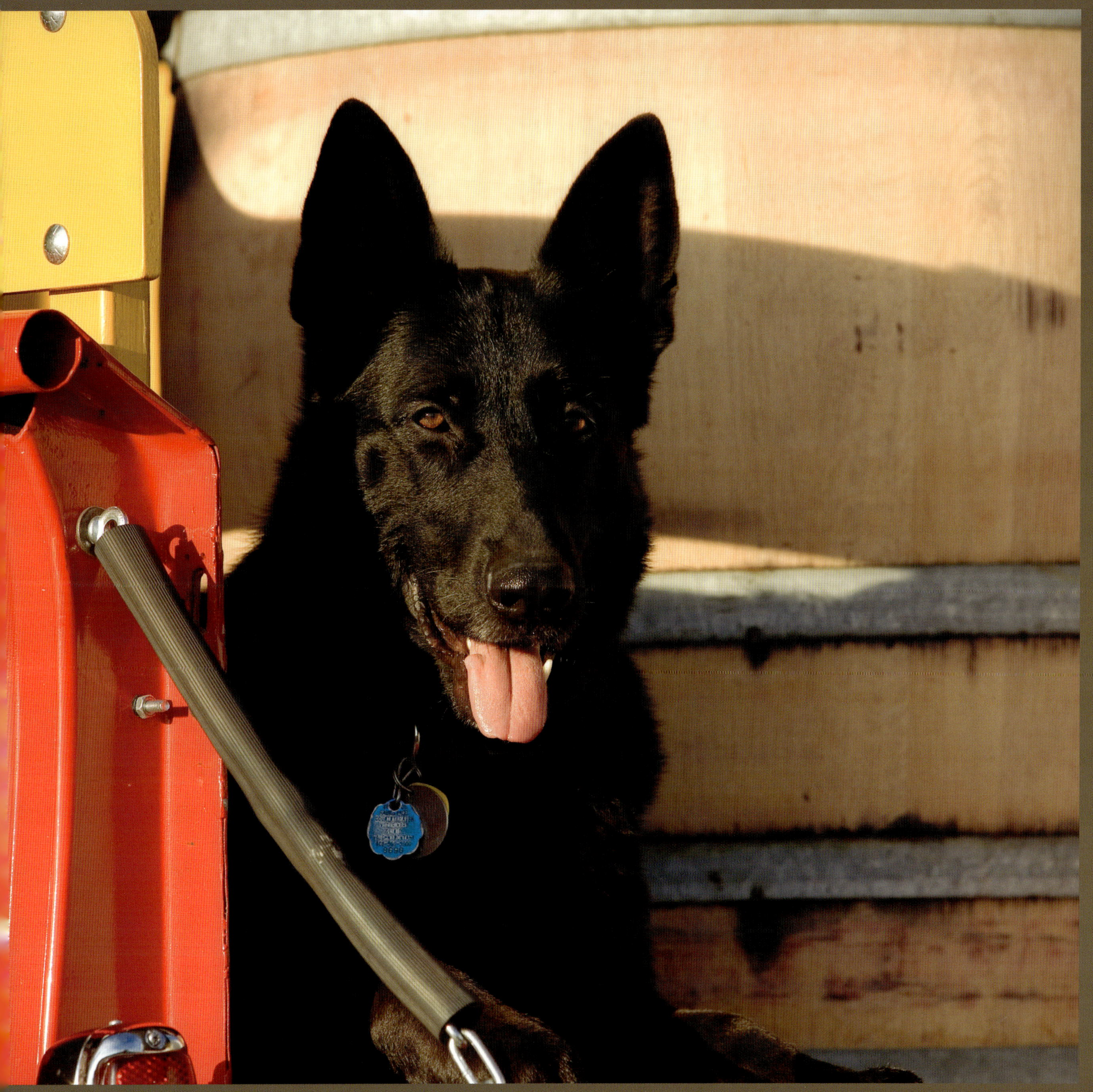

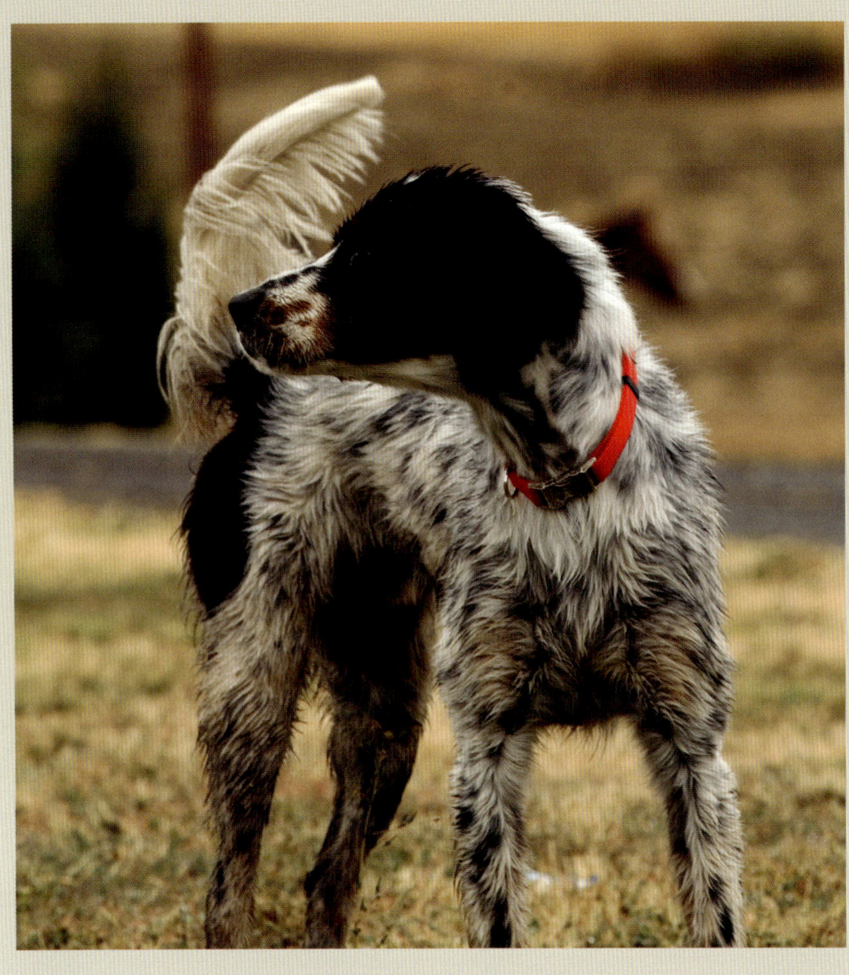

Rocco

Couvillian Winery

Our faithful companion, Rocco, came all the way from Baghdad, Kentucky, a 2,000 mile flight away. Of course, we didn't bring him all that way for the fun of it. He has important responsibilities.

Because of his "hunter backgound," Rocco, a Llewellyn Setter, is in charge of winery security. Any unwanted or unannounced feathered creatures must be personally screened.

Secondly, he is in charge of athletic training. Rocco periodically leads the crew on high speed walks up and down the valley road. The crew chooses not to go with Rocco, but maybe in time they'll get up to his speed.

Rocco is the best motivator on this farm. He keeps everyone's spirits high with his goofy little "smile" and his unbounded energy. And whatever the adventure, Rocco expects everyone to keep up and enjoy the day like he does.

When we have guests, he is curious, but courteous and positions himself at the front door to greet newcomers with a warm welcome.

Jill and Craig Noble

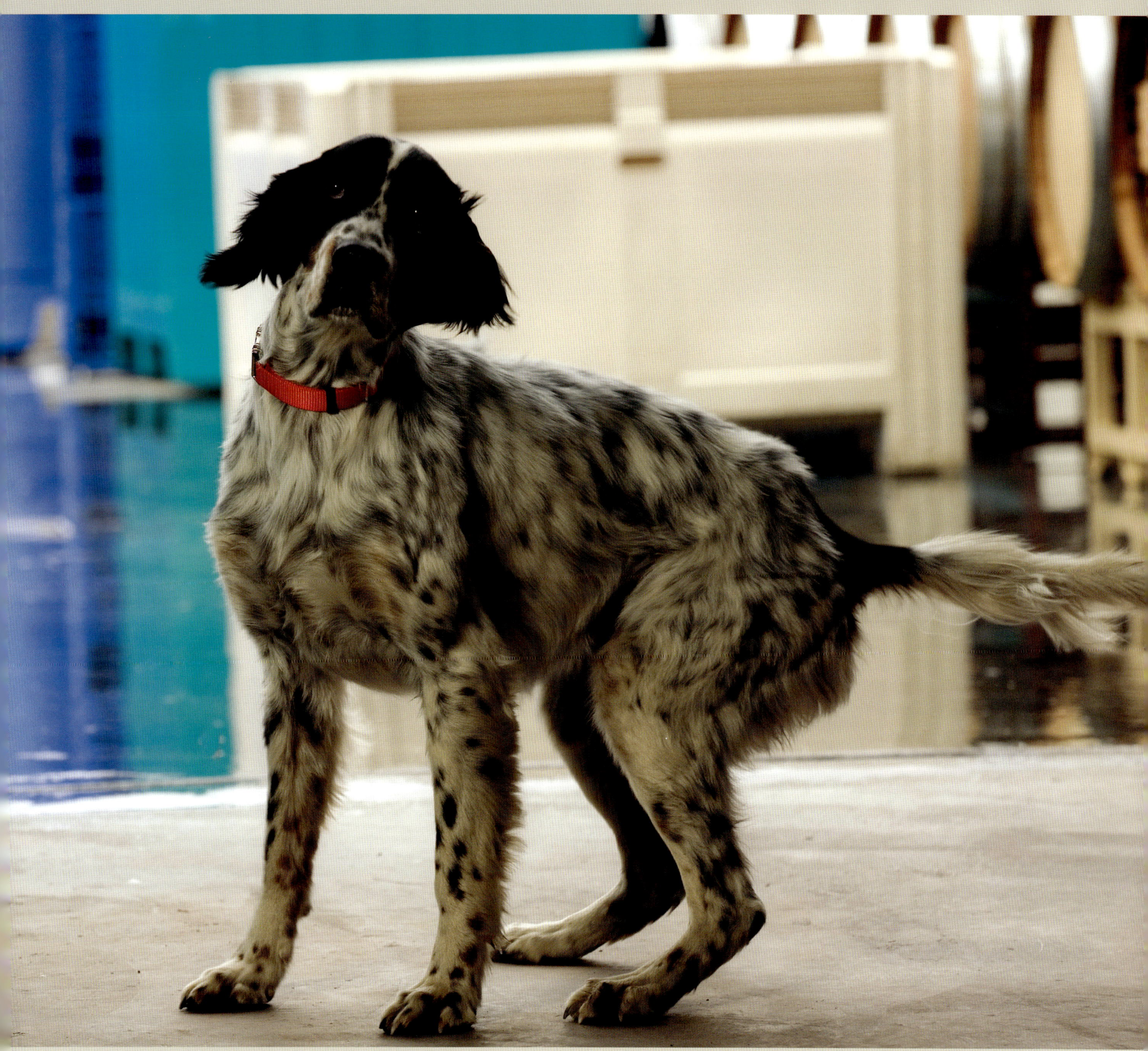

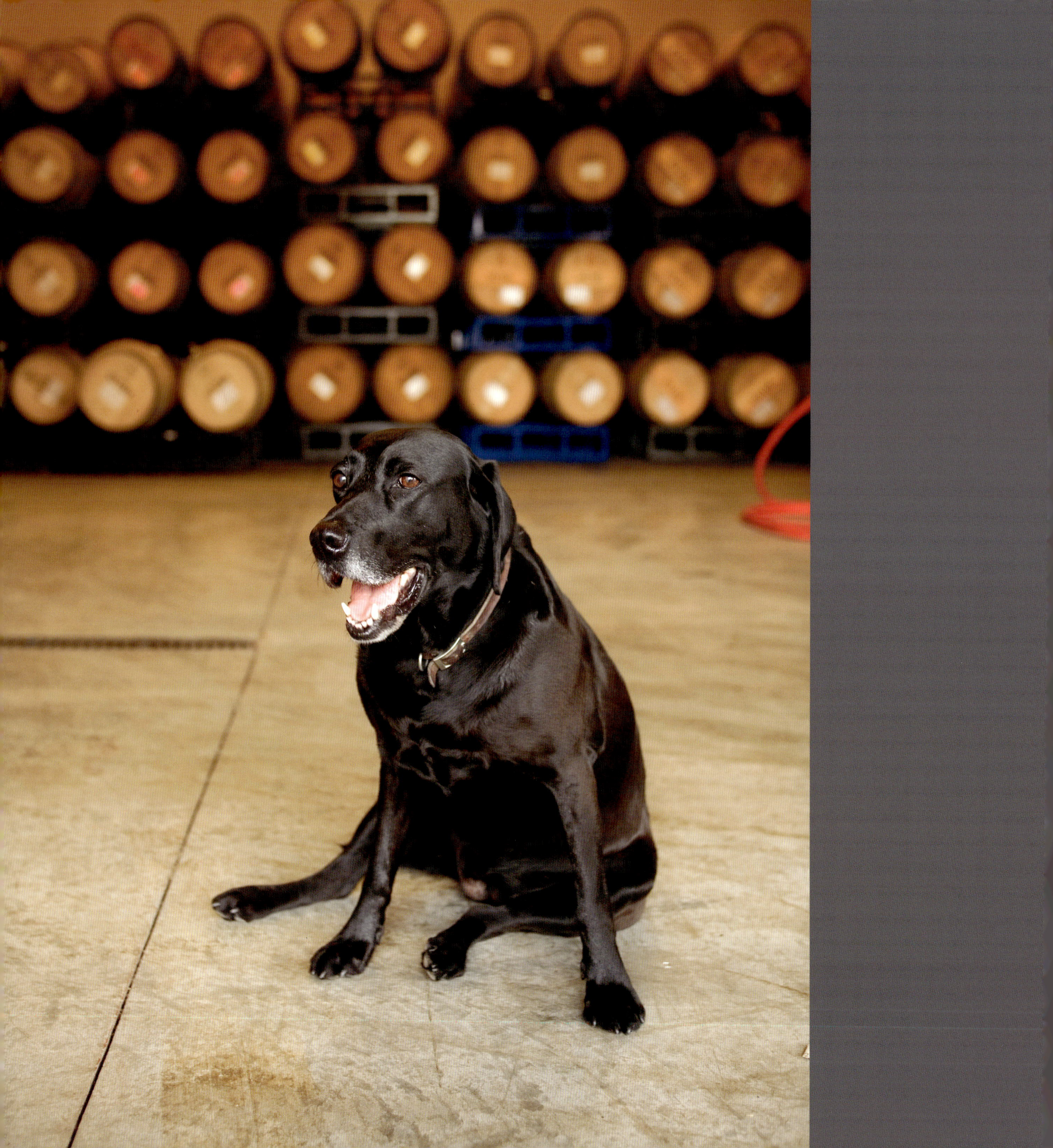

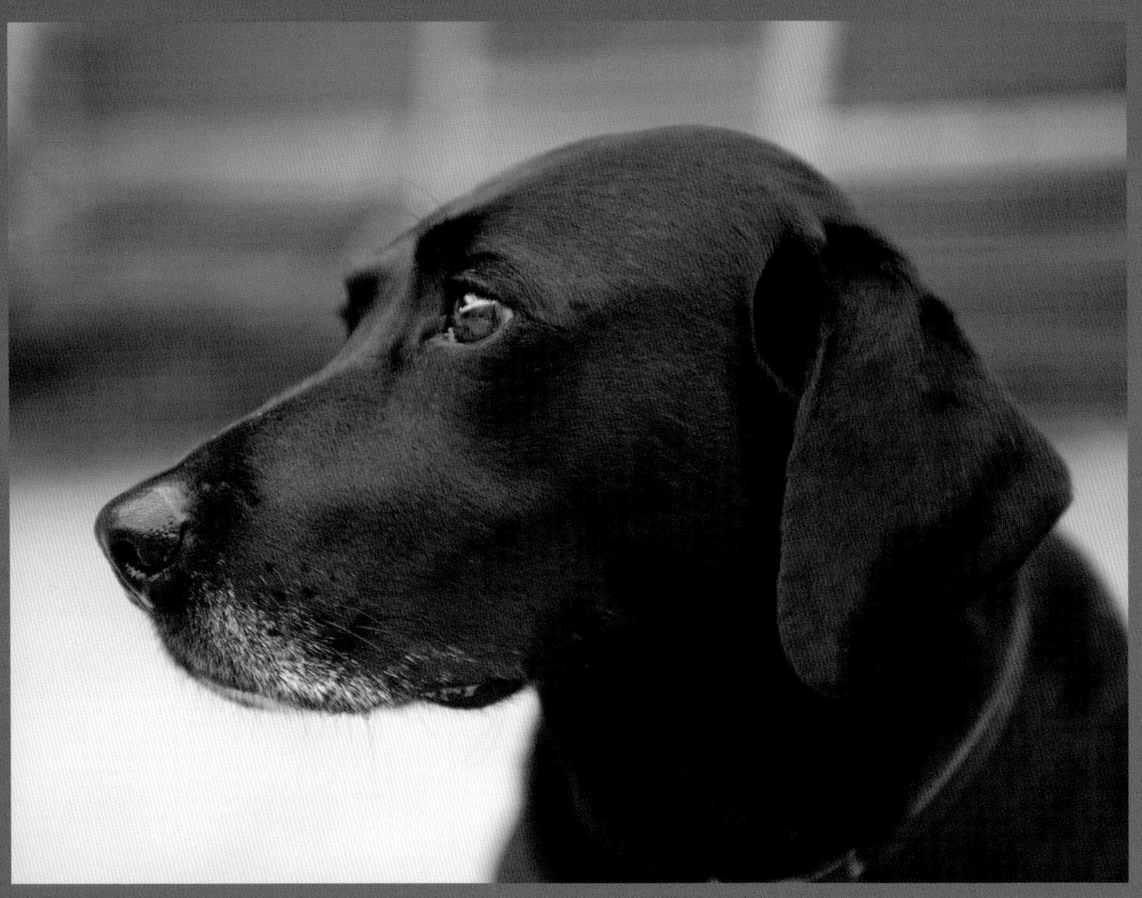

Salsa

Forgeron Cellars

I found Salsa in a vineyard 10 miles North of town and close to a state park where people "dropped" unwanted animals. The dog came back day after day because work crews fed her. But, they all had pets so nobody would take her home.
They did name the dog "La Rena" (the Queen in Spanish) as she was well mannered.
I never ever wanted a dog, but decided to give this one a try.
After getting comfortable with us, La Rena started showing her real personality – jumping up and down when we went out, running around fast when we tried to get her and demonstrating other puppy behaviors.
When it was obvious that our La Rena was not so well mannered, I renamed her "Salsa" because she was pretty hot (and she was in heat when we found her).
Eight years later, Salsa has mellowed, but she can still jump quite a bit!

Marie-Eve Gilla

Gabi

Ensemble Cellars

Gabi is an 8-year-old Beagle owned by our youngest daughter, Melissa.
Gabi is a wonderful companion dog, always ready for a walk or treats! She loves chasing the squirrels around our home vineyard. Her perfect day is a snooze in the sun 'til noon, a short walk, a big treat and slow squirrels.
At the end of the day we are always happy to be greeted by Gabi with a wonderful smile.

Craig and Bunny Nelson

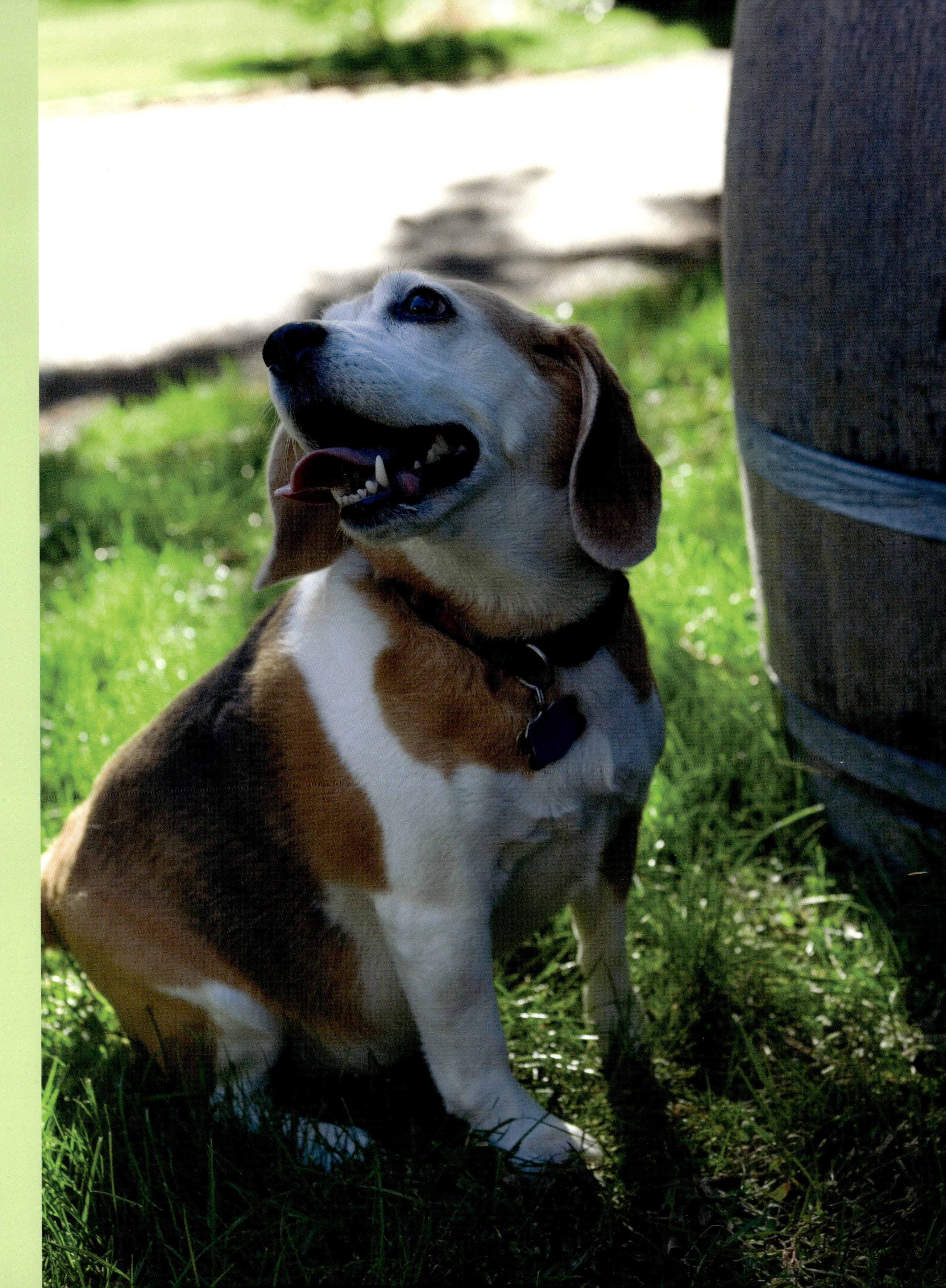

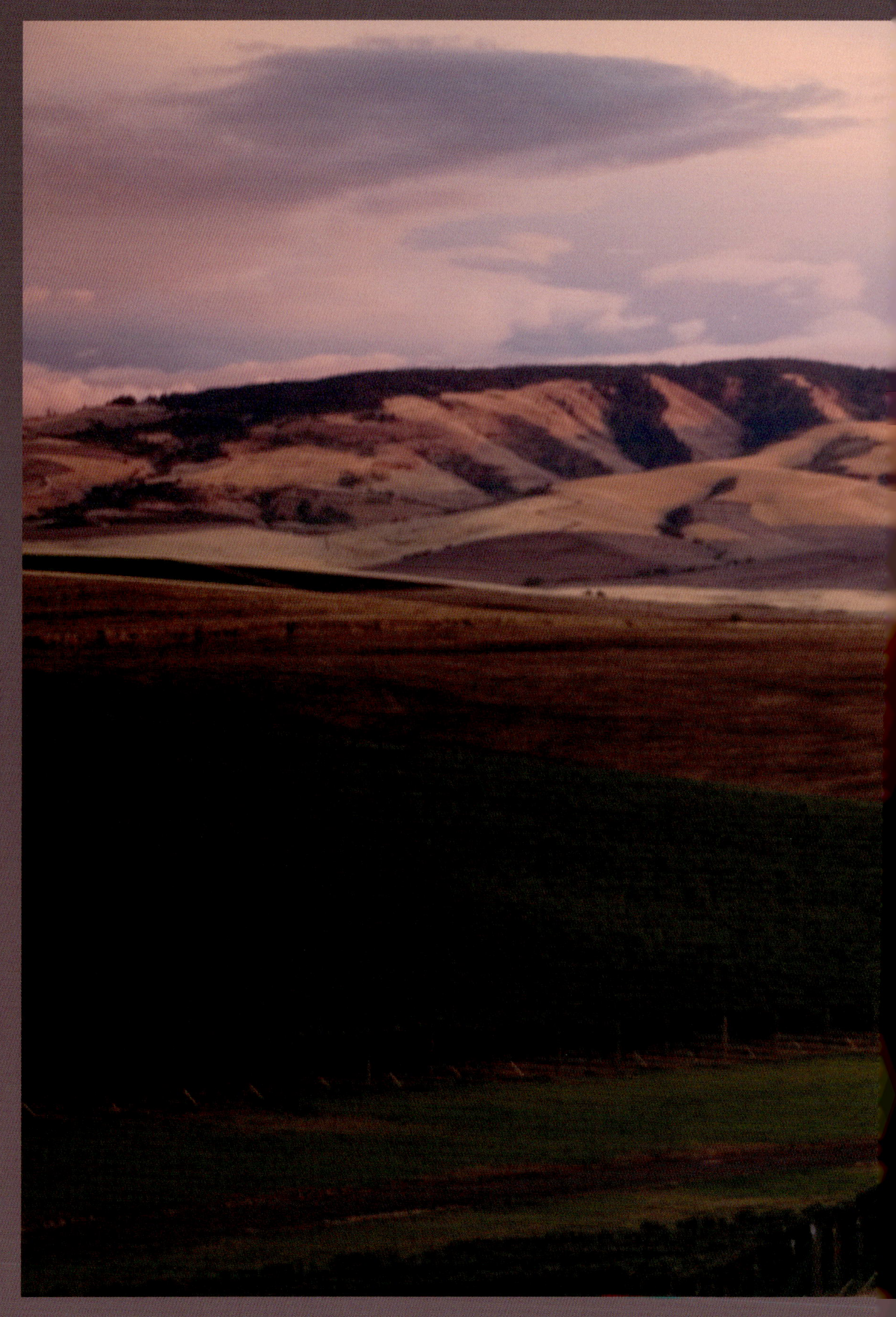

Vineyards at Dusk

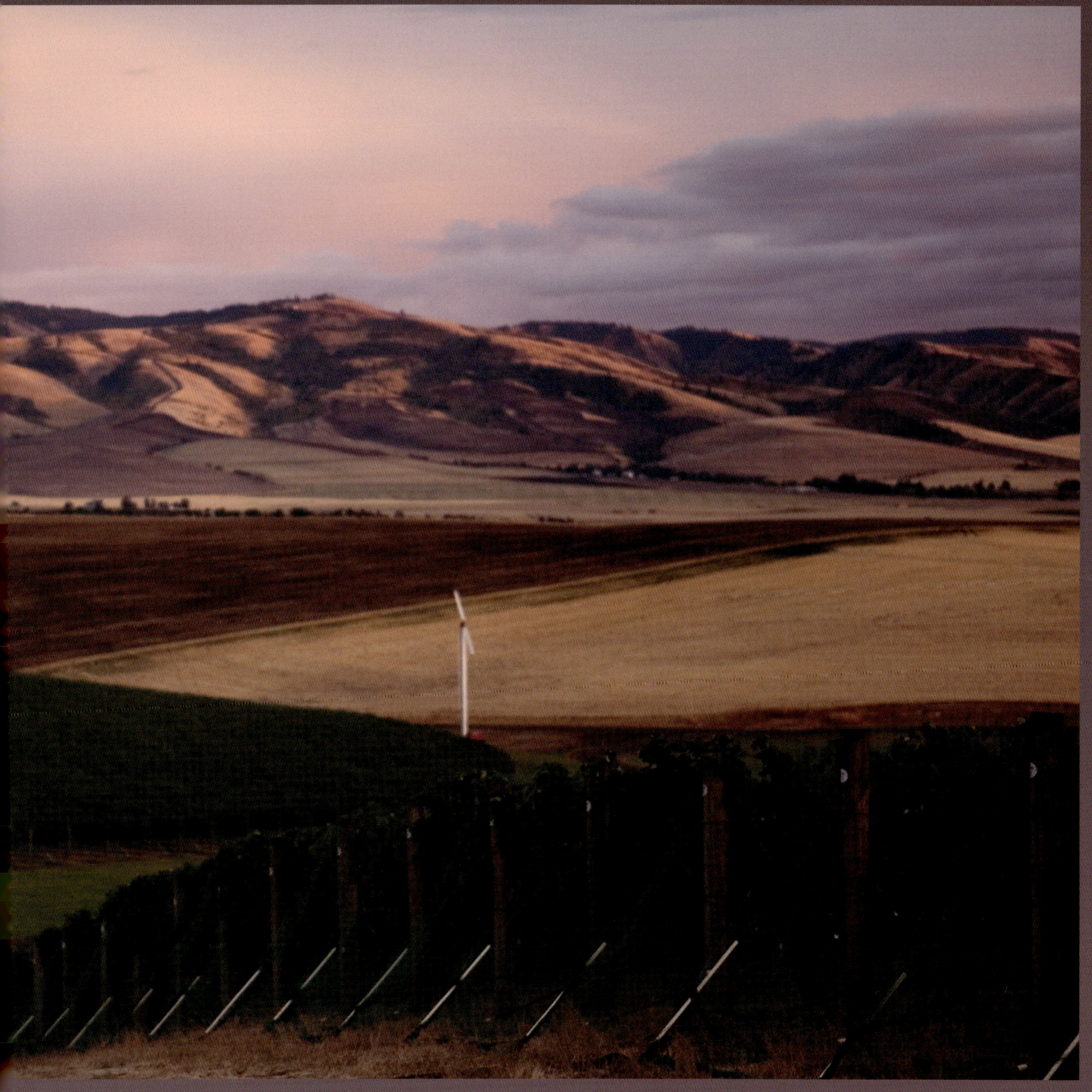

Winery Roster

Abeja
(509) 526-7400
2014 Mill Creek Road
Walla Walla, WA 99362
www.abeja.net

Adamant Cellars
(509) 529-4161
600 Piper Avenue
Walla Walla, WA 99362
www.adamantcellars.com

aMaurice Cellars
(509) 522-5444
178 Vineyard Lane
Walla Walla, WA 99362
www.amaurice.com

Amavi Cellars
(509) 525-3541
635 North Thirteenth Avenue
Walla Walla, WA 99362
www.amavicellars.com

Basel Cellars Estate Winery
(509) 522-0200
2901 Old Milton Highway
Walla Walla, WA 99362
www.baselcellars.com

Beresan Winery
(509) 522-2395
4169 Pepper Bridge Road
Walla Walla, WA 99362
www.beresanwines.com

Bergevin Lane
(509)526-4300
1215 West Poplar Street
Walla Walla, WA 99362
www.bergevinlane.com

Canoe Ridge Vineyard
(509) 527-0885
1102 West Cherry Street
Walla Walla, WA 99362
www.canoeridgevineyard.com

Cayuse Vineyards
(509) 526-0686
17 East Main Street
Walla Walla, WA 99362
www.cayusevineyards.com

College Cellars of Walla Walla
(509) 524-5170
500 Tausick Way
Walla Walla, WA 99362
www.collegecellars.com

Cougar Crest Winery
(509) 529-5980
50 Frenchtowne Road
Walla Walla, WA 99362
www.cougarcrestwinery.com

Couvillion Winery
(509) 520-3369
86 Corkrum Road
Walla Walla, WA 99362
www.couvillionwinery.com

DaMa Wines
(509) 525-2299
45 East Main Street
Walla Walla, WA 99362
www.damawines.com

Dumas Station Wines
(509) 520-1156
36229 Highway 12
Dayton, WA 99328
www.dumasstation.com

Dunham Cellars
(509) 529-4685
150 East Boeing Avenue
Walla Walla, WA 99362
www.dunhamcellars.com

Dusted Valley Vintners
(509) 525-1337
1248 Old Milton Highway
Walla Walla, WA 99362
www.dustedvalley.com

Elegante' Cellars
(509) 525-9129
839 "C" Street
Walla Walla,WA 99362
www.elegantecellars.com

Ensemble Cellars
(509) 525-0231
145 East Curtis Avenue
Walla Walla, WA 99362
www.ensemblecellars.com

Five Star Cellars
(509) 527-8400
840 "C" Street
Walla Walla, WA 99362
www.fivestarcellars.com

Forgeron Cellars
(509) 522-9463
33 West Birch Street
Walla Walla, WA 99362
www.forgeronecellars.com

Gifford Hirlinger
(509) 301-9229
1450 Stateline Road
Walla Walla, WA 99362
www.giffordhirlinger.com

Hence Cellars
(509)529-4010
4122 Powerline Road
Walla Walla, WA 99362
www.hencecellars.com

Isenhower Cellars
(509) 526-7896
3471 Pranger Road
Walla Walla, WA 99362
www.Isenhowercellars.com

JLC Winery / Spofford Station
(509) 529-1398
At the Airport
Walla Walla, WA 99362
www.jlcwinery.com

Leonetti Cellars
(509) 525-1428
1875 Foothills Lane
Walla Walla, WA 99362
www.leonetticellar.com

Long Shadows Vintners
(509) 526-0905
1604 Frenchtowne Road
Walla Walla, WA 99362
www.longshadows.com

Lowden Hills Winery
(509) 527-1040
1401 West Pine Street
Walla Walla, WA 99362
www.lowdenhillswinery.com

Nicholas Cole Cellars
(509) 525-0608
705 Berney Drive
Walla Walla, WA 99362
www.nicholascolecellars.com

Northstar Winery
(509) 525-6100
1736 JB George Road
Walla Walla, WA 99362
www.northstarmerlot.com

Otis Kenyon Wine
(206) 463-3125
52744 Burris Lane
Milton-Freewater, OR 97862
www.otiskenyonwine.com

Patit Creek Cellars
(509) 522-4684
325 "A" Street
Walla Walla, WA 99362
www.patitcreekcellars.com

Reininger Winery
(509) 522-1994
5858 West Highway 12
Walla Walla, WA 99362
www.reiningerwinery.com

Sapolil Cellars
(509) 520-5258
15 East Main Street
Walla Walla, WA 99362
www.sapolilcellars.com

Seven Hills Winery
(509) 529-7198
212 North Third Avenue
Walla Walla, WA 99362
www.sevenhillswinery.com

Seven Hills Vineyard / North Slope Management
(541) 938-8941
83501 Lower Dry Creek Road
Milton-Freewater, OR 97862
www.sevenhillsvineyard.com

Skylite Cellars
(509) 529-8000
Highway 12 and Campbell Road
Walla Walla, WA 99362
www.skylitecellars.com

Spring Valley Vineyard
(509) 525-1506
7 South Forth Avenue
Walla Walla, WA 99362
www.springvalleyvineyard.com

Stephenson Cellars
(509) 529-8200
755 "B" Street
Walla Walla, WA 99362
www.stephensoncellars.com

Trio Vintners
(509) 529-8746
596 Piper Avenue
Walla Walla, WA 99362
www.triovintners.com

Va Piano Vineyards
(509) 529-0900
1793 JB George Road
Walla Walla, WA 99362
www.vapianovineyards.com

Walla Walla Vintners
(509) 525-4724
225 Vineyard Lane (off Mill Creek Road)
Walla Walla, WA 99362
www.wallawallavintners.com

Waterbrook Winery
(509) 522-1263
31 East Main Street
Walla Walla, WA 99362
www.waterbrook.com

Waters Winery
(509) 525-1590
1825 JB George Road
Walla Walla, WA 99362
www.waterswinery.com

Whitman Cellars
(509) 529-1142
1015 West Pine Street
Walla Walla, WA 99362
www.whitmancellars.com

Windrow Vineyard
(541) 938-8376
52015 Seven Hills Road
Milton-Freewater, OR 97862
www.windrowvineyards.com

Yellowhawk Cellars
(509) 529-1714
395 Yellowhawk Street
Walla Walla, WA 99362
www.yellowhawkcellars.com

Zerba Cellars
(541) 938-9463
85530 Highway 11
Milton-Freewater, OR 97862
www.zerbacellars.com

My thanks to each and every winery that participated in the production of this book. All of your dogs are wonderful! Neither myself, or my photographer suffered from a single bite. All the dogs enjoyed the attention and turned out to be quite the performers and stars. I recognize and thank you for the privilege of meeting each of your dogs and for your enthusiastic cooperation on this project.

Each of the stories and scripts are the winemakers or vineyard owners own words. Each one original and written from the heart.

ENJOY and SHARE . . .

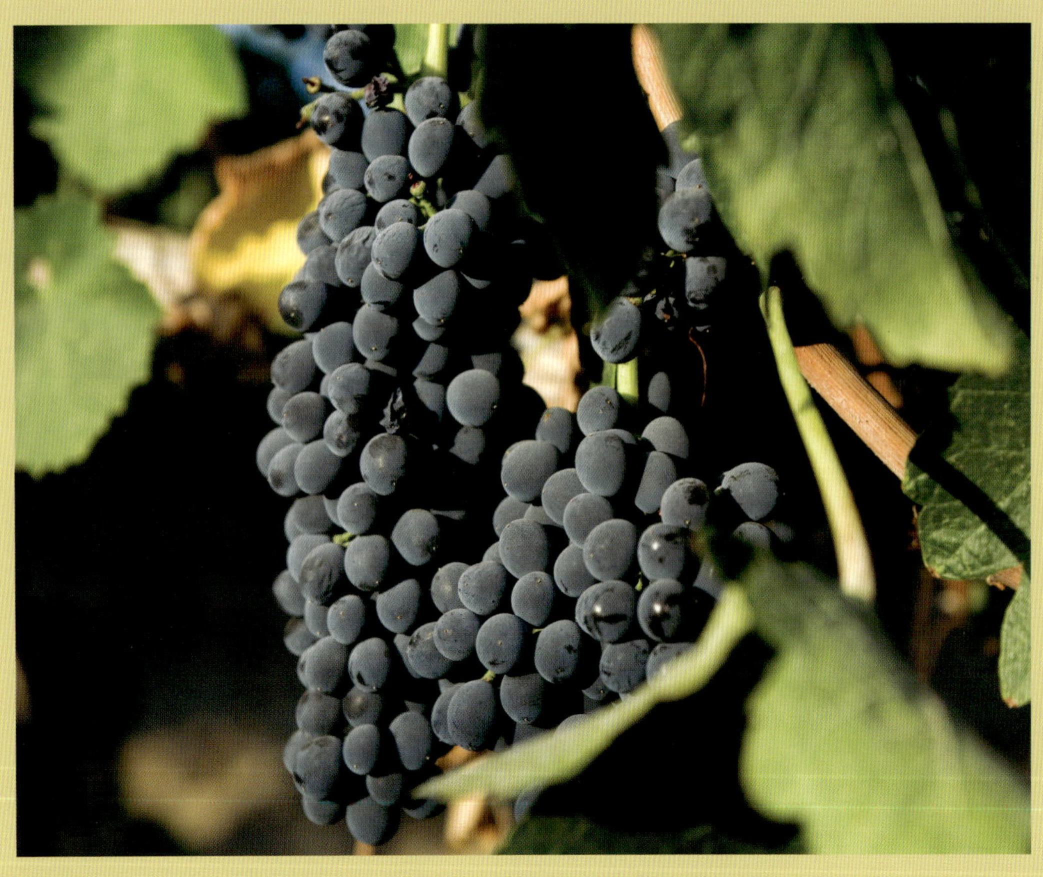